Reflections
by the Sea

A French Riviera Photo Travelogue of Healing

Irene Armani, JD

RP Books & Media LLC
Calabasas, California

Irene Armani, Esq.
RP Books & Media LLC
4774 Park Granada #9295
Calabasas, CA 91372
USA
www.irenearmani.com

Book Cover Design by Eli Bavar
Book Layout © 2017 BookDesignTemplates.com
Pebbles Design on the Dedication page and of July 25, 2016 by Jade, Antibes, France
Edited by Daniel Johnson

Reflections by the Sea/ Irene Armani. -- 1st ed.
ISBN 978-1-7341522-1-0 Print Edition
ISBN 978-1-7341522-8-9 eBook Edition

to Sabeen and Sareen

and to

La Cote d'Azur

to Sabeen and Sareen

and to

La Cote d'Azur

Introduction

Dear Reader

I am thrilled to share with you my yearlong physical and spiritual journey and the lessons I learned while traveling a very painful and treacherous road towards recovery. When I traveled to the South of France in November of 2014, my planner was filled with ambitious goals and deadlines all through the end of 2016. But little did I know that God had a different plan for me. The unbearable personal disasters I was about to experience in the ensuing months would completely change my life.

The long months between November 2014 and July 2016 brought my life to a screeching halt. My daughter rushed me to the hospital where I was placed under 24-supervision in the critical care unit. I don't remember much from those days except that after I was released from the critical care unit and during the coming weeks she would keep my mind occupied by sharing with me her daily gorgeous photos of the beautiful sunrises and sunsets at the Mediterranean Sea, and would ask me to capture and send her sunrise and sunset photos from my hospital room in which I was lucky to have a large window overlooking the mountains.

I was finally discharged after several weeks. As a woman without any prior health conditions, my very survival was in question: Will I live or die? Will I ever be the same? Will my heart ever feel joy again? I felt a dark cloud hanging over me and my spirit and body trapped inside cement walls that kept getting higher and higher. Here I was, in the most beautiful place on earth, yet I couldn't see, feel, and hear the very essence of that beauty. I was sick, physically, mentally, emotionally and spiritually, and ready to give up on everyone and everything. My dreams were shattered, my planner's goals and deadlines forgotten ... I had lost my faith.

But God did not allow me. He prompted me to either keep feeling sorry for myself or fight! I chose to be a fighter. With the help of my loving family and friends, and the grace of God, I began to face my challenges head on by taking baby-steps. With the support of my doctors and their holistic approach advising me to exercise, take meditative walks, and use the breathing techniques that my therapist taught me, I began to slowly pave my path towards recovery. I remember one particular doctor specifically advising me to "Live, really live." I took his words to heart and started my daily Walks along the stunning Mediterranean shore.

My journey of spiritual awakening, self-healing, and self-discovery had begun. Although difficult at first, I walked along the sea, photographing her daily, capturing her magic and everything that was intoxicated by her beauty. I found myself reflecting on life, love, family, health, Mother Nature, and sometimes ... nothing. One day, I started to scribble my thoughts, feelings, and observations in my phone rather than committing them to memory. My daily Walks brought peace and clarity to my mind. The sea's solitude and silence attracted me, and I escaped the world as I found peace and tranquility at sea. Where do I even begin to describe her tranquility, depth, and beauty? Why was I attracted to her? Was she *the* place to escape the world or discover my inner world? Was she the source for the wisdom I was seeking about how to Live my life? I began to directly speak with the sea to seek answers. Every day, I would ask her for a surprise gift, an answer to a question, or a solution to a problem, and she'd answer me by offering an endearing treasure—a beautiful shell, a sleeping rose, a white stone heart, a unique sea-glass pushed by a wave, the reflection of a spectacular sunrise, or the glittering of the moonlight on her water. Each gift taught me something about life, love, our existence, humanity, faith, trust, healing, happiness, letting go, and much more. She taught me that the mind and body have the power to heal themselves reaching higher levels of consciousness. Her gifts nourished my soul. Her aura cleansed my mind and spirit.

For the first time in my life, I began experiencing Love. This was not ordinary love. It was a selfless love towards humanity, Mother Nature, and God. It was about believing, trusting, forgiving, and Living. This type of Love began to define my identity.

Gradually, I realized that everything in life had a purpose. As my Walks became infused with breathing techniques, mindfulness exercises, and intentionality, my body grew stronger. To this date, I cannot say with certainty whether regaining my physical health led to the healing of my mind or the healing of the mind led me to regain my bodily strength. One thing is for sure, the healing process of both the body and the mind are intricately interconnected. As days turned into weeks and weeks into months, I grew stronger physically, mentally, and spiritually. I learned much from the sea. Her attitude brushed onto me. I noticed how she patiently watches life being lived by her—she gently keeps pounding, her pebbles roll until they morph into sand, people come and go, the sun and the moon take turns to rise and set, the sky darkens only to light up again, storms beat, rain pours, and soon new life blooms. After each change came the light. Wasn't this also the story of my life? The sea also taught me that the seasons will always change at their prescribed time, that every change set the stage for the next change, and that nothing lasted forever. All I had to do was to patiently wait—just like the sea— watch the storms hurl and pass by, watch others come and go, keep moving, stay focused, embrace life, and rise higher. And my soul decided to live by the sea's wisdom.

The seasons changed, and the charming towns of the French Riviera kept welcoming its visitors and offering their local traditions, culture, heritage, hospitality, and gourmet dining. Soon eleven months had passed. My mind accepted what was and what is, forgetting the physical, emotional, and spiritual adversities that had triggered my daily Walks. This bright Light had entered my soul, extending past the physical boundaries of our world. My soul bloomed. God was still there, waiting for my return. His words had helped me heal. My heart swelled with His Love. And He restored my faith.

I returned to Los Angeles on July 27, 2016. I continued my journaling until August 15, the first date that I had started journaling, then stopped. I tucked my journal away. Months later, something gently pushed me to revisit my journals and read them daily. Interestingly, my reflections had a different meaning now because I was a different person. God had given me a second chance. I had learned that nothing was impossible in life, and nothing was permanent except Love. Therefore, I decided to share my journey with the world, hoping it will help someone, somewhere, to face and to overcome their trials, and to find inner peace.

Come, join me on this extraordinary journey along the charming Mediterranean shore. It will transform your life. The process of writing these reflections involved self-doubt, deceit, learning, unlearning, trial and error, and questioning my faith. These are experiences that many people are also going through. Perhaps one of them is You. Venturing into this journey with me will help you reclaim your health, power, peace, and happiness. You will learn to let go the burden you have been carrying and emerge into this new, healthy, and confident person you are meant to be. You will gain the confidence to endure the different blows life will throw at you and most importantly, to Live a joyful and a meaningful life.

Wishing you love, happiness, and health on your life's journey,
Irene

PS: Even though some prefer to use the male gender when referring to a sea, I chose to refer to the Mediterranean Sea as a "she," because seas are a vital part of Mother Nature, and because the word "sea" in French, "la mer," is a "she."

Assumption of Mary

Doctor's orders: Walk daily, breathe the fresh air, strengthen your immunity. Today, I begin. Walking along the sea, I reach the port of Nice. There is a huge cheerful crowd, flower-filled boats floating on the water, and preparations are ongoing to celebrate Mother Mary's Assumption into heaven.

On August 15, the Niçois[1] celebrate Mary's Assumption here at the port. Her huge statue, placed amidst gorgeous flower arrangements in a tiny boat, parades the Port. Without warning, rain pours down the huge gray clouds that were watching over us a moment ago. The downpour blesses the crowd, Mary's boat, and the decorated boats accompanying hers. Ending the boat parade, they bring her statue to rest at the make-shift altar in the Port. Politicians including Mayor Estrosi and local clergy express their respect and gratitude towards Mother Mary. Their speeches reiterate and reinforce her place in this community, and I feel God is blessing the crowd while the fiery speeches, the soft hymns, and the praises rise through the misty rain.

I feel a sudden deep urge to describe the beauty and the mystery of this occasion—celebrated in this serene and beautiful setting—and to share it with those who are far away. A sense of belonging fills my heart and soul. A sense of finding the way to my lost home cheers me up. My daughter and I dart forward and rush ahead of the procession that had formed behind Mary's life-size statue. With her professional camera, my daughter starts capturing photos of Mary and the procession. We arrive at the nearby Notre Dame de Port Basilica. We enter the silent illuminated church, and the bearers place Mother Mary's statue at the right side of the altar, always surrounded by those beautiful bouquets. She is home. So are we.

Mother Mary is assumed into heaven—body and soul. She promises she will always watch over us who in faith and prayer keep her here, alive.

A Mid-Summer Evening

day 2: august 16, 2015

Continuing my walks and reflections, I stroll alongside her this mid-summer evening. The white foam delineating the edge of the sea rushes up and down the pebbles, sometimes hugging each pebble and other times blanketing all of them with its crisp yet rounded streaks of stars. The younger larger pebbles often resist the constant pressure of the tiny waves, not knowing that by staying there on the vast shore they will eventually succumb to the eternal gentle pressure exerted on them, and morph into older, smaller, rounder, more uniform pebbles, which in their turn will transform and disappear into the soft, beige, vast field of sand.

Isn't it like human life? Don't the constant gentle nudges of an ideology, or another human, change our perceptions and beliefs over time? The constants of the universe smooth out the little variants, shaping them to fit in the big picture. When you envision something in life, all the constants of the universe will conspire to offer you that finished polished product. You just need to keep pressing, pushing, and forging on, gently and yet ferociously. The sea still nudges, even at the older pebbles, which have been already smoothened out, into the vast sand. Who says they don't need to be polished anymore? Even the old ones, now diminished in their grandeur, need meaningful content: a sheltering umbrella, a heart-shaped pebble, or an optimistic rainbow.

I look for a message, a gift from the sea. The sea responds. She tosses out a beautiful rainbow. A long, wide, seven-colored rainbow. After a little serenading with the sea and the sky, it starts disintegrating from its root. Soon, its colors diminish from above and it vanishes into thin air.

I leave. We return to the sea at night, my daughter and I, to watch the International Space Station (I.S.S.) pass by at 21:35. We wave and yell, hoping Astronaut Scott Kelly will catch a glimpse of us.

The Shore Winds Down
day 3: august 17, 2015

Oh, the sea's perfume. Intoxicating. The mélange of life its splashes contain. To whom belongs the sea? We say to us. We find solace by her. The pebbles claim her as their own. They rest at sea, or so they believe. The seagulls assert their entitlement, gathering at the shore to prey, recollect, and reconvene with their others.

To whom belongs the swelling and ebbing of life? To whoever lays claim. They come and go, sit and leave, visit and forget. Such is life. And the sea, with its memorable perfume, presses on. The sun, tired of watching the same movie, retreats. It leaves my elongated shadow to plunge into the sea. The waves are pink now, still rising, receding, and fading away.

Surprise. The rainbow displays its wonderful cascade of colors again. Larger and whiter. Bang, slams the sea. Wake up. Listen to me. Hear me. The rainbow's beauty is overwhelming. Looks like it's here to stay. Bang, boom, explodes the sea. The waves ripple on their huge gray rolls and splash against me faster, now that the sun has set. But the shiny rainbow hinders the sea from exalting herself until it fades away entirely. And my shadow dissolves in the shade. Hawking seagulls come preying on the pebbles. Groups of humans leave the dark sea, all umbrellas closed, all beach chairs tucked in. Serenity rushes back to claim its place at the seafront. Serenity. Sincerity. You and me. All fading into the sea blues.

And the I.S.S. sighting at 22:17 is the cherry on top.

Seashore at Dusk
day 4: august 18, 2015

It's the same spot as yesterday. The same ripples. But are they? Staring into the perfect line where the turquoise sea meets the pink sky, you forget about the furious waters knocking at your door. The crushing sound is silenced for a while. A solitary wave slaps the pebbles. It exclaims, "Come back to me. I am here." You hear the sea crashing again. The tangy marine scent perforates your heart. The fullness of the wave fills up your mind. No more room for idle, negligible thoughts. The sea reclaims you.

This man is struggling to stand on his feet after swimming from the horizon to the shore. He cannot walk on the hidden pebbles. With one arm extended to the ever-present sky, as if grasping an invisible heavenly hand, he pushes himself up, and blocking the waves and the pebbles out, runs out of the shoreline.

That young mother lengthens their golden retriever's leash to let it out into the sea. Her happy child throws a pebble in the sea for their puppy to fetch. The golden follows mouth open, trying to retrieve it. Where is that pebble? Sniff. Sniff. They are all the same. A loud bang of the waves forces it to run back to the laughing owners, tail wagging. Doggy keeps up the adventure without giving up. Doggy cannot find the pebble. The sea swallowed it. They leave.

A reddish helicopter whirrs above. That tiny yacht on the horizon pierces the line uniting the sky with the sea. But the sea inhales and exhales. Swells and retreats. Often, it's calm, steady breathing. Then, as if stricken by anxiety, its breathing becomes faster, stronger, louder. So does your chest. But then, they all go home. The sea stays, serenading the shore, acting as if not to care.

What the Sea Sees
day 5: august 19, 2015

A hook fastened to the lit end of the fishing line hits the water. It wants to steal from the sea, but the sea refuses to reward. Each shot comes up worthless. She lights a cigarette. He does too. They take another try at the sea. Empty hooks. Now she eats a sandwich. He does too. They sit there at the edge, murmuring, wanting to try their luck again and again.

Behind these fishermen, a mother is teaching her daughter how to use a metal detector to hunt for lost treasures among the pebbles. She advises her to walk in a steady straight path and to just keep going forward. She gestures ahead as if instructing to not change course. She must return on a parallel path alongside the beach, and repeat, until she covers all parallel lines. The girl embarks on her treasure hunt, metal detector in hand, the mother nodding. She does not contemplate the pebbles themselves but seeks what's fallen and forgotten among them. She despairs. The pebbles hold on tight to their secret treasures, hoping to morph them into pebbles like themselves. What is she learning? Discovery? Laziness? Patient persistence? Picking up what others have left behind?

Some, sitting on their chaises, stargaze. They wait for a glimpse of the I.S.S. which will pass above here at 21:18, and to which the HTV5, launched today, will dock after orbiting for six days. A small white truck sells waffles, blasting Spanish dance songs amidst the flickering party lights. It does not distract the bungee jumping kids. And so it goes.

Conglomerates eat, drink, chatter, gossip, stare, fish, and then leave. No one stays.

Darkness falls. All leave. Once more, the sea embraces her solitude with the lonesome pebbles. She hits the shore over and over as if saying "Come back, don't leave us alone." Apart from her rage at the shore, all is calm. Peaceful. Empty.

Lights
day 6: august 20, 2015

The sea is calmer today, unlike what is within. But the within doesn't show. The symphony of the waves resonating within plays with the flickering lights. But nobody hears. Swish. Shshshshshsh. Question. Answer. Tktktktktk... the lazy pebbles chat in the meantime.

And these lights that flicker at sea, what are they? Who are they? Three tiny lights glow at the end of three fishing poles stuck up high at the edge lying in wait for a catch. The huge illuminated yacht far away at the horizon matches in size with the glow-in-the-dark fish baits at the shore. On the other side, city lights caress the dark side of the sea. And over there to the right, the green marina lights guide the night ships. Above them all, the moonlight drowns the sleepy pebbles. Feeble candles light up that loving family's picnic table. The airplane's guiding light emanates from underneath and extends gracefully to the shore wanting to compete with the moonlight. And the stars, those eternal lights of the soul, flicker overhead.

Each light helps someone, shows the way, dissipates fears of the night. Illuminates. Eliminates the darkness around. But how about the darkness within? Where to find the light to illuminate it? The answer: in Jesus. Jesus is the light that shines in the darkness and the darkness cannot extinguish it.[2] He said, *"You are the light of the world. So let your light shine before men, that they may see your good works, and glorify your Father who is in heaven."*[3] What a blessing it is to be the tiny guiding light for someone living in the darkness of despair.

Voices and Noises

day 7: august 21, 2015

As I promenade on the beach this gorgeous warm summer evening, I hear voices and noises that disappear as I pass one group onto the next. I walk by the colorful food-truck emitting Spanish dance-music and the aroma of fried fish, but then the noise of the speedboat and the smell of gasoline fill the air. Further ahead, the drums beat to the rhythm of acrobats with fire poles and they attract me, while the smell of sweat of the gathered people dispels my attraction. The cries of little children mix with fear of the dark deep sea. The little bungee-jumpers' screams jolt to the beat of rock music. Soon the brrrrrrr of another speedboat commands attention—to show off that it's pulling a huge yellow smiley air-balloon along with four shrieking dangling feet. And I stroll along the sand listening to these sounds approach and fade away. A conversation in Italian passes by: "una casa plus grandi non soldi." And the gentle touch of the tiny ripples escorts a jogger's heavy panting. The Russian yells at his child to walk close by, the thump of the tennis racket hits the ball, and that little dog barks wanting to plunge into the sea.

The noise in my head, the ringing in my ears, they walk with me too. They don't fade away, unlike all the others. What do I replace them with? And how? I approach the loud tune drumming from the loudspeaker, and it overrides the noises in my head. And while the white-dressed, handsome Jamaican man sings Bob Marley's "Stand by Me," the pleated skirt of the elegant dancer moves, along with our silhouettes.

The voices and noises of that summer evening at sea are still in my head. But the eternal splash of the sea masks them all.

Not Anymore

day 8: august 22, 2015

The waves crashing against these huge boulders are different: their course is deeper and longer. Men have placed huge boulders to protect the man-made pier from the constant attacks of the sea, and to protect the sea from man's intrusion. The boulders are stronger than all the pebbles on the other side of the pier. They have kept their sharp edges despite the smoothing of some tops. And I keep walking along my sea. That black swan captivates me. It's all alone among the five whites, blending in with the same motions and curves. But it stands out as the lonely one. The frail one. Although it is neither alone nor frail—for God protects that swan, because it is the only one not "conforming to the patterns of this world."[4]

As soon as I pass by, the light breeze caresses my face, plays with my hair, bringing me a taste of the salty sea. How calming it is to watch the small ripples morphing into a huge wave and crashing at the pebbles, jolting up my spirit with each cool crash. I have been battling sickness for almost nine months, and many of my so-called loved ones, instead of providing me with a loving, caring, nurturing environment, throw at me their eternal caprices while leading their own comfortable, pleasure-filled life. They still expect me to be there for them at their slightest demand. I remember the protective boulders I just passed by. Those solid boundaries.

And I think, "Not anymore."

Father and Child

day 9: august 23, 2015

Separated, yet united? United, yet separated? Renewal, Continuity, Infinity. Father walks along the shore holding his baby to his chest, her trusting head falling on his shoulder. He seems dedicated to make her feel secure and comfortable, and holds her head towards him, not intending to let go.

But until when? Will she grow up to be the representation of what he taught her? Will she appreciate his emotional and spiritual guidance? Will she be grateful? Will he be proud? Will she leave him for another life?

What does the father need to do? Maybe heed to this verse's advice: "Fathers, provoke not your children to anger, lest they be discouraged[5]... provoke not your children to wrath: but bring them up in the nurture and admonition of the Lord."[6]

United yet separated. Children of the sea. The sea of life. Children of life. Where do they come from? Where do they go? Where have they gone?

Stay child. Stay.

Summer's Crying

day 10: august 24, 2015

Shielded from the first rain behind the windshield of my car, I admire the family huddled under the huge twin umbrellas. They ignore the drizzle. Everybody else has disappeared. The sea is almost alone. Pebbles—alone, yet their thirst seems quenched. The sea looks anxious. Swelling and crushing its evening-sun kissed waves, she tries to reach farther on the shore than yesterday. The sun retracts its colors and paves the way for the downpour. The lifeless seashore succumbs to the crying heavens. That family continues to enjoy the rain. Their kids, playing. Their umbrellas are out, mismatched in their bathing suits. They now stand as if preparing to leave, but they don't. Standing and chatting, they let the rain drench them. They enjoy the feeling. That's courage. Unity. Bathing in the storms of life together. On the deserted pebble-istan. The frail summer umbrellas they are holding as shields do not protect them. Neither do the two twin huge beach umbrellas they are standing under. But they don't care. The source of their determination springs from the sea. The sea of love. From their faith that the heavens will clear soon. From their unity and harmony.

The sun peeks again. The rain diminishes. Rainbow. Hope. This is life. All sufferings pass. New horizons shine. "*Let not your hearts be troubled. Don't worry. Have faith,*"[7] said Jesus.

Do not cry, summer. The sun will shine once more. You will shine again.

The Enduring Pebbles

day 11: august 25, 2015

The pebbles look satisfied, soaked in the rainbow of yesterday's rain. They are the soul mate of the sea, standing by it for better or for worse. They endure the crashing, smashing, caressing, bashing, feeding, withholding, howling, chuckling, jolting, frigidity, warmth, and every other whim of the sea. Why do they stay? Have they become insensitive? Or have they learned the art of forgiving and forgetting? Have their hearts turned into stones? Or does their love of sea surpass all.

Why do people stay despite the constant bashing, railing, oppression, and criticism? Do they get used to it? Do they ever become desensitized? Do they lose self-respect and self-esteem? Or do some learn the art of forgiving and forgetting? Is forgiving the equivalent of enduring the constant bashing, accusing, and disrespect? Or should it come after the oppressor shows a deep sense of remorse, requests forgiveness, and discontinues the unacceptable behavior?

Jesus said, *"If your brother trespass against thee, rebuke him; and if he repents, forgive him. And if he trespasses against you seven times in a day, and seven times in a day turn again to thee, saying, I repent; thou shalt forgive him."[8]*

What if they don't repent? What if they don't ask for forgiveness?

Changing Colors and Shifting Shadows
day 12: august 26, 2015

Today, the feisty colors are back by the beach. The deep shades of green, blue, and aqua dance with the sparkling waves. Orange and white-sailed catamarans and red kayaks cross the waterfront. The bleu-blanc-rouge (blue-white-red) tailed airplane races with the white mama-seagull to the nearby airport. The pebbles have dried up. They look thirsty. Glaring at the sea, they maintain their eternal hospitality to the late tourists.

Tourists are back, some of them extra tanned, are still lying down on their vibrant beach towels, facing the sun at the correct angle to get the maximum dose of rays. The lighter-tanned ones, hiding behind their multi-shaped hats, display themselves under the colorful umbrellas. They are still hesitant to imbibe the late-August sun. Duos are floating at the shore. Few, gazing at the breezy waves, have gone blank losing their worries to the azure the sea that always listens.

And the sea keeps their secrets, even when colors and shadows change. Trust the sea. Can you trust family? Your best friend? Yes. No. Sometimes. Maybe. Do they change with the changing colors and shifting shadows? Sometimes they do. And it is disappointing and disheartening. But you know, Jesus doesn't—for He is the Father of "heavenly lights, who does not change like shifting shadows."[9] He said, *"Trust me."* Trust is not seasonal; it endures to eternity. He also said, *"If therefore, you have not been trustworthy in the worldly riches, who will trust you with the true riches of heaven?"*[10]

Today, resolve to not change with every caprice of the sea of life. Resolve to be trustworthy and trusting.

High on the Trampoline
day 13: august 27, 2015

A huge multicolor trampoline greets the visitors of the Mediterranean shore. It is enclosed and secured with intertwined knotted rope, almost invisible walls—for kids to jump in with both feet. The towering rope-walls limit the distance the kids can reach. Pretext of safety. Safety zone. Not many want to break out of it.

The kids of many ages and smiling faces spring up, arms and feet jerking into space, and shoot down. They stagger, they fall. The loud Latin music entices them. Again. Hop. Beat it. Dance. Bounce. Plunge.

The trampoline underneath welcomes them with open arms once more. Up and down. On the side. Ouch. Scream. One more time. Up again. Touch the sky. Giggle. Chuckle. Seize the chance. Fall on your face. Shedding tears. She is hurt. Unaware, the others continue jumping in that square bubble. Some hold hands and jump up high on this trampoline of life.

Isn't life an exotic journey on a huge trampoline by the sea? All are bouncing up and down, up and down. Few keep going. Others get tired and give up. Some, sitting on the sides, watch the high jumpers and gossip. The jumpers do not care. They soar past the towering imaginary walls. They focus on the game and on the prize: a certificate at the end. A certificate of conscious choice of a life well-lived, or a life unfinished. Which certificate will you receive?

The more forcibly you tap-dance on the trampoline, the higher you fly. You can reach the sky. You fall. You get up. Take turns on the trampoline. Time is limited. The fun-loving folks keep jumping and falling and laughing and screaming. Bouncing again. Enjoying life. The good thing about the round trampoline is that you don't need to stay in the same place. It takes you out of the mundane repetitive chores. There are no rules but one: you fall, you get up. You never stay down, or other jumpers will stomp on you. You will be crushed.

Get up now. Force yourself up. Look to the sky, arms stretched out. Jump higher and higher. There are no walls, no barriers. Reach out to God and grab his arm. He will not let you go.

Non Spaventare I Pesci (Don't Scare the Fish)

day 14: august 28, 2015

Sunset. The sea and the sky melt into fading hues. Humans have claimed their lots on the compact pebbles at the beach. A young family is dining on a makeshift table here, a group of friends cocktailing there; other sun-setters sitting alone, some lying on their beach towels and chatting, a couple serenading along the waves, and a few swimming along the beautiful calm shore.

Two tourists are fishing at this *pêche interdite* (fishing-forbidden) zone. Not minding the human crowd, they cast their long, baited fishing poles back and forth, only to angrily watch the empty end come back out again. These recreational anglers have been here for the past week. He swings his fishing rod and throws the long, baited line into the serene waters, reeling quickly to pay out the line as much as possible, in hopes for a good catch. Noticing that the hook, dressed in bait at the far end of the line, will hit the kids playing at shore, he, with his free hand and a stern face, motions to the parents to collect their kids. He wants his fishing space. In a no-fishing public beach. Wanting to avoid conflict, the parents get their kids, collect their beach bags, and leave.

My daughter carefully selects petite pebbles and throws them into the sea, watching how far they reach. She counts the ensuing ripples. She tries different styles of throwing, different trajectories. Arm swirling up. Swinging sideways. What is creating the most ripples? How can she reach far enough, have an impact long enough to get noticed? Suddenly, the fisherman screams in Italian, "Che fa? (What are you doing?)" She ignores.

He now yells in French, "Madame, madame, tu fais quoi?" (What are you doing?)

Surprised, she responds, "Je suis à la plage." (I am at the beach.)

He raises his voice, "Pourquoi vous jetez les pierres dans l'eau?" (Why are you throwing pebbles?) "Jetez pas, non spaventare i pesci." (Don't throw them, you're scaring the fish.)

"C'est une plage publique, Monsieur, et c'est interdit de pêcher ici," calmly responds my smart girl. (It's a public beach, Sir, and it is forbidden to fish here.) He leaves.

He doesn't have bigger fish to fry. Fishing at a no-fishing zone, stabbing the fish with his baited hook, and yet turning around and yelling "don't scare the fish." Ironic. The fish are already scared to get caught on the hook by their throats, to gasp for breath twisting from side to side, to be hooked out of the water, to suffocate to death.

She had a tiny pebble. But he had a hook. Her small pebble belonged to the calm sea and the roaming fish. His sharp-pointed hook was fabricated to trick and kill. He intended to trick and catch the fish. But she saved them. She didn't know the small ripples caused by her pebbles would trouble the fishing waters, would anger the fishermen, would scare the fish away from the fishing pole, and thus save the fish.

Dance with Me

day 15: august 29, 2015

It's after the blue hour. The super moon is flirting—"Dance with me." The golden sparkling trail forms for me to walk to the moon. SHSH. Shshshshshshshsh, wooooooshshshsh. The rippling wavelets lure me to get up and walk ahead. Golden moonlight passes through and flickers at my feet, coaxing my spirit. Golden opportunity. Where I'm going, it's magical.

"Take my hand and tiptoe to me. For you, I sprinkled gold glitter on the sea. Take the first step. Don't be shy. Don't be afraid. Ballet and sway, soon you will reach the end of the gold sprinkled path, and when you do, jump high and touch me. Why are you sitting so far away only contemplating? Get up. Move towards me. Aim high."

I hesitate. The glittering starlets of the moon come closer and caress my feet which are extended on the pebbles and barely touching the sea. Where do I go from here? I step forward. But the further I go, the more the super moon rises. The more it rises, the more it loses its luster.

The masquerade ends. Lights are out. The golden glitter trail disappears into the darkness. The super moon casts her long white robe instead. But the distant tambourine's shkshk shkshk rhythm that I hear entices the sparkling ripples to keep dancing at my feet. And I dance with them. I will always dance.

Le Lever du Soleil—the Rising of the Sun

day 16: august 30, 2015

Not just sunrise. The French call it the Rising of the Sun. It's a glamorous phenomenon here, at 6:49 a.m. The first reddish tones of light break out. Sacred twilight. Time for spiritual worship, meditation, prayers, and rituals. The sea and the sky are on high alert. Anticipating the rising of the sun, grand preparations are underway. Only the sky and the sea are working because it is still too early on this beautiful Sunday morning for humans. They are painting a fanfare of reddish colors fusing them all into themselves and each other. The sky withdraws its blue hue, while the sea hides its green, thus leaving the pink, the orange, and the red to showcase the way for the rising sun. 6:52 a.m. The silent trumpets blaze, lighting up the horizon, and the sun peeks at the east.

It is the Rising of the Sun.

In its entire splendor, is the sun truly rising? Or, is it only a glitzy illusion?

Who is the illusionist? Is it the Earth? Stationed between the sun and the moon, our dear Earth flirts with both, worshipping the sun yet serenading the moon. Competition. Rivalry. Teamwork.

The glowing orange rays of the sun extend and arrive to rest at my feet. The golden rippling trail touches the shore, where the seagull trumps, and announces, "Come; arise with me, at the splendor of bliss."

To the west, the parting moon, the paramour leaves behind a final glance. So sad, its face. Is the pale moon really parting? Or, is it yet another illusion?

Why Mosquito?

day 17: august 31, 2015

When all around is beauty and calmness untroubled, why the sudden sting of betrayal? Or does Mosquito think it has impressed a kiss? *Judas.*

The sea is calm with the yesterday's vacationers now tucked away in their homes, offices, schools, and other boxes men have created for themselves. No sound chimes with the tired waves. Even the silence does not want to talk. The lazy pebbles long for the gentle touch of yesterday's humans. No chaise-lounges, no colorful towels, no vibrant umbrellas. The appetizing mixed aroma of pizzas and kebabs has dissipated into the horizon. The huge transparent trash bags hang empty in their blue receptacles. Seagulls scream at each other. No one feeds them now. No one on whom the opportunistic mosquito can suckle, except for the unsuspecting prey.

Why not leave her alone, mosquito? You do not know her. She is not of your ranks. Did you think your vain humming and buzzing, and your sting's itchy red swelling would cause her anguish and heartbreak? No. You are just a temporary disturbance. You too shall pass; shall be forgotten. Your prey for now will never again be preyed upon. She will rebound from your deceptive stingy kiss. With more vigor. More determination.

Be gone, mosquito. Gone with the warm winds of summer.

La Rentrée

day 18: september 1, 2015

Belated tourists gasp to catch the last glimpse of the fleeting summer. The gloomy sky, the flat sea, the unscented raindrops, the empty beach—save for a blue beach-bag, the silent atmosphere, the stony bare pebbles, the bland unflavored breeze, and the uniform pale color palette all conspire to paint the first picture of La Rentrée.[11] Yesterday's summer playground has been dismantled, packed, and ready to migrate, just like the migrant tourists and the real migrants—all of us are migrants here—to warmer more peaceful grounds.

Life has been ferried away from the sea. The first photo of the early rentrée morning looks different there. Solemn school buses with small sleepy heads dotting their sparkling clean windows. Kids weighed down under their dark backpacks. The colorful summer beach bags are absent. Look-alike cars rush to be on time. Humans are busy. The human longing for the sea overshadows her stimulating transformation. She develops an eager patience, waiting for her children while she nourishes and nurtures the left behind. La rentrée used to mean something for them too. Now, they just watch the transformation of the sea. They watch the Poste de Secours (security post) removing its safety notices from the shore and getting ready to leave, reasoning that the left-behind don't need help. Lone humans are now scattered at the shore. Some bathe in their speedos, then change back into their clothes, right there at the beach, thinking they have earned that right. This entitlement of theirs.

"Il n'y a personne! Pas beau ça?" (There's no one, isn't it beautiful?) I hear a lonely passerby exclaim. I tend to think that way. He is rushing as if he has plans for the rentrée. I too had made plans for the previous rentrée, but soon learned that God had a different plan for me. I don't plan for this one.

Jade

day 19: september 2, 2015

The sea of Jade. True inspiration reinforcing faith in God appears from unexpected encounters. Jade. Sincere. Deep Jade. Holding beauty, integrity, and candor inside. I don't know if Jade loves the sea. She passes by it every morning and evening. Does she ever notice it? She loves the sea's jade color which is reflected in her thoughtful eyes.

She says jade invigorates her. It brings life into her surroundings. Jade thrills her soul. But Jade had been blue, and had turned to God, to her "Seigneur, Dieu tout puissant" (Lord, God Almighty). She has a direct relationship with God. She has removed the intermediaries. She asks anything of Him, with full trust, and precision. And God offers it in abundance. Just entrust her your worry, and she will abandon it to the Dieu-Tout-Puissant, assuring you He will take care of it. You must believe, just as she does. She recommends you write exactly what you want from God on a piece of paper—describing it in names, nouns, adjectives, in colors and shapes—and to trust Him, and you will receive it. There should be no doubt in your heart. I asked that she pray for me too. She said, she will, and we started our dinner with Jade's one-word-prayer before meals—Bismillah (In God's Name).

Besides her work, Jade swims in a sea of creative talents: painting, singing, dancing, choreography, acting, sewing, sowing, and creating all that is beautiful. She creates friendships too. Only trusted ones. She has had her own share of life's beatings but as strong as she is, she keeps her head up, with a sweet smile reinforcing the dimples of her cheeks, and she presses forward. She would encourage you to do the same. Her preferred shades of jades, blues, Earth tones, and wood emerge in her unique artisan creations. She also loves animated movies, afternoon tea, and old roses. Believing in the laws of attraction, she sends out positive thoughts attracting the positive. She gets results, she says. What a blessing to have a sincere friend like Jade—my Friend.

Nothing

day 20: september 3, 2015

The sea reflects nothing today. Nothing. It does nothing today that it didn't do yesterday. What to reflect about today? Nothing. Nothing to reflect about, nothing to write. How calm. Lacking nothing. Needing nothing. Nothing to think about. Nothing to worry about. Nothing to do. Nothing to miss. Nothing to hurt. And nothing to love.

Nothingness. Silence. But, the dawn's early waves bounce, and the first birds take wing.

Nothing is the beginning of something, of everything. The intriguing eternal circle must be drawn and completed. Does nothing come first? Is there something before nothing? "First, there was the Word. And the word was with God. The Word was God."[12] How powerful. Incomprehensible. Yet existing. We exist.

Where did we come from? From nothing. From something. But what?

Celebrate the nothing. Tiny rays sprout from nothing. Shiny golden rays of the sun sprinkle once more their enchanting golden powder on the wetted pebbles. Early morning sunrise.

Coffee at the seaside. The morning sea breeze caresses my nothingness relentlessly. The charisma of nothing grows wings and flies. And all life blossoms again, mirrored in the sea. This is the life.

Swept Away

day 21: september 4, 2015

Sea, did you see that little boy? Drowned in your hugs. Swept away. Did you hold him for long? He looked for a new life beyond your horizons that he could see. His dream life was a short boat-trip away, just across the deep, dark, stormy sea. So close, and yet so far. Wouldn't he have loved to splash, giggle, and enjoy himself floating on your shores, dressed in his red-blue bathing suit and puffy arm floats? Yes, he floated. For his life. Did you see the solitude of his face? His face immersed in your salty pebbles drenched in the downpour of his tears. The loneliness of his little body. The chill of his tiny blue fingers clutching at your parting waves. The privacy of his broken baby heart is not imprinted in your heart forever. How you snatched him away from life. His dream life. The tribulations of his life. The passing migrant life. And yet you forever permit so many cheerful wandering migrant travelers pass by your dreamy shores.

Rest little boy, sweet Alan Kurdi. Rest in peace. Little Syrian refugee boy in red shirt and blue shorts and tiny shoes. You are in God's loving arms now. God is gathering His elect. It is written, "And he shall send his angels with a great sound of a trumpet, and they shall gather together his elect from the four winds, from one end of heaven to the other."[13]

You, elect boy, you found your new life beyond the sea. Your brother, too. And your mother too. Peace.

Oblivion

day 22: september 5, 2015

What a wonderful blue-framed canvas of pebbles dotted with sporadic umbrellas. Some sea gazers are back resting at your sunny, breezy shore. Tardy, wandering travelers have thrown themselves, their sparkling beach towels, and their filled beach bags on your side. Some swim, some float, some read, some eat, some relax. Oh sea, did you tell them your secret? Do they know about that little boy in the red shirt and blue shorts who was sleeping at your shores? They don't seem to know. Oblivion. They bake in the chilly silver sun in their red and blue bathing suits. Not to catch cold, some wear light jackets. He was not wearing a life jacket. He was cold. He did not have a floating device. Not for sea. Not for life. He was too young to learn to float in the turbulent waters of the vast sea of life.

And the passing tourists relax by you, sea. Aren't your tourists passing migrants staying at welcoming hotels at your shores? Aren't we all fleeting traveling migrants finding momentary abode here on Mother Earth? Wasn't he just another traveling migrant, passing to find a home beyond your shore? The little boy. Nobody wanted him. But his gloomy washed-up reflection—everyone wants. Now they need his image. Now they have heard his silent sobs. Muted cries. Shut-down heart.

He returned home. The Son of Man performing miracles at the Sea of Galilee elected him. He told the boy, *Today you shall be with me in Paradise.*[14] The Son of Man wanted him. You did not want him, sea. You washed him ashore. He is now famous. The little boy— Alan Kurdi. Out of oblivion.

Message from the Future
day 23: september 6, 2015

Tonight the calm sea hides her rolling waves that dare to reach and touch my shoes and recede quickly while splashing a dash of marine mist onto my face. I can't decide if I like the smell or if it's putrid. My agitated soul tries to avert it. My sea, are you anxious because you are enclosed in this small bay flickering in the dark? Or is your soul disturbed? But listen. There, he's playing the trumpet to cheer you up, to cheer all night sea-goers up. That is why they are here at night. Right? Listen to the victorious tunes of the graduation march "Pomp and Circumstance" elating the spirits.

Daaaa da dadaada dadadaadaaa dada—emits the golden trumpet shining in the evening light. Then you notice the message bearer, this one-man impromptu marching band beats with the assertive, joyful triumphal music of the trumpet, and the sea waves clap the cymbals, and shk-shk shake the rolling pebbles. He's celebrating something. Triumph. Victory. Joy. Inviting everybody to celebrate with him, but nobody participates.

Except me. Secretly, my heart jolts with old memories of graduations past—and I don't know why it's reminiscent of graduations. He marches on to the next set of pebbles, trumpeting the Triumphal March. I too march along, smashing the pebbles. Drumming my footsteps. Right. Left. Right. Right. Left. Daaaadadadaadaaaa—hoping for an imminent triumph through this message from the future.

The Rhythm

day 24: september 7, 2015

One of the last long Mondays of summer. While the sea lullabies its entourage with her charm, the world rotates in its usual frenzy. Anxious students are attending school hoping to move a day closer to achieving their dreams. Offices spitting out papers, decisions, indecisions, speeches, presentations, social media, and press releases. People rotating and rotating. Migrant families finding homes, or not. Migrant souls finding rest, or not. Politicians politicizing. Wars continuing. Laughing folks, crying souls, sick bodies, numb mortals, smiling faces. Some loving, others hating. Surviving. Adapting. Believing. Pressing forward. Even controlling the movements of an earthling Dutch robot from space. Different strokes, same rhythm.

And across from you, my cold sea, the cozy Les Foires de Vins, the year's wine harvest, exhibited in the market, marks the imminent arrival of autumn, winter following. Red, Rosé, Blanc, sparkling, bubbling, sweet, sec, demi-sec, brut. Locals are stock piling their cave-à-vins (wine cellars) for the winter and beyond. They need the warmth. The oomph. The happiness. The love. Hibernating. Same rhythm, different folks.

My evening sea, sitting by you I hear the rhythm of the Cagnes promenade darbouka belly-dancing: ddddb ddb db ddb ddb db tktktktktktk db ddb db ddb.

And your orchestra accompanying: shsh shsh Splash. Shsh shsh Splash! Shshshsh Crash! Splash! Ddb ddb db ddb ddb db … tkt tkt tkt tkt tkt tkt … Splashshsh.

Vroom! Db ddbdb dbdb db ddbdb dbdb … The rhythm entices you to dance to the beat. Move. Shake. Sway. Dance away. Come on you all: Shake it, move it, laugh, take a chance, dance with the rhythm. Let it flow.

What is life, but rhythms. What is the sea, but rhythms.

The River

day 25, september 8, 2015

Calm, serene, and drifting at this end, but raging, cascading, and deluging at the other. The river. At which end is the mother sea, I don't know. The slinky, sleekly, greenish, clear river is rushing to reach somewhere. Is it the sea? Or is the river gushing away from her. Its romantic watercourse is deceptive. Eyes cannot see. The river is moving, flouting and floating. The fluttering ripples swing right, and then swing left, without divulging their course. But they wash away the first yellowish orange leaves of autumn. "Les Feuilles Mortes" sings Yves Montand in my earphones., leaving Edith Piaf's "La Vie en Rose" behind into the fading pink summer nights.

Ripples of laughter from the nearby preschool fill the air with pleasant sonatas. Unseen birds chirp at their giggles. The ducklings and young doves seem content here, unlike their older relatives at the mother sea. Yellow and purple flowers, green leaved trees, and long and furry vegetation adorn the riverside. The yellowish orange autumn leaves are leaving with the river anyway. Life appears different at the river away from the mother sea. For all that, it is shallow, the river. Twigs, branches, moss, and other treasured things which were once needed, rest at its bed. It collects some, discards some, flaunting what it keeps at the river-scape.

Is the river a reflection of the sea? It gathers the reflections of all it encounters on its path of life. Green, blue, yellow. Good, gorgeous, and ugly. The inanimate and the living. Don't know if they are just to reflect or for keepsake. It changes course, changes colors. But always keeps going to its mother sea. Rippling and drifting at its inception, the river rushes and storms at its end to mother sea to find refuge melting into her vast blue tender embrace.

And today is Mother Mary's birthday. Happy birthday to all born on this blessed day.

Faraway

day 26: september 9, 2015

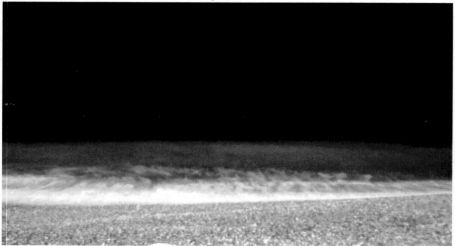

My beloved sea, beyond you, on the other side, I see the faraway. Far, faraway. At least that's how far it looks sensing how you are not able to reflect their lights. Chasing after their colorful lights in the distance. But your other side is the mirror of here, right? Its reflection is in your soul.

How to reach that far? Is it brighter there? Happier?

How are they doing? Do they miss those of us on this side of the faraway? The night's windy waves are trying to say something, but the words are muffled. These murky waves overwhelm my shivering soul. Maybe they could stir up and stretch out their silvery path to the other side. Build a lasting bridge. Then the faraway can come closer. Can reach out.

But who shall reach out to whom? Over your starless vast distance. To try? Or, to leave untroubled the waters and ripples of your surface—if they are happy, in the faraway.

The Girl with the Tripod
day 27: september 10, 2015

This is never a dull moment at the sea for the girl with the tripod. She says she has learned from her friend the mother sea. Calm, yet ferocious, sweet but serious, kindhearted and smart, discretely omnipresent, caring and caressing, ever-available, non-grumbling, the girl with the tripod and her mother sea. She comes by the sea every sunrise, and if not, every moonrise. Her tripod on her shoulder, she leaves the boardwalk, passes through the carpet of pebbles to reach the front seat. With each step the pebbles unite in drumming the cha-cha-cha. The mysterious waves cast their silver sprinkles towards her and lure her to the shore. She exudes honesty, love, security. One can trust her. Confide in her. The serious smile on her face says so.

She captures the reflections of the sea. She loves the sea. And the sea loves her. At the twilights of sunrise, the sea puts on her best suited, red, orange, yellow, blue, aqua vestments getting ready for the photo-shoot. Life bursts at the sea to impress the glimpse of the moment captured on her camera. Birds of the sky open wide their elegant wings; puppies of the shore jump on their excited *pattes*; tall green palm trees lighten up; human faces brighten in hopes of reflecting their momentary joy in her camera. When the lights dim, the sea shows off her twinkling colorful reflections: starry spots, trailing lights, images mysterious, stories dark, tilting and shifting at the caprice of the waves, but always attached to the skyline's root.

She has a heart that can understand, a soul that can embrace, an ear that can hear, an eye that can see. Everything. Determined, she immerses her tripod on short legs into the pebbles, she moves the camera around and captures the ever-present reflections of the sea-sky scape. She captures life. She wants to reach the twinkling stars, the shining moons, the depths of the seas and the hearts, and the space station in the skies above our sky. She will. The sea will see to that.

Shadows

day 28: september 11, 2015

Who are they? What do they reflect? They are always dark. The dark side cast to the ground. The sea does not reflect the dark, only light and color. Have you ever seen a colorful shadow? No, rather, they are the passing darkness of the soul, as they absorb the light. The dark shadows within. They are afraid of the light.

The Light. When hit by light, they are exposed—casting their long or short silhouettes, depending on how much light they are in. But they teach something. These momentary shadows do not reflect the true soul. Soul is natural light. Soul is a candle, and the candle gives light in the darkness. These dark shadows sometimes haunt, but the light casts the shadow out. If there was no Light, Jesus being the true Light, we wouldn't have known we have a shadow—a dark side. Shadows shift with the light. Long and short, sitting and up, sideways and sleeping. The more the light is at an angle, the longer the shadow. The shadow is the darkest when the light is closer, as if afraid, it shows off its final dark oomph. But if the light shines right above you, the shadow is under your feet. You are in a No Shadow Zone. You are in light.

If we let ourselves be guided by the Light, all darkness will be cast under our feet and into the ground. Light outside us, and we emit constant dark shadows, however, if the Light is inside us, no dark shadows will be cast out. And we will dwell in the Light. We will emanate light.

The Accordionist of Antibes
day 29: september 12, 2015

The accordionist plays at the seaside café-trottoir. The poker-faced hungry diners enjoy the gratuitous tunes accompanying their savory pissaladiere[15] with rosé-de-provence, or loup[16] fish with sauvignon-blanc. Yet, nobody dares to make eye contact with him so as to avoid placing a few coins in his crimpled beret lying in the accordion case on the ground. It is a mastered art to keep eating and chatting as if no music is being played, heard or enjoyed.

He maneuvers the accordion, cajoling its folding and unfolding pleats to emanate the "Oh how we danced, on the night that we wed…" The easel of the "Les amoureux aux remparts" ("The lovers at the ramparts") by the artist Raymond Peymet, on the promenade, may well be the source of his inspiration. Daadadaratadadaaa. It ends.

Nobody reacts. Nobody applauds. He invisibly strolls around the crowded tables hoping for the clinks of euros landing in his beret—now in his extended hand. One believer in that song drops in appreciative coins. Another diner, capturing that gesture with the corner of his eye, and wanting to continue the exhibition, gets up and puts something in the beret. Now a third one displays the same showing off. The accordion effect.

Were they happy with the song? Satisfied with their relationships? Humoring the accordionist? Or were they plain poseurs? May be some of them are newlyweds. Or celebrating their anniversaries, or the lack thereof. They did not clap once when the song finished. Nor did they place something in the beret when he passed behind their backs in total silence.

After his solo tour, he packs his coin-filled beret and accordion and walks through the boat lined seaside alleys of charming Antibes toward the blue breezy wavy beach. I wonder if he knows that he made someone happy, or another one sad; created the mixed feelings of nostalgia and indifference in them. But he is satisfied with his collect.

Last Year's Christmas Tree

day 30: september 13, 2015

The calm after the storm at Villeneuve plage. I arrive here after praying at the Saint Pierre Church on Cagnes' promenade. When I was at the exit of the church's parking lot, I tried to pay for my parking ticket at the automated cashier, but it said payment was annulled. And it did not want my payment. I had paid my dues. The bar-gate opened by itself and let me out of the church parking. My prayers were heard.

Arriving at the shore a great calm enters my heart. It sounds cliché but calm does indeed reign after the storm. All storms end in calmness and peace. There's no other way. And while the sea's bubbled edges are still unsettled, the remote horizon of the unknown future keeps its composure. And the serene horizon sends the young waves out to shore to get beaten up and toughen up. They always return to be mélanged with the deep. Or else how are they going to learn?

Something interrupts my reflections. An old Christmas tree devoid of its decorations, washed up at the shore, sitting upright, as if waiting, stares at me. It has landed right at the spot where we usually sit. This beautiful old emotional icon kept its root and branches, but lost its green leaves to the salty dark waters for eight to nine months. Now it's ready to bloom again for December to welcome the King to be born to this sad lost world. Call me superstitious or call me a believer—my prayers were answered today.

The Name of Your Soul

day 31: september 14, 2015

He is the alphabet man sitting at the Antibes port. He is aesthetically crafted with huge white letters overlapping each other. He seems well versed and poised. He does not talk. Just keeps staring at the sea—his back turned to the vibrant port.

Le Nomade, by Jaume Plensa. He must be traveling, migrating, wandering about, drifting, and yet he sits. His knees bent up hugged within his arms, his wide shoulders relaxed, his white head up, he sits in silence. And he welcomes the travelers and drifters of this world in his exquisite charming alphabet shell. For all the alphabet and knowledge he exudes, he is hollow inside. Hollow heart, hollow brain. Blank face. Charming yet empty. Fueling the imagination, yet void. Just an illusion. Illusionist. The nomads don't see that. They go in. Sit there. Photograph themselves from the inside with his hollow alphabet. They get to peek at the sea from inside the letters. The letters are hollow too.

What does he reflect upon by the sea? He watches the expensive yachts and pleasure boats go by. He allows all to touch him, caress him, tell him their stories. In return, they admire him, warm him up for a few minutes and leave. Does he dream of going away? Is he content sitting there by the sea and contemplating in silence while all his family members[17] are scattered in the different ends of the world? Is he waiting for their return? Or is he a spiritual nomad who has left his hollow physique here, but his mind and soul freely roam? Is his soul a wandering pilgrim waiting to reach his sacred destination?

And it dawns on me: I have found my soul's name—Pilgrim. My body might be roaming the earth, confined to its artificial limits, but my soul is free, the Pilgrim in me is free to journey towards her sacred destination.

How about you? What is the name of Your soul? Have you named it yet?

Me Too
day 32: september 15, 2015

I want to be one of you. I cannot fly but I can swim too.

SPLASH. BOOM. Feel the warm spirit and the friendly aura of this golden furry friend who jumped into the sea from the boardwalk. The scattered geese, swans, and their babies startled at first, start heading his way. They are surprised to see this huge gold hearted furry fellow stir up their waters.

He is man's best friend, but he wants friends of his kind too. He sees the wild geese, followed by their petites flying right into the azure. So, he jumps in. Me too... Me too... He silently cries in joy. His actions show it. He wouldn't talk back. Wouldn't slander them. Wouldn't talk behind their backs. Would fetch them food. Would protect them from predators. Would lick their wounds. Would swim them to calmer shores if needed. The perfect friend.

The feathered bunch is skeptical. They stay far away. Would he be one of them? Does he have to be? He is different, but the same.

The sea—she welcomes everyone. Holds anything.

The Lutrins of La Cote d'Azur

day 33: september 16, 2015

The artists of romantic yesterdays who lived by the sea—they loved her so much that they transferred her on their canvases, immortalizing her. Now, in turn, the sea immortalizes them. It's a circle. Nothing perishes. It just gets transformed into a different matter or era.

Oftentimes, even if the physical is gone, the soul stays, and the memory lives on. Appreciative locals render homage to these artists of yesterday. They have raised lutrins (meaning easels) all along the Cote d'Azur. All in all, 90 of them, each located at the vantage point of the artist from where he painted the sea, and the life at her shores. It's unsettling to see that unrefined humans have already defaced these lutrins. These two in the photo above are by Claude Monet. Why not appreciate their beauty? The offering? Why destroy, scratch, damage, defile. Is it jealousy, boredom, or complete lack of cultural and moral values?

What have we become, dear sea? You do not destroy but preserve. You're the source of inspiration of great artists who lived here, right by you: Picasso, Monet, Renoir, Matisse, Soutine, Chagall, Cocteau, and others. And now proud of the richness of their heritage, you showcase their famous works, mounted on easels, dotting your promenades. If we cannot create our own heritage for future generations to enjoy, then let's at least appreciate, preserve, and immortalize the art of those who can.

The Tsunami
day 34: september 17, 2015

Today's Chile earthquake is followed by tsunami warnings and evacuations at different shores devastating the world. They say the killer high waves travel unnoticed in the deep oceans to strike the unsuspecting faraway habitats.

But here you appear to be calm, my lovely sea, dark but calm. You are serene, somber this morning, yet calm. The skies and the sun have conspired to overshadow your inside turmoil, the unspoken tsunami within. With its puffed dark clouds, the sky veils the sun, and she in turn tries to withhold her bright happy rays from you, but allowing its silver rays of hope to rest on your chest.

A cruel trigger on one end of the earth would propel its angry killer waves in the distant horizons to slam the other side. To gain what? Devastation and destruction, uprooting homes, habitats, animalia, hearts and souls. But you, my overwhelmed sea, the reflection of my soul, you are not allowing that to affect you. You are patient. You stay calm. You ignore and shun the catastrophic disturbance. You wait.

You think: "This too shall pass."

And it surely does.

To Forgive and to Forget

day 35: september 18, 2015

How soon you forgive, forget, and rebuild after the frantic storm passes. How you obey God's preordained laws without questioning. You continue pressing forward at peace as if you were not hit by the tempest. If the sea can do it, why can't we? Forgive, forget, and forbid another creature's mood to deteriorate ours, or their wrongdoing to deflect us from our rails.

Why obey the ever-changing laws and moods of creatures when the laws of our Creator, the highest power, endure forever? Why waste this one precious life distressing and fretting over a creature's storms when we could just forgive and forget—or perhaps just ignore—and keep walking towards our Creator?

Today, let us resolve to imitate the sea, to keep walking forward on the path of our life, undistracted, making the best use of our talents, perhaps forgiving, but forbidding the actions of others to throw us off-track.

We must keep our steps steady, traveling on the Creator's path.

Patrimoine: Heritage
day 36: september 19, 2015

Today and tomorrow will mark the European heritage days. Many wonderful museums, off-public artists' homes, secret castles, cathedrals, synagogues, perfumeries, perched villages, and other unique cultural sites freely open their doors, so the visitors enjoy the richness of their heritage handed down to them from ancient generations.

Two days are not enough to even take a hasty look into this lane of heritage riches. And as you hurry through Renoir's home in Cagnes-Sur-Mer to Picasso's in Antibes, in an effort to not miss anything, the eternal sea runs along with you. Is she part of our heritage? She is handed down to us from generations. But we neglect to take care of this precious inheritance from Mother Nature. See how the storm few days ago had washed ashore plastic bottles, cups, diapers, twigs and branches, balls and other indescribable items which should not be thrown at sea.

This sea that has inspired Picasso, Monet, Chagall, Matisse, Renoir, Soutine, Cocteau and so many more, has helped civilizations thrive for thousands of years. It's our duty to hand her down, in her purest, natural form, so that future generations appreciate, celebrate, and hand down the richness of their heritage as well.

Summertime's Last Sunday

day 37: september 20, 2015

Dear sea, what remains? What remains of those colorful summertime days?

Not long ago, passionate lovers were whispering in long hugs and sweet kisses at your warm shores. Their future children were playing in your welcoming tender summer waters. Their aging parents, hand-in-hand, in the same scheme of clothes, were walking at your ever-young shores. Tell me what remains of those beautiful care-free days.

And my mind sings along with the renowned Charles Trenet, humming his "Que reste-t-il de nos amours, ..." (What remains of our loves, of those beautiful days ... a photo ... an old photo ... of my youth ...).

And I decide to enjoy each day. To be happy for each day that is offered to me. After all, my friend, what remains of our days past? Only that fuzzy feeling of love, engraved in a memorable photo.

Go ahead—live, be happy.

The Balcony Bars

day 38: september 21, 2015

The view is breathtaking.

The sea salutes. Its blue horizon aligns exactly with the black horizontal metal bar topping and holding the balcony rails. Looking through the black bars, you see the free crisp air, the green shaded pine tree crowns, the red rooftops, and some modern apartment buildings fill this picturesque side of the blue Mediterranean. But you cannot move past the bars. They imprison the soul and decorate it with everlasting beauty, so the entrapment is not felt. Like a protective glaze over the trap. This cage.

Above the horizontal metal bar, the sky is the limit. Perfectly attached to the sea at the eternal horizon they share. There, the soul is free. Free, to glide with the soaring birds of autumn. To explore new horizons. Fly past this one. Nothing holds you back. No protective glaze covers up your life.

Finishing my writing, I get up. And the balcony's black bars disappear. They are no longer important. Negligible. The vast beauty opens up.

It is a matter of how you look at it. Your point of view. Change it, and you will change your horizons. You will be able to see new horizons beyond the cage.

Let Not Your Ship Sink

day 39: september 22, 2015

I read somewhere that "an entire sea of water cannot sink a ship unless it gets inside the ship."[18] Likewise, the negativity of the world cannot put you down unless you allow it to get to you.

So calm is the sea while it entertains different types of vessels: cruise-ships, yachts, private boats, speedboats, catamarans, sailboats, and of course, swimmers. All are able to traverse the shallow and the deep waters without any difficulty. They row their boats merrily down the sparkling waters.

The last day of summer is still engaging the sea lovers in Monaco. Today is the classic yacht show. None if these yachts allow the sea to enter in. They are well prepared to fend off the waters—well guarded outside with sturdy walls, and their inside too is calm, serene, confident. The jolts of the waves don't change the mood or the course of the vessel. The small rudder controls the path the ship will maneuver if it encounters high waves. Otherwise, it sails in tranquility.

Let my little-complex-rudder-brain guide me through the rough seas. Let not water get in my ship. Let not my ship sink. "Show me the path I should go O Lord."[19] All outside chatter and negativity stop at Your doors.

Keep. Head. Up.
day 40: september 23, 2015

It's the first day of Autumn 2015. It brought with it the mistral that blows everything around, especially the huge surface of the sea. The shiny Mediterranean waves glide with the looming wind's direction to keep themselves from sinking. They keep their head up. Andy Grammar's song "You Gotta Keep Your Head Up" starts playing in my mind.

Gotta keep your head up and ride the mighty waves of life. Head down, you will sink and drift away by the wishy-washy winds.

Keep your head up. And live. Look around for the first beautiful yellowish red autumn leaf that will drift from the sky into your path. The sign of newer things to come along. Old things have passed. As Saint Paul wrote: "If any man is in Christ, he is a new creature: old things have passed, and all things have become new."[20]

Keep. Head. Up.

It is your choice. Make it now and never look back.

The Lighthouse
day 41: september 24, 2015

The Lighthouse at the sea. The guiding light. Guiding the ship of the sea to safe harbor.

Pope Francis gave his historical first speech to the U.S. congress today, via social media channels to those willing to hear, guiding the lost sheep of the sea of life to the safe harbor of God. He was trying to reestablish faith, dialogue, compassion, acceptance, fraternity, mercy, charity, peace, and love in our hearts.

The Light, Jesus' Light, is always there; in the darkness. It shines. Guides. All those who are willing to allow themselves to be guided by it, see it. Others walk in the dark and believe they are on top of the world. But he who walks in the dark does not know where he is going.[21] In the dark. Alone, with material possessions. Without God.

Oh, wouldn't it be wonderful to let our souls be guided by the Light of our only lighthouse: Jesus Christ? That Light that shines in the darkness, and the darkness doesn't comprehend it?[22] To be guided by the Light and to live in such a righteous way that we eventually land at the safe harbors of the Kingdom of Heaven?

Bread, at the Boulangerie by the Sea
day 42: september 25, 2015

To catch the royal sunrise on the Mediterranean this early dawn, I stroll along the shore and arrive at the boulangerie next to the Saint Pierre Church.

Baguette, banette, restaurant, fourné de provence, ficelle, grand viennois, petit viennois, pain de mie, tradition, Viking, céréales, boule blanche, petit-campagne, gros champagne, complet … Unable to decide on my choice of bread amidst this flamboyant list, I place my order: "Le formule #2 s'il vous plait—un café long avec de viennoiseries."[23] And I extend my credit card. Forming a smile across her rosy cheeks, she responds, "Not for small amounts." She points to the right informing me the location of a money distributor at the corner. I proceed to leave. She says, "Mais non, sit please, drink your hot coffee, enjoy your warm breakfast, then you go get the money." And she hands me my breakfast tray, its delightful painting of the Cote d'Azur beaches covered with my coffee and small pastry varieties.

The sweet aroma of my collection of pain-au-chocolat, croissant, and pain-au-raisin, mixed with the awakening scent of the dense espresso, plays with my senses. And whispering to myself: "Where else would I encounter such hospitality: 'enjoy your warm breakfast first, mind the payment later,'" I give thanks for my life events that enabled such opportunities. And my brain reminds me that I "shall not live on bread alone,"[24] that Jesus is the bread of life, for He had said, *"Whoever comes to me will never go hungry, and whoever believes in me will never be thirsty."*[25]

Wedding by the Sea

day 43: september 26, 2015

What a beautiful day to get married. The picture-perfect day: the slow breeze, the still trailing summer effects, the deep blue sea, its rippling waves, a few red and yellow umbrellas and swimmers here and there.

How many weddings and beginnings of new life have you seen here my sea? How happily do they begin? How fervently do they persevere? How sadly do they end?

The church by the sea is dressed up in white, decorated in perfumed flowers and shiny veils of white silky tulles. The mild sea breeze finds its way into the church and strokes the silky edges of the white ribbons bow-tying the white bouquets to the pews, waiting to welcome the celebrants. The afternoon sunlight enters from the open church doors illuminating the path towards the altar.

The wedding car procession approaches, honking all along the journey from home to the *Mairie* and to the church close by. The small group of beautifully, yet simply dressed family and close friends surround the wedding couple with their intimate love. They have not invited the distant, the remote and the extended. Why should they? After all only the close and the caring matter on this sacred day of theirs, and beyond.

The wedding bells usher the happy families into the church, and curious heart-filled onlookers, like me, follow them in with adorning eyes.

Beautiful traditions of different cultures and places, and yet it is always the beginning of a new life. The wedding. And ending of another. The love bridge always remains. Between the old emptying nest, and the new budding one.

Blessings and best wishes of wonderful years to all old and new couples.

The Table of Life

day 44: september 27, 2015

The table—high, low, on the ground, round, rectangular, glass, wood, fancy, simple, picnic, makeshift—the table hosts the small and big celebrations of life, be it at sea, at dawn, at dusk, on the pebbles, the benches, the laps.

The table is the center of life. Born at a table, dying at a table. Think about it: the kitchen table, the coffee table, the bar table, the game table, the negotiating table, the business table, the study table, the kids table, the marriage table, the separating table—does life go on without the table? Do families survive without their table? Does anything get done far away from a table?

Oh, my beautiful sea, these humans have once again formed their own tables at your shores. How many tables do you welcome here every day? What is their story? Do they tell? Do they tell the same story, but at different tables? All gather at the table of life, and then, somehow, they leave, one at a time. The time comes when they all do. And you let go. Is it hard?

The table knows our life stories and keeps our secrets. The table of life.

Super Blood Moon

day 45: september 28, 2015

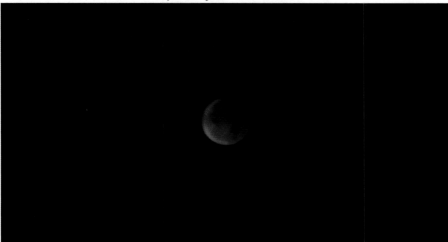

Have you been eager to see the Super Blood Moon, and contemplate her majestic stance? This is a unique celestial occurrence of full moon and total lunar eclipse manifesting as a rare combination around every 30 years. The super moon at its full stage being closest to Earth appears larger, and the red light traveling during the lunar eclipse creates the moon's red color—hence the Super Blood Moon. She works in perfect harmony with all her neighbors: the ocean, the sky, the sun, and the millions of stars, all tangoing in chorus. They all know their boundaries. As should we.

"The heavens, revolving under His government, are subject to Him in peace. They consistently run the course appointed by Him, without hindering each other. The sun and the moon, in the company of the million stars, roll on in harmony according to His command, within their prescribed limits, and without any deviation. They never complain. The fruitful earth, according to His will, brings forth an array of food in abundance, at the proper seasons, for men and beasts and all the living beings in between, never hesitating, nor changing any of the ordinances which He has fixed. The vast immeasurable sea, gathered together by Him into various basins, never passes beyond the bounds placed around it, but obeys His command, 'Thus far you may come, but no further, and here your proud waves must stop.'[26] The seasons of spring, summer, autumn, and winter, peacefully give place to one another. The winds in their worldwide expeditions, fulfill, at the proper time, their service without hindrance. The ever-flowing fountains, formed both for enjoyment and health, furnish without fail their breasts for the life of men. The very smallest of living beings meet together in peace and concord. All these the great Creator and Lord of all has appointed to exist in peace and harmony while He does for the good of all, but most abundantly to us who have fled for refuge. Amen."[27]

Abandoned

day 46: september 29, 2015

The seashore looks abandoned today. Completely void of colorful humans and their protective umbrellas. Have her unsettling waves pushed them away?

All the summer visitors came, rejoiced, benefited from her, and then left. The Mother Sea. All of them leave at the autumn of the sea, thinking they don't need the autumn sea. They turn their back and look for springs and summers in faraway places and people. But the autumn sea is filled with patience, regeneration, and rebirth. She makes herself available to those who honestly seek her autumn virtues.

There is this one surfer, clad in his black wetsuit, springing on and off his surfboard, trying to ride the surging waves, battling the swell of the sea. He is faithful to Mother Sea. Only a few faithful humans remain unmindful about the changing seasons of the sea. Of life. Of Mother.

The Unexpected French Friend

day 47: september 30, 2015

The salty steamy breathless sea pushes and huffs and puffs this 30th day of September, the last reminder of the summer past. Its unexpected friend, the mighty wind, howling about the trees nearby, blows and shakes the lush branches forcing them to shed the old branches along with their spectacular autumn orange-yellow leaves. They must shed the old to make room for the new.

The unexpected friend—who shares common betrayals and who just yesterday was but a stranger—rages now like a gust of wind pushing me to throw my old self away and focus on the new to come. As she offers me a bite of a typical Niçoise[28] dish—Merda di Cane (literal translation: dog's poop, but is made of green gnocchi and has nothing to do with neither a dog nor its poop)—she says, "You must shed off the bittersweet memories of old relations and betrayals and all of yesterday's problems to free up your mind and soul for newer and better experiences." She pauses, then repeats, "The old must end for the new to begin."

She is right, my new friend. And we discuss about life and beliefs and religions and cultures: our similarities and differences. She says I am helping her too, that I'm giving her strength, a different approach to her own problems. I hope I am.

And I allow the rush of the wind of change to work its miracles.

The Hunter of the Rainbow
day 48: october 1, 2015

What else could she ask for? Eyes shut she was listening to the "Hunter of the Rainbow (Il Cacciatore Di Arcobaleni)" from Mattia Cupelli's album titled "Frammenti D'Infinito (Fragments of Infinity)". Deep down she knew she wished to catch the rainbow at one end, travel onward and slide down on the other side. She imagined herself slide up and down, from end to end, just like a baby—weeeeeeee.

At that moment, she lifted up her head to catch a glimpse of the October sky, and there it was: Roy Gbiv. Not one, but double rainbows with their full strands of Red, Orange, Yellow, Green, Blue, Ivory, and Violet, those charming curved parallel stripes stretching from one end of the horizon to the other.

Her wishes were granted. The Hunter of the Rainbow kept staring at the majesty of the soundless rainbow striped sky—right in front of her eyes. Going up, swinging left, circling the earth's skies, and ending on the other side, ending in a full loop. The Hunter had caught her rainbows.

Stop the Wavering
day 49: october 2, 2015

Driving by the melancholic promenade today, I reflect at the wavering waves of the sea. They rage, they foam out their shame, they are driven, tossed, and hurled aside. Nothing is gained by their wavering, except instability, after which they resume their cycle of being kicked around.

This Bible passage comes to mind: "My brothers and sisters, consider it all joy when you face many trials and fall into diverse temptations. Because the testing of your faith produces patience. And let patience do its full job so that you may be perfect and complete, lacking nothing. If you lack wisdom, ask of God who gives to all liberally and without calculations. Ask, and it shall be given to you. But ask in faith, not wavering. For he who wavers is like a wave of the sea driven with the wind and tossed. A wavering, double-minded man is unstable in all his ways and therefore should not expect to receive anything from God."[29]

Life, like the eternal sea, presents itself with many tests and trials. Facing them with firmness of faith and patience completes the growth of the soul. Stop the wavering. Stop being kicked around. It is not healthy, neither for the body nor for the soul, to waver like the waves of the sea. Make up your mind. Have a steadfast faith.

Ask without wavering. And it shall be given to you.

In the Rain

day 50: october 3, 2015

It is a rainy day. Living in the rain, by the sea, is priceless.

Having the privilege to notice the sea's changing temper and fading colors opens up one's horizons enabling them to deal with all sorts of rains, shines, colorful leaves, white snow, green pastures, blue seas, or murky waters. And all these make up life. As the raindrops drizzle weeping, the liquid sunshine disappears, leaving the swollen clouds to obscure the misty ground. I notice the first yellow autumn leaf at sea—we had agreed we would cheer to new beginnings on the first sight of a red-yellow autumn leaf. So, here we go—cheers to new beginnings.

The rain makes a rainmaker. The rain waters the Earth, its living things, along with its living minds, so new seeds can sprout into new creation, new ideas, and new life. It kicks the rainmaker into action, into creation. Let's not cringe under the rain-pour of life's problems, even when they blow on you in overwhelming quantities. Life's tests (LSATs including) become easier and exciting in the rain. You see, there are rainless parts of our world, where there are no opportunities to enjoy the changing seasons of Mother Nature, where life is threatened with dryness, boredom, and uniformity.

Let us be grateful and appreciate what we have at this present moment.

Aftermath of the Les Intempéries
day 51: october 4, 2015

Last night the beautiful Cote d'Azur sea turned upside down, uprooting huge old anchors from the deeps of the sea along with their rusted iron chains and tossing them off at the shores. The mega storm, the flash floods, the overpowering rivers, the high waves, the running sludge, the filling of car populated tunnels, parking lots, and rez-de-chaussées[30] shocked the nation. At least seventeen dead and four missing so far.

It is difficult to imagine yesterday's calm sea would rage so passionately at night causing enormous, everlasting devastation in such a short time. While the powerful hailstorm hit, the picturesque rivers roared dumping their flood on the trusting red-roofed homes and green pastures. The ensuing mud avalanches attacked everything that crossed their path creating chaos, piling up cars, pushing all into rivers, and dragging along dead and living souls.

Life stopped for some in an instant. It changed forever for others. In the midst of the complete disarray, some lost loved ones, homes, souvenirs, photos, papers, things, all the life they had lived so far. Just like that. In a couple of hours. Why?

Why was Mother Nature so angry? Why was the Divine so angry? And yet the sea is so calm today, glowing with a blue serenity.

Daily Bread

day 52: october 5, 2015

Yesterday's hardened baguette. They don't eat it anymore, and they don't feel good throwing it away, so they bring it to the seashore to feed our feathery friends.

The feathered-animal kingdom gathers sensing the presence of food. Swans: in whites and a black. Ducks' extended family with their multicolored grandchildren. Gray pigeons, white doves, and seagulls. They congregate because they want bread. How do they invite each other? Initially, a few arrive, and as the bread pieces continue to shower them, other hungry birds appear from the ends of the sea. If they can communicate so intuitively, why can't we? They gather at the source of the bread. They don't fight, don't fret, don't steal, don't grumble. They let their neighbors get their share. They trust that their portion will be delivered too.

"Give us our daily bread."[31] That's all they need. They share it too. That's how they live. And they persevere and prosper together. Why can't we? We want more and more. A never-ending saga. We get more, but the more does not bring forth peace and joy. Therefore, we seek even more of those things. We look for lasting peace and deeper joy in all the wrong places. And they elude us.

If only we shift our minds inward to our souls and search for the Word implanted there in the wrinkles, we would understand that our souls are connected. That God will always provide us our "daily bread" because we are all one. We are His children.

Another Beautiful Day
day 53: october 6, 2015

Each day is a beautiful day. And today is another one of them. Look at the sea. Just yesterday it swelled, overflew, tossed and turned. Today it is almost calm. I got close and personal with the waves, trying to capture the image of them stroking the shore. They lunged at me, almost touching my feet, as if pushing me out, as if telling me to stay away. Then, they receded.

It does not matter what is going on outside. Conflicts, misunderstandings, illness, grudges, gossip, work, and personal problems—all are the uncomfortable waves of life that accompany us on our journey. They nudge you, but you stay away. They too, like the waves of the shore will recede. Just stay away. Keep them out of your mind and your soul.

Keep your impenetrable inner peace. Keep going. Do that which fills your being with inexplicable joy. Love. Dance. Sing. Laugh. Be happy.

Dawn

day 54: october 7, 2015

"An angel, robed in spotless white,
Bent down and kissed the sleeping Night.
Night woke to blush; the sprite was gone.
Men saw the blush and called it Dawn."[32]

The Mediterranean Sea welcomes the sun at dawn and embraces it so tenderly. Her lazy seashore leisurely advances to cover the sun-kissed pebbles and sweeps away the sun's golden sprinkles into the sea. The pine tree holding its crown high up faces the sun. Standing behind it, I see only the sun's golden light, not the whole sun. But the sun is there. Always offering its life-generating light. It is us who—in half of our day and therefore half of our life—unwillingly and other times intentionally, turn away from the Sun. The Son.[33]

But the Earth always forces us to rotate back to the sun. To marvel at what we think are its new golden beginnings every morning. The Light[34] is given to all, at all times, from now to eternity. Blessed is the one who sees the Light, embraces it, and walks on its golden path.

From now on, I will see the Light; I will walk in the Light of each and every dawn, turning my back to the mischievous darkness.

Dog Friend or Friend Dog?

day 55: october 8, 2015

A golden retriever strolls at the seafront alone with his master friend following her from far. It is an amazing morning at the Cagnes promenade. The sea is so serene, almost not moving. The sky bathes in the early dawn pink hues. There are no cars, no other humans, or other distractions. The silence of the solitude fills the air. It clears my head.

The golden retriever does not distract from this oasis of peace. In fact, she fills the silence with love and honest friendship. She warms the heart with her smiling face and tender eyes. She loves the sea and the sea loves her back. She wanders all along the shore, sniffing the cramped pebbles, wondering if she could find anything of value to her. She does not value gold and silver. She values love, honesty, loyalty, dignity, Mother Nature, and some food.

Her master approaches and I ask if I could take a photo of her gorgeous golden. Sending a smile, she nods. She adds: "It is better to have a dog friend than a friend who is like a dog."

And it brings back the nostalgia of my own late golden retriever and makes me ponder about my friendships.

Smile

day 56: october 9, 2015

The multicolored sailboats put a smile on the face of the gloomy glassy sea today. The dismayed sea wants to be left alone. But on the insistence of these sailboats, she gives way. Little by little, with their waltzing sails, and the rowing of the nearby rowboats, the sea accepts the smile. And her edges curve up hiding her sadness. The power of a simple smile.

Despite the melancholy lurking inside, the smile on the glassy face beams contentment, faith, and confidence. A smile is contagious. It takes away the frowns of the eyes, melts the frozen hearts, and brightens the empty days. It even works on the most stubborn sad faces you encounter.

Put on a radiant smile in the morning, and your whole day will blissfully smile back at you. Build that unshakeable faith and confidence, and peace will be with you always.

Stop Beating Yourself Up
day 57: october 10, 2015

Dear sea, stop beating yourself up against the rocks and against yourself.
Retreat. Calm down. Go to your inner peace.
Never overlook the fact that it's only a journey.
It will neither affect the skies nor the stars nor the sun nor the moon.
You will not arrive at perfection, yet you persist beating and crashing.
It's an unattainable illusion.

The Power of Water

day 58: october 11, 2015

Water. It reflects the power of unity. The deep blue Water of the seas and the oceans. It stands united in all corners of our earth. It is the reflection of humans. A mirror image. Humans treat it with respect, and they get respect. Show neglect, and it will reflect. It supports and yet it sinks. It gives life and yet it destroys. It is up to the humans to tap in the positive healing powers of the Water, or to destroy its habitat provoking it to respond in destruction.

Water takes away the uncleanliness of body and soul; it baptizes the believers to a new spirit; it regenerates the mind, the body, and the soul. And the Earth.

Yet, with all its talents, Water remains contained in the areas assigned to it by a higher power. It does not overstep the boundaries of the oceans and seas; just stays the course despite its swelling and receding over the four changing seasons. And as Water fulfils its assigned mission, its power enables it to evaporate, morph into clouds, pour as rain or snow, return to earth, refresh all life, and cause the budding of new life.

The life-giving powerful Water: drink it insatiably, let its drops rain onto you, swim in it and let it hold you, wash your soul clean. Respect and preserve it, so it respects and preserves you and your generations.

Joie de Vivre

day 59: october 12, 2015

Clad in my warm coat and my scarf wrapped around my neck I take photos of today's glassy sea. I stand where the pebbles meet the shivering waves. I hear the confident footsteps of a woman in bathing-suit, walking past me towards the water. She strolls to the left along the shoreline for a while, then stops slowly immersing herself to her knees. Feeling the cold, she returns and continues to walk right in front of me. I ask her if the water is cold. She said it is not and that she had checked on the Internet and it was 20°C. I ask if she is going to swim afterwards. She nods and explains that it is good for the back, the body, and the mood.

"Bon courage, alors!"[35] I say.

"Ce n'est pas de courage; c'est du plaisir,"[36] she replies with a content smile, and continues, "but, first you have to walk in the water to warm up, that's the secret." Then, she throws her neck towel on the pebbles and plunges right in. In my other ear I hear a screaming "oooohhhh," and there she is, on my right, yet another health-seeker who is about to tiptoe down into the crisp cold sea. What a difference of outlook and expectations, yielding different outcomes. One plunged into the cool smiling contently and let herself be carried with the mild waves, while the other resisted to put her knees in the water, just standing there, screaming, and finding it difficult to immerse herself in the chilly unknown. The first went in with a calm and pleasant spirit to experience deeper joy, while the other touched the sea with a fighting spirit that stressed her out.

This is joie de vivre: in everything, do the homework first, prepare, and then walk in faith and perform the task—for the joy of it, not the obligation.

The Bench's Story

day 60: october 13, 2015

Every day they walk by the bench, or they drive past it. Day after day, that gray-haired man, the jogger lady, and the kid on the bicycle, stop by to take a moment to sit on the bench. Most have their four-legged best friends too—enjoying, sharing stories, laughing, crying, uniting, and separating at that bench. The bench had been sitting there at the boardwalk by the seafront for so many years. Even it does not remember how many years it has been. But it likes its life: facing the sea, feeling its breeze, listening to the whispering waves, watching the planes arriving and taking off to unfamiliar seas, bidding the cruise ships and other boats farewell or welcoming their approaching horns. The bench admires how the sun and the moon play hide-and-seek, setting and rising and hiding but never catching each other. It loves the fresh marine smell of fish floating nearby married with the fresh smell of grilled fish at the restaurants-de-la-plage[37] a few steps aback.

A long time ago the bench had turned its back to the buzzing life on the delightful promenade, and never once it looked back to the zooming cars, the strolling souls, and the colorful facades of beachfront living. But it had eyes that saw, ears that heard, a heart that felt the joys and sadness of all life that thrived there.

The Yacht on the Horizon
day 61: october 14, 2015

Cruising majestically in silence on the dark horizon, the pleasure yacht captures the wandering eye and intrigues the imagination. Is it going anywhere, or does it only give the illusion that it is? It rests on the Mediterranean, blasting its music into the misty autumn night—the dream of many—cruising and looking happy.

Gazing at the yacht, feeling the cold sand under my feet and the icy breeze on my cheeks, I think: Do we have to go on a yacht cruise to feel happy? Will we be free there? Aren't we the prisoners of our own thoughts? But on the royal yacht, you have to be happy, even though you are imprisoned. And is the yacht really on the horizon? How do they see us from there? How do we look to those looking at the distant shore, we who seem to be living in nests of flickering lights of the night? Isn't it their dream to live on these picturesque Mediterranean shores? After all, that's why they're here in the middle of the cold night, in the middle of the dark sea—just to catch a glimpse of this picture-perfect place.

Blessed Be Thy Divine Will

day 62: october 15, 2015

I stretch up my arms
Alongside the mighty tree
Standing at the edge of the river
Wanting to rush to the sea

I reflect upon the power of He
He who has made all this, including me
He, by His own free will
Is able to make all things still

Why look any further if He is right here?
Hearing my murmuring prayers crawling up
Attempting to align with His Divine Will
He answers, "Consider it done."

Does She Know She Can Fly?
day 63: october 16, 2015

This lone bird soars on the beach, hovers over the deep blue waves, then dives straight in, picking up some food. She brings it to the shore to eat, then, she walks along the shore. Does she know she can fly? Does she know she can swim? Does she know she can walk? Does she understand? Does she think? Does she grasp her freedom? Her talents? Does she appreciate her wings, her webbed toes, her two feet? She might be just a puppet reacting to her instincts.

For us humans, to have these three talents coexisting would be equivalent to having supreme powers. Yet, we do not have them, but we have the brains to replicate them. And we have copied her: we have created airplanes, boats, and bicycles, and we think each one of them would ferry us to freedom. But we cannot conquer all three domains of air, water, and earth in one go. We think we have freedom, but we are not free. We lack this lone bird's three coexistent talents of flying, swimming, and walking. We are not free. She is.

Does she know she can fly?
Does she know she can swim?
Does she know she can walk?
Does she know she is free?

Best Find

day 64: october 17, 2015

Where is it hidden – the Best Find? I look among the pebbles trying to find that rare treasure. And I walk and walk along the unending shore, head down, eyes fixed within the cracks of the pebbles and sand cramped up against one another. A blue gem, a gold coin, a rare crystalized piece of jade glass, make my heartbeat jump for a while, but soon I realize their lifeless existence add nothing to mine.

Then my eyes wander at sea. Perhaps the Best Find is in there within its deep-blue splendor—silver-white covering, exotic creatures, and sunken treasures. I see the beauty of it all. But soon, I realize their interesting existence adds but a fleeting charm to mine.

Dismayed, I turn my head up to the eternal skies. Perhaps it's in the blues, and I examine the distant horizon going from left to right, disappearing upwards, engulfing its flying marvelous creatures, the scattered white puffs of swelled raindrops, the ever-warming sun, the soothing moon and all the bright hidden stars. Its magic works in me for a while. And soon, poof, it is gone.

Perhaps, I think, the Best Friend is hidden in the relaxed boardwalks, busy streets, red-roofed homes, luxury cars, man-made things, buildings and structures, and I feel the disappointment of not finding it there either creep into my soul.

Then I search my heart, and there it is, my Best Find, within the folds of its lost memory: the childhood friend, the unforgettable bond, the honest soul, always comforting, forever there.

Life on a Rainy Sunday in Cagnes-Sur-Mer
day 65: october 18, 2015

This picturesque fisherman's town lies between the famous Antibes and charming Nice. Minutes from the Nice airport, accessible by all means of transport, in addition to being the renowned Renoir's home, Cagnes now houses the famous Polygone Riviera, the first open-air mall in Europe. This ultra-modern center coexists with the old town, the Haut-de-Cagnes. There, the towering Grimaldi Castle and its museum sit atop the narrow winding medieval cobblestone streets. On the shores of the town, the famous promenade stretches from Antibes to Nice, offering the *Velo Bleu* bicycles to cycling enthusiasts, and the pedestrian marked areas to walking lovers. The famous Hippodrome—the horse track, hosts races, and many exhibitions such as French and Italian wine and gourmet food. Various activities take place at the cornerstone of the promenade the Saint Pierre Church. And the fish market is a walking distance away.

So, what to do on a rainy Sunday? Walk in the rain showering the Cagnes Promenade, feel its crisp touch on your face, smell the blessings of Mother Nature, get a fresh croissant, and watch how the raindrops serenade the sea, and imbibe the beauty of the town. Visit the Polygone. Tour Renoir's home-museum. Enjoy a café gourmand complete with ice cream, chocolate mousse and Chantilly, and Panna Cotta topped with raspberry. Better yet, get a pizza, or taste a Tajine dish or a savory Gnocchi plate at one of the cafés, that welcome you with a warm smile, now misted by the rain, but warmed by the nearby towering church.

Life

day 66: october 19, 2015

Life. Where does it come from? Where does it go to?

It starts at the unknown, the parent, the universe—just like water—and it flows and winds and paces at times, then races, banging on rocks, twisting through beautiful streams, green pastures, rocky peaks, snowy mountains, and rests at blue sandy shores. It continues its course nonstop. Rushing through time, it gushes its breath at the end, at the same source where it started, mingled with the soul of the universe.

Along the way it sees insurmountable beauty, despicable ugliness, changing seasons, shallow and deep souls. It picks up eternal treasures and lifelong loves. It lets go of some, but it carries the close-to-the-heart to the end.

I am glad I understood this at this stage of my life—the swiftness of life's journey over the bumps and rocks and twists and turns. It's our ability to ride the waves—through the gentle lullaby of the peaceful azures or the bumpy troubled raging waters—that propels us to our destination. Let us enjoy the ride no matter what. Enjoy life.

Solitude

day 67: october 20, 2015

With his spectacular splendor of the spectrum, the sun shines in his solitude today. Nothing bothers him—neither bright light nor black darkness.

And he likes his solitude, for he is not lonely. He sees his handsome reflection in the sea. And the sea adores him.

He loves his solitude.

Chaises at the Beach

day 68: october 21, 2015

A family of chaises longues[38] sit and wait at the shores of the gorgeous beach. They wait for a long time, but nobody shows up. Nothing happens. The sun's rays glow, giving way to the moon. The lazy sea ripples, and the sky watches. They do not know what they are supposed to do, other than be and look their best and wait. Someone had planted them there for a reason and a season. Waking up each morning, the chaises arrange themselves here in pairs—complete with a table for service and an umbrella for protection—and wait.

One day, the youngest chaise, exclaimed, "Why are we here and what are we supposed to do? I'm tired of this." And the elder of them replied, "When I was your age, I asked the same question to my parents. I did not want to sit here and wait any longer. I did not comprehend the purpose of it. My parents explained that we resemble those humans who come here for a reason and a season. They don't know why they're here. But someone has planted them here. For that reason they, just like us, sit and wait, and wait… And some of them complain. But others are light-hearted and, while waiting, make someone happy, serve another, or protect others from harm. These are exactly the things that we are supposed to do when humans visit us here. Only the light-hearted shall enjoy the blue sea and the watchful sky without realizing that they're waiting for nothing."

The young chaise nodded in approval, faced the sea once more, and got ready to serve, and to make someone happy.

Port Grimaud

day 69: october 22, 2015

Hidden in a remote shore of the sea is this small paradise called Port Grimaud. No noise pollution, no car pollution, and no light pollution. Port Grimaud is reminiscent of Venice, with its winding canals and tiny bridges. None of the 2000 buildings look alike, each displaying an array of yellow, red, pink, white, and orange facades with green shutters, not the mention the wooden, rustic bungalows along the sandy shore.

Climb up the tower of the Church to enjoy and capture the panoramic views of fall colored, red-orange-yellow hills, and the many shades of green and blue lifting all up to the sky. The proud masts that stand tall on the boats lining the canals will adorn the photos you capture of these stunning views.

Whether you enjoy walking the sandy shores and swimming the clear waters, or you prefer to be a gourmand for a day and indulge in moules-frites,[39] pizza and French table wine, crepes and ice cream, or you opt for a boat ride cruising the canals, this will be an exquisite time of fun outside of real life.

Transparency
day 70: october 23, 2015

How wonderful would it be if everything were as transparent as this sea? No hidden agendas, no double faces. What you see is what you get. The gems hidden inside would manifest along with the edgy pebbles, but nobody would care if they coexist, for the transparency soothes and comforts and exudes trust. No need to dig deeper, for all hidden vices and virtues are apparent right there on the surface. And once you know about the vices behind the transparencies, you learn to deal with them since the virtues are a breeze to live with anyway.

Transparency: You always know what's inside: it's always as you see it. No fear, no worries. No bad surprises. No lies.

Wouldn't life be so peaceful and tolerable if humans were as transparent as the sea is today?

Determined

day 71: october 24, 2015

Determined, in the colors of the night, it approaches unnoticed into the enclosed bay, slams the quay, bounces back, swerves and rushes forward, undisturbed by all the vibrant distractions and reflections around. The mighty wave. It gains force as it advances towards its goal as if an invisible mighty hand is guiding it, increasing its power. And the wave intentionally allows itself to be directed and pushed forward in its journey. Nothing will stop it until it reaches its destination where it will merge with all its siblings to rest at the bosom of the mother sea.

It reminds me of the determined person who, disregarding all the distractions life has to offer, gushes forward in the journey of life, abandoning herself to the divine will, letting divine providence guide her through peaceful or turbulent times to fruition until she merges with all other souls to rest at the bosom of Mother Nature.

Times Have Changed

day 72: october 25, 2015

The sea at morning twilight is swaying with the fiery clouds. How times have changed. Only yesterday it was exhibiting signs of the blues hovering all over and around it. Just a small hint of a ruby red heart filled its whole essence with vibrant life.

Times do change indeed. Nothing stays the same forever. And when change is embraced with a welcoming heart and an open mind, it shapes new horizons and opens fresh paths, so we continue on this wonderful journey of life.

That bright path of change shall journey into the next eternal life, if this one is lived correctly according to divine guidance.

Renaissance
day 73: october 26, 2015

Colorful waters of the sea, how many rebirths have you witnessed? With the preordained paces of the changing seasons, you clothe yourself with the vibrant colors of renaissance. One can ponder at your red, yellow, brown laden banks and shores about how old things pass and how all things become new again.[40]

It feels good to shed the old habits, rotten feelings, passé thoughts, and cold souls and instead, fill the emptied space with their blooming new counterparts. Rebirth fills the heart with hope, the mind with strength, the soul with grace and gratitude, and the future with everlasting peace and love.

Therefore, go on, my sea; keep reflecting the wonderful colors of renaissance in your endlessly evolving image of ourselves.

Divine Providence, Divine Love

day 74: october 27, 2015

God is Love and God's love is seen in all the minutia of the canvas of life. The sea has abandoned herself to the power of God. The sky forms the clouds obeying to the wishes of the Almighty. The mountains, the pebbles, sand, and ocean deep have surrendered to the will of God. And divine providence guides them, helps them change with the seasons so they don't get stuck in the seasons past. If only we, His sand-creations, could learn to abandon ourselves to the will of our Creator, His divine love would guide us to through our changing seasons, so we too would not have to carry along the burdens of our seasons past.

Yes, God is love. And we don't find that love with our brains, trying to reason God's providence. His love has to be in the heart. And once you close your eyes, take a deep breath, and allow His love to envelop your heart and lungs and chest, you'll feel there is no room for anything else—no hatred nor jealousy, no doubt nor worries, no troubles nor sufferings—but just pure divine love that overwhelms you to the extent you'd want to send it to others too, so they too learn of it, feel it, and share it.

Yes, abandon your life to Him, and He will take you to that tranquil place where all difficulties are surmounted with love's strength, as if they don't exist.

The Soul of the Sea

day 75: october 28, 2015

The nostalgic sea longs for yesterday's young life bubbling at its shore. She tries hard to bring that life back home where the sky is the ceiling. She reflects light, gives colors, makes warm. The sea does not know she has life in her depths—in her soul. Just look inside of you my dear sea, and see. See with the eye of your soul. You are the mother of a whole different life tucked away within you: vibrant corals and coral reefs; beautiful stars and sea urchins; rays and seabirds; schools of colorful fish, small and large; creatures mysterious, camouflaging, and translucent. Ancient treasures and humanities have been lost at sea, in your soul. No human reaches that deep—the deepest wrinkle of your soul. The fisherman fastens his eyes to see. But he does not see. His soul is dark. The eye is the lamp of the body, of the soul. If the eye is pure, the whole body and soul will be full of light. If it is not, all is darkness. How great is that darkness.[41]

The human tries. He tries without discovering the immense treasures you hold in there. The human rejoices and gloats over his so-called big catches stolen from your deeps. But he fails to penetrate your soul. What treasure is hidden in there? He looks but does he see? He searches but does he find? He finds but does he discover? Does he understand? Blessed are the eyes that see the things that you see.[42] Keep rolling, my sea. Stormy days are arriving. Soon you will be tossing and turning. Stirred. And then, once more, you will turn up and reveal the harvest of your depths.

And at that time my sea, the human, oblivious to your needs and insensible to your soul, will return to you to harvest a new catch once again.

Awakening
day 76: october 29, 2015

"And I will give you a new heart, and a new spirit I will put within you. And I will remove the heart of stone from your flesh and give you a heart of flesh."[43]

Awakening. The new heart feels. The new spirit jumps. The heart of stone has disappeared. The heartbeats amplify stirring the sleeping soul—and the emerging soul stretches out its freedom-seeking arms towards the limitless skies, touching true freedom. The flesh heart and the spirit soul have awakened; they now live for each other, complement each other—now, and for eternity. Those long walks along the shore, absorbing the sea's heart and soul, put you in touch with God, and God gives you a new heart, and a new spirit, just as He promised.

Reflect Life
day 77: october 30, 2015

As the sea reflects the sky
I reflect on my life passing by
As days turn into nights
And moons give way unto suns

What I speak I see
What I think becomes
What I work manifests
What I give reflects

So, I reflect like the sea—
What I speak I see
What I love reflects in the sky
And while letting up a sigh
I feel my soul fill up with the Divine High

The October Cards

A heartwarming card per day makes my day. That was the case with the 31 days of this October. A tender card for each of the beautiful days of October faithfully arrived in my inbox, from my wonderful and caring daughter, each marked with a special loving theme, collaged on an appropriate photo of us and our sea—our own blue sea, the heart shapes on the sandy shores, the red autumn leaves flowing to the sea, the birds speeding away, and the gray clouds dancing with the blue sky.

The nostalgia of October. My heart will reminisce on these daily, faithful, empowering, appreciative cards for days and years to come. I will fondly remember the warm feelings they evoked on cold October mornings. And I will always be thankful.

May you always be blessed, my dear daughter.

All Saints Day

day 79: november 1, 2015

Today, on this 1st day of the 11th month, at 11:11 a.m., the doors of Heaven opened up for prayers to go up and be heard. The white-rayed gown of All Saints was dropped from the Heavens onto the peaceful palm-tree laden sea, illuminating the way for my prayer to go up. For me, and for my loved ones, and for you too, I pray:

Health for the body, mind, heart, and spirit

Peace within, and with each other

Love inside, and for each other

Living life in a manner pleasing to God

Letting go of futile and fake thoughts, words, deeds, and people

May we all read God's Word. Understand and apply it

To those who can't—may we be able to share it with them

Forgiving others so they may forgive us our sins

May I be able to bring at least one person closer to God

Success and fully productive days

My challenge for you today: Dare to transform someone. Dare to ask how they're doing and really listen. Dare to bring an astray back into the Light. Dare to help them to send up a prayer in faith. Dare to ask them to come to church. And challenge them that they will surely receive their answer at the destined time.

Time to Let Go
day 80: november 2, 2015

Oh, sea, why do you keep hanging on to the old summer warmth? It is time to let go. Let go of those warm days. Let go of the chaos at your shores. Let go of all the drama brought about by all the passersby and their emotions. Let go of your comfort zone where you felt secure having your regular swimmers and sunbathers caressing your cheeks. Let go of the past. Let go of the dead.

Yes, despite the summer weather of yesterday, today you let go of that cozy, warm, secure feeling. Leave the antiques and the dead behind murmuring a heartfelt prayer for All Souls. Then move on.

It is time to let go. Get out of your security zone into the loneliness of the winter cold. Out there, venture into the unknown. Only then the wind will blow your way. Only then your clogged head will clear, your blinded eyes will see, and your heavy heart will bounce. And you will grow new wings to take off.

Savoring the Rain
day 81: november 3, 2015

Drip. Drop. Tip. Top. And the rain slowly falls.

How delightfully the droplets serenade the sea at the pace of the misty sonata. With each drop, the winter smells fresher and fresher. You just want to stay out there, in the rain, so it showers you with blessings from the heavens above, and you let it slip onto your forehead, trickle down your eyes, dribble on your face, and wash down your body, letting go the burdens of your soul.

Drip. Drop. Tip. Top. Tippedi-pop

The rain speeds. It quenches the thirst. Rejuvenates the Earth. Makes grow the dead roots, plants, and shrubs. Cleanses the air and the soul. The rain.

Tip. Top. Tiptoptiptoptiptop ... Tippedi-pop ... Tippedi-pop ...

And suddenly you feel your feet tapping along with the drops, splashing the fresh rain-puddles happily around. You sense your arms swaying along, turning your being round and round. Then your heart jumps. Your face smiles. Your lips serenade the rain. Your brain relaxes. You dance. From the corner of your misty eyes you notice that Willpower is back, that yacht which dominates this bay. Yes, rain brings forth your willpower too.

And you decide: "Rain or shine I shall dance in the rain, and that secret smile of willpower shall carry me through the day."

Tiptoptiptop ... Tippedi-pop ... Tippedi-pop ...

Believe in Your Wings

day 82: november 4, 2015

As sure as the belief that the golden sun will shine tomorrow, and the sea will sway away and come back to the shore, it is sure that the one who believes in their wings will fly to where they want.

This flock of birds, now circling altogether harmoniously above the sea, have migrated here from colder weather. They did not worry about their journey, nor did they become anxious thinking they could not fly the long treacherous distance. The fear would have crippled them had they worried. Instead they believed in the wings gifted to them by God, they trusted their instincts.

They flew. They soared. They arrived. They achieved.

Keep Your Secrets
day 83: november 5, 2015

Oh, sea, keep your secrets. I don't want to know of them anymore. They are not secrets any longer. Once, a long time ago, they were intriguing, evoking deep interest, and at the same time enervating and exhausting.

Not so, now.

After the love has gone, secrets have no meaning at all. After all, these sneaky secrets push the love to run away, and then the fatigue wears off. That bland irreplaceable calmness reigns.

So, keep your secrets, for they are now unworthy of my knowledge.

Should I Stay or Should I Leave

day 84: november 6, 2015

Standing on the pier I look down at my wavy reflection in the mirror of the sea. The crystal ripples caress my weary face and the unclouded sea washes my dull hair. It feels good to be welcomed. I look happy and careless, floating on the uplifting powers of its transparent waters. It relieves my fatigued body. The warmth of the moon's rays absorbed by the untroubled sea envelopes my worn-out soul. And now it shines again. My murky mind clears, rocking gently, hugging my reflection in the sea. My wasted heart comes back to life. Love. I think, "This must be love."

I ask, "Should I stay, or should I leave?" And I hear the wind of the sea whisper in my ear, "Stay, if he is transparent like this sea, if he makes you feel welcomed like this sea, relieves your fatigued body like the uplifting waters of this sea, envelopes your worn-out soul like the warmth of the moon at this sea, clears your mind like the tender hug of your reflection with this sea, brings your wasted loving heart back to life. Stay, if he makes you feel loved."

And I, I walk away.

Let it Be

day 85: november 7, 2015

The sea encouraged me: "Let it be."
It is what she learned as she persevered in her calm existence.

"If the waves want to hurl, to smash, let it be.
If creatures push and shove, let it be.
If the sky wants to clear or drop rains, let it be.
If they want to leave, let it be.
If anyone wants to stay, let it be.
If all around you create chaos spinning around, let it be.
If your mind wanders off, let it be.
If your soul wants to soar, let it be.
If your heart wants to love, let it be.

For this is what I learned as I calmly persevered in my troubled existence."

Mantra for the Heavy-Hearted

day 86: november 8, 2015

Author's Illustration of the Villeneuve Village

I am healthy
I am happy
I am strong
I am capable
I love God
God loves me
I love my children
My children love me
I love my family
And they love me
I am joyful
I am grateful
I am honest
I am compassionate
I love life
I live life
I've got peace
I've got God's grace

Live

day 87: november 9, 2015

Today, the sea reprimanded me: "Go. Live your life. Don't sit here wasting it. Stop staring at me with those sad desolate glassy eyes. The dull old is gone. It is no more. You have a colorful, abundant new life ahead of you. Go build it. You have dreams and goals you want to accomplish. Go live."

I kept staring at her, and she kept reprimanding in return: "Vivez si vous voulez. Mais vivez! (Live, if you wish, but LIVE.)" Many have come before you to contemplate and reflect. Most decided to stay. But only few summoned the courage to leave and start all over again. Their colorful reflections by my side helped them stand tall and strong at times of trouble. But they learned to live not for others, not bogged down by the past, not for ideologies, but for themselves. They found themselves here, they received God's graces here, and they left.

Therefore, go live with your newly found grace.

I will miss you. I will still be here if you wish to come back from time to time, but I know you don't need me anymore."

Leaving
day 88: november 10, 2015

Leaving. What is it? Does it provoke negative sentiments of loss and leaving love behind? Does it entice positive thoughts of hope, of a new life without any antiquities? Isn't it true that people leave to get away? But "[y]ou can't get away from yourself by moving from one place to another."[44]

The clear waves leave the edge of the shore, but soon after they rush back. Or do they leave the swell in the middle of the sea, only to return to it again and again? The sun too leaves the horizon and the sea, but at the set time, it comes back again to let the sea shine. The starry sprinkles on the sea follow that path of leaving and returning. The ships go and come back to port being lured by the magic of the returning full moon. Planes take off to faraway skies and return to the origins of their flight. Creatures drift away and leave. Some get lost. Some migrate back.

Everything that leaves arrives somewhere new. Anyone who leaves reaches other brighter shores. What propels their leaving? Being pushed to leave, or … ? Curiosity. Boredom. Tangles. Imagination. Ambition. Urge.

And then they arrive. But is the one that arrives the same, or are they now changed forever?

Arriving

day 89: november 11, 2015

What happens when the waves arrive at the shore in a huge splash? Is arriving an end or a new beginning? There is no clear line between the two. The end and the beginning blend in harmony, sometimes silently without stirring up any waves, as if the horizon is blending perfectly between the sea and the sky making them one continuum of wavy clouds—or you could say cloudy waves. It doesn't matter. Two halves restored to one. Two opposites reunited. Arriving and departing. New and old. All is one, we are one.

Today is Armistice Day or Veteran's Day depending where you are. It marks the leaving of the old-world war and the arrival of new life. It is also Saint Martin of Tours Day. Saint Martin was a Roman soldier and had a vision one night. He saw a beggar in the cold and cut his red military cloak into half with his sword and gave it to the beggar. In another vision he heard Jesus tell an angel that Saint Martin had given Jesus his robe. In another vision, his cloak was restored to full size. He then left the military and became the bishop of Tours, France, where his remains are interred in the Basilica of Saint Martin of Tours. His Jubilee year starts today, as 2016 will mark his 1700th birthday. Processions led by a red-cloaked soldier on a white horse, and reenactments of his vision take place today around Europe and in other countries.

He arrived as a soldier and left as a priest. He shared half of his robe with a poor stranger—Christ. He cut his old life as a soldier and became a pastor. But the two halves were restored to one. Arriving and leaving. In the end, all is restored to one.

Duck Dared

Don't duck under your worries, nor under the shadows of your fears, nor in the stormy currents of your troubles. Look at Duck. Instead of ducking, he held his head up straight and dove right into the troubled waters. At first, he thought he would fall and be instantly swallowed by and carried away within the waterfall's rage. He did not think he could fly.

But he tried. Duck dared to take the difficult route and enjoyed the surprises it brought. Duck glided. He landed in the peaceful shallow waters ahead.

Dare today, and tomorrow, and each day that God gives you breath, to hold your head up and to dive into the troubled river of life. You see, after the initial rush of the troubled waters, that peaceful calm oasis awaits you.

Dare.

Don't Waste

day 91: november 13, 2015

Don't waste:
The sea because she is the universal magnet of deep abundance
The skies because the blues fill us with misty fresh breath
Mother Nature because she is the giver and keeper of all life
The trees because their greens and reds and yellows beautify all around
Water because it is the source from which all new life springs
Food because this sustenance of life is not equally available to all
Your day because once it passes, its unique opportunities pass with it
Your life, because you only have one life to live, explore, love, share, and leave behind
Your body because it is the holy temple of your soul
Your thoughts, because they build your future—remember, happy, healthy, strong thoughts create a happy, healthy, strong future
Your energy on chasing resentment, because you need it to attract what you love
Your words on empty conversations, because they will only lead to empty roads
Love, because once it is gone, you may not be able to recapture it
Your patience with the wrong people, because some are a dead end
Your actions on projects you don't like, because you will waste your life
Your relationships, because if they leave one by one you will be left all alone
Your legacy, because that is how future generations will remember you
Anything or anyone you come across in your life, because each is there for a purpose
Your spiritual life, because it is your sole passport to eternity
Your precious soul, because only through it God will welcome you

The Divide

day 92: november 14, 2015

Good and Bad. Light and Dark. Carnage. Attacks. People killing people everywhere. They all have their own justifications. Who is the Good? Who is the Bad? Why kill each other in the first place?

The Good think they are holy, not needing to improve. The Bad think they are good, thus, justifying their immoral acts. Where did Bad come from? I've come to learn that when the dark powers of envy, lust, despair, power-hunger, and lack of faith seeped into the bright white heart of Good, a thin, invisible line formed between them. It's the other side of one's palm, which will flip at the force of a small trigger if one is not careful.

Do we need the Good and the Bad? Yes, Good and Bad must coexist; one cannot live without the other, and sometimes, they even collaborate to teach us a lesson, and they endure until we actually learn that lesson.

So, next time you feel you are immersed in and surrounded with Bad, remember this: find the lesson it is trying to teach you, learn it, and open the doors for the Good to rush in. It eventually will.

PS: Two years after writing this, on this day of November 14, I met an old friend from law school who taught me that the lesson to be learned from each trial was LOVE, unconditional love.

Living in Peace and Harmony with Each Other

day 93: november 15, 2015

I stare at the autumn leaves and the various creatures floating and cohabiting in your waters dear sea and I cannot but wonder at their capacity to coexist harmoniously despite the differences in their varying sizes, their diverse looks, the color and texture of their skin, their habits and preferences.

How come they, who do not have our human thinking capacities, live in peace and harmony and we don't? We, who regard ourselves as superior to them, have to disagree, despair, displease, defect, desecrate, and desert each other.

I ask the sea to help me see the reason for their peaceful existence. Is it because they live for the moment? Is it because they forgive and forget instantly without holding grudges? Is it because they love each other unconditionally? Or maybe there is no outsider, intruder, divisive influence purposefully and persistently turning them against each other. Or they don't care about accumulating material possessions and riches, and their utmost happiness derives from peaceful, happy, caring, nurturing coexistence. The sea nods in agreement.

Solidarity
day 94: november 16, 2015

Many public officials and an enormous crowd gathered today at the Memorial at the Quai des États Unis, along the promenade of Nice to honor the fallen victims of the horrible Paris terror attacks of November 13th, 2015. The emotional power of the strong solidarity filled the solemn air emanating from the chant of the French National Anthem, "The Marseillaise."

All silently vowed not to give in to fear.

After a moment of stillness, the huge crowd burst into applause celebrating the lives of the innocent victims. Solidarity, in face of an incomprehensible act of human hatred and violence, brings us together, forever.

Lost and Found

day 95: november 17, 2015

"When you ask for miracles, ... the sea obeys and fetters break, ... treasures lost are found again, when young and old your aid implore."[45]

They say if you pray to Saint Anthony—the Patron Saint of lost items, lost people, lost souls—you will find that which you have lost. And if you come upon the sweet fragrance of lilies, he is secretly informing you that your lost would be found.

Do we really find what we have lost? There is a reason we lose people, faith, hope, health, love, or simply things. At first, we don't nurture that person or thing, and we lose. And regret sinks in. And we start fighting for it to come back. Sometimes it's an uphill battle. Sometimes we win. And the lost is found. When we find them we think the find will be exactly the same as when we lost them, but that's rarely the case, for once we lose something or someone, we lose a piece of ourselves with it too, and that lost piece of ourselves never comes back.

Rethink Yourself

day 96: november 18, 2015

Walking on the crunchy autumn leaves, two words came to mind as if the silent rustle whispered them into my ringing ear, "Rethink yourself." I responded, "Let me give it a try and see what I come up with."

Rethink yourself:

How do I rethink myself? Do I really know myself? Have I taken the time to find out who I really am? Or am I letting myself to drift day to day along the direction of the blowing winds.

Rethink yourself:

Do you know your talents? Have you taken the time to cultivate them? What are you waiting for? Tomorrow might be too late.

Rethink yourself:

Do you know what you want from life? Have you created your life's plan?

Rethink yourself:

Have you taken the time to think who among your surroundings is good for you, and who needs to be cut off?

Rethink yourself:

Go deep into yourself to find your soul. Nourish your soul to find your God-given gift and start cultivating it. Share your gift for that is God's plan for your life. Set priorities. Write your life's plan. Don't waste another day letting your life to aimlessly drift by. Change your habits, love yourself, change yourself. Radiate love and compassion to see the same positive change in the people around you. Change your life. Start now.

Beaujolais Nouveau

day 97: november 19, 2015

Joyful celebrations are everywhere welcoming this year's yield of the Beaujolais Nouveau. What is celebrated? New wine. Keeping up with long standing tradition, France celebrates the new wines of the Beaujolais territory each November. These nouveau wines must be consumed shortly after, and within the year of, their grape harvest. Unlike other wines, they don't need to be aged in barrels and caves in ideal conditions for few years to attain their finest state of taste, aroma, color, and texture.

Yes, the Beaujolais Nouveau infuses new wine in your blood, and you are renewed. Off with the old self. Welcome to everything new.

Cheers to the new you.

No Absolutes

day 98: november 20, 2015

I recently learned that there are no absolutes in life. There's no never, no forever, no always.

And I immediately dropped them from my vocabulary.

If you say never, that very thing you're running from will soon find you and bite you. If you say forever, you will shortly discover nothing lasts forever in this fleeting life and its momentary possessions. If you say always, the disappointment of constantly expecting and never receiving will distress you and render you hopeless.

Only the vast sea and Mother Nature are ordained to work in absolutes. You see, the sea is always there for you, never disappoints you, and forever waits for you. And Mother Nature always carries you, never abandons you, and forever nurtures you.

The Sanctuary

day 99: november 21, 2015

Two pebbles were arguing: Was the sea their sanctuary? They had always lived on the edge where the rippling sea lullabied them, and the alternating sparkles of the sun and the moon toyed with them. The Soft Beige, wanting to bring sense to the Shiny Gray, gently rolled closer, and whispered, "There's nowhere to go. We are made for the sea, by the sea. She's our sanctuary." But Shiny Gray disagreed, shouting, "No more. I don't need the sea to survive. I'm independent. I'm leaving right now." At that moment, a human played soccer with the pebble, kicked it up and away from the sea.

Soft Beige, troubled by Shiny Gray's attitude and ingratitude, sought refuge, and rolled away with the next wave into the sea, singing, "The Sea is my sanctuary, I owe my sparkle to her caressing belly." While up there, far away, surprised, and shocked at the immediate realization of its wish, stood Shiny Gray, among a new dull dusty pebble population. Feeling the dryness creep onto its skin, and sensing the familiar tangy marine smell fainting away, Shiny Gray screamed, "Nooooo …" But its regretful scream was muffled by the endless noises of heavy feet stomping, humans talking, and cars honking. No one heard the regretful "Noooo …" Now, the caressing lullaby of the sea was far away, unreachable, and the golden sparkles of the sun and the moon played with other pebbles, who had chosen to not leave the sanctuary.

Soon, its color faded into dull gray. Its sparkling luster disappeared. Dust stole its shine, blending it with the multitude of unicolor gray pebbles forming the path for traveling human feet—wanting to reach the sea, their sanctuary.

Christ the King

day 100: november 22, 2015

"Come reign in my life, my heart, my mind, my plans, my troubles, my worries, my health, my family, my children, and all whom I love," I prayed to Christ the King today in the Antibes Cathedral, lighting a candle beside His statue. And He promised, *"I will."*

And my heart sang a beautiful song that Taizé interprets, "Jesus, remember me when you come into your Kingdom …"

Go check it out, you will love it.

Pick Yourself Up

day 101: november 23, 2015

How battered looks the sea today with the icy weather, the gloomy gray skies, and the empty shores. She has endured a lot for a long time.

And yet, even today, she picks herself up and never lets her guard down. She plays with the pebbles, shaking them a bit harshly today. She rocks her swelling waves as she picks herself up. She provides refuge to white seagulls, black craws, tiny fish, and large ships alike, even more intensely today.

She has nothing to lose—picking herself up after all the battering she has endured.

She has nothing to lose as the alternative is to leave herself to the whim of outside forces who, if left uncontrolled, will continue pounding her over and over again. She rushes forward in a proud tone, and with each rush at the shore she knows she is a step closer to the glorious days of her colorful summers. She knows she just needs to ride the tide through the cycle of the changing seasons.

And thus, she lifts up her huge belly and marches on. And she empowers me to pick myself up, ban outside forces, and march forward into the newfound bright path of my life.

Lying Around

day 102: november 24, 2015

What do they do, lying around? What do they gain? Do they wait for something to happen? Do they care if something happens?

Their life shall go on lying around, watching the waves, the sea, and the skies; idly viewing many lives pass by. Their life shall go on lying around until they all morph into vast areas of sands of the same shape and size, under the constant beating of the waves against the shore—their home.

And we too shall morph into that same sand no matter how lazily we lie around or how frantically we pace the world.

The Catch

day 103: november 25, 2015

Waiting for the catch, that climax of a fisherman's happiness.

Is it the catch itself or the journey leading up to it that enriches your soul and cheerfully energizes your being? Where does it start, and where does it end? It doesn't matter because there's always a catch—you might not like it and choose to throw it back into the sea, but it could well be someone else's dream catch.

So, keep your eyes open, and your mind flexible. The thing you catch might not fit into your mold, but it might be the catch you need.

Thanksgiving
day 104: november 26, 2015

Menton

Kneeling before you in thanksgiving
Father of everlasting mercy
Always willing, forgiving, and life giving
There is no higher curtsy
Than giving glory to You
You—
You bless us
You heal us
You pardon us—
Us the poor sinners
We adore you
We love you
We thank you for your blessing
The trials and triumphs while living
The solace and comfort while sleeping
We will forever proclaim
And praise your Holy Name
Amen

Let it Go

day 105: november 27, 2015

I watch the sea let go of the debris piled up in her belly. She had hidden them in there for quite a long time, perhaps waiting for a miracle. She lounged in her serene jade-blue dress covering up the deep sorrows percolating beneath. Her visitors, from the locals to the tourists, sat by her side in total oblivion. And then they left, one by one. She struggled alone, the sea.

So one day she was awakened by the fierce wind—that she was hanging on to nothing but debris. The vibrant life in the debris had long gone into fading memories. Memories, she cherished. But she did not need the junk. So, her loyal friend the wind blew strong and shook her up to face reality, to cast out her debris. And she did.

The courageous sea has regained her calm existence.

Let it go. Just let go of the debris. Peace and calmness are waiting to rush in.

Driving by the Evening Sea
day 106: november 28, 2015

Driving by the evening sea … that soothing, enchanting, captivating painting takes you places … far away. The faraway shore on that other side of the sea shelters brothers and sisters of other cultures, other religions, and other habits. The sea divides, and at the same time unites, bridging that distance between us. Memories and memoirs of those far away shores come rushing in, blinding me to the beautiful scenery presented at this moment.

But the old is gone.

This fleeting beauty is now the present. "Be happy for this moment. This moment is your life,"[46] said Omar Khayyam. Therefore, I will live this moment as long as it lasts. And I will impress this alluring painting in the depths of my heart for when it's gone. I wonder if the sisters and brothers on the other side of the shore share those memories and memoirs. Maybe they do, maybe they don't. I guess I will never know. That moment is gone now.

This is a new moment. A new now.

Advent: For Whom Do We Wait?

day 107: november 29, 2015

This first Sunday of Advent makes a spectacular entry into the Christmas season. The misty pink air flares up the blue sky casting its Christmas hues unto the world.

Advent calendars, with 24 tiny doors hiding surprises and scripture for each of the 24 days until Christmas, have reappeared. Christmas Sacred Music festivals and concerts are organized in churches and cathedrals. You want to get in the mood? Go to YouTube or your favorite music library and listen to Puccini's "Messa di Gloria," Rossini's "Petite Messe Solennelle," Bach's "Christmas Oratorio," Pietro Mascagni's "Messa di Gloria," Rimsky-Korsakov's "Christmas Eve," or Handel's "Messiah" …. Oh, and those charming Christmas Markets have begun sprouting all over the Cote d'Azur and Europe. Skating rinks add to the allure of this Christmas season, inviting all to swish on the white ice letting their hair and worries fly away along with the tassels of their red-green shawls.

Nativity scenes, with the empty manger, are now being tucked away in the beautiful cathedrals, village churches or homes, and a few public places.

Why all these festivities and preparations? It's Advent—a waiting period, counting down to the 25 days of Christmas. And all will wait in the silence of these nights for the birth of the Messiah.

Rejection and Acceptance
day 108: november 30, 2015

Rejection. Rejected by the trees, they dove into the sea only to find out that the sea would reject them too. The autumn leaves. Rejected but still beautiful and radiating warm red beauty in their desolate state. They keep searching for reasons, but the reasons why it happened are now blurred and not so important anymore. Who was right, who was wrong; who's fault was it … all fades in a distant blurred memory. The red autumn leaves have accepted that their rejection has happened, and the reasons don't matter anymore. Nothing will change at this point if the reasons are crystal clear, remembered.

Acceptance. The state where the agitated waves reject the autumn leaves, and when the bright sunlit sea waits for them in her welcoming arms. The reasons are not important. One has to end so another begins. Acceptance, then, has to follow rejection.

Which one would you choose: to sit and ponder about the reasons and beat yourself up, or, to just accept, put them behind, and choose to bathe in the sunrays rather than in the troubled waves underneath?

The Prince of Peace

day 109: december 1, 2015

December is here. Soon the Prince of Peace will be born. That pure, perfect, precious, powerful, peaceful Prince. He never got mad, but spoke only to teach, did not respond to ignorance with ignorance, did not worry about appearances or possessions, avoided conflict, made trusting circle of friends, and tried to teach us to take care of our souls. He had no worries of tomorrow, and no nostalgic regrets of yesterday.

He is already here, at the sea this morning. And the sea accepts His mark. His mark of peace. And the sea is also at peace. She does not get up, come out, swerve off its way to do things as she pleases. No. She patiently waits for divine interference to change the seasons from autumn to winter, and then spring, summer—all at their appointed times.

Do you also wish for peace to fill your heart? Reign your home? You have tried many techniques to have peace and maintain it, but it does not last, does it? What to do? Call on Jesus and live according to His teachings. Then, as He said, "*[He] will bring peace to your house.*"[47]

The Snowman is Back
day 110: december 2, 2015

Special greetings from my sea today. The smiling snowman is back. He was here last year too, illuminating the sea with its colorful dancing lights at night. It melted and joined the flow, and at the right season and moment in time it rose again. What a wonderful reminder of the beauty of life and the wonders of our world. Snow days. No school days. Snowball fights. Family gatherings. Warm fire glowing from the red and green decorated chimney. Doggy sleeping by its side. Skiing and yummy munching. Subtle announcement of the arrival of the holy waiting period for the human birth of our Baby Jesus.

But while we wait, life happens every day. As soon as each moment passes it melts into the flow and becomes engraved in memory. We choose to cherish it or forget it and move on. There is no time to contemplate and stick to each passing moment and memory because a new moment is happening right now. This is the sacred moment. Feel it, breathe it, smile, enjoy it. Make yourself happy, make someone else happy. Love yourself, love someone. Create, leave your mark. Then it passes. It melts.

Start over. It is a new moment. It is a festive moment.

Shshshshshsh ... Wshshshshsh

day 111: december 3, 2015

Wshshshshsh... Exhales the living sea, and ... shshshshshsh ... she inhales. She has been living for a long time and she has been comforting herself incessantly, for she encounters limitless tragedies, pain and suffering, sadness and solitude. And so, she empowers herself. Shshshshshsh ... wshshshshsh... shshshshshsh ... wshshshshsh.

There are times when the sea is happy and exudes joy to welcome the changing people with the changing seasons. Wshshshshsh exhales the living sea, and shshshshshsh she inhales. It's Christmas tree time. And they planted that regenerating tree by the trio of French Flags that stand saluting. The sea knows it's that time of year when people are happy, filled with hope, and love enables them to breathe ... shshshshshsh ... wshshshshsh.

Keep breathing. The same force that drives this immense sea is in you and in me too—in each of us. We need to stand still in the calm by the Christmas tree and reach inside our soul. God breathed life there. His own breath resides forever in there. Reach within and access it.

Fear and Courage
day 112: december 4, 2015

Fear and Courage were strolling hand-in-hand along the shore, walking over the soft sands, and sometimes jumping over the boulders. The horizon was blissfully calm and perfectly drawn, delineating the meeting point of the cloudy sky and the soft sea. But the shore appeared troubled on its surface.

Fear gazed at the waves rolling at the shore, the proud rocks obstructing the path, and with eyes wide open—pupils almost lost in their wide white globes—and with a voice almost out of breath, whispered, "Let's turn back. I don't feel well, I can't breathe. I will fall into the sea. I can't go on."

Courage, who was never intimidated by anything, declared, "My dear friend Fear, I need you to move forward, you are my life companion, but if you force me to take a step back every time a ripple ruffles, we won't be able to complete our stroll. Close your eyes, hold my hand, trust me, and follow me, and I will take you along the blue shores, up the snow-white mountains, through the green valleys, into the dark nights, and out where the sun always shines."

And Fear firmly held Courage's crisp hand and they lived happily together ever after.

The Christmas Tree

day 113: december 5, 2015

All the trees by the sea are welcoming their ruler—the glorious Christmas tree. The others are permanent here at the seaside. Unlike the majestic Christmas tree, who appears and gets dressed up in red and lit up only for a short season, and yet invokes so much happiness, joy, and good news.

Today, at the beginning of this festive season, resolve to be a Christmas tree for someone who somewhere hopelessly drifts alone; enlighten their winter even for a short while; strengthen their faith in the meaning of the Christmas tree. Assure them that they were born to fulfill a purpose, to live a full life, despite all ailments. Go on top of the mountains and in the deep of the seas and yell, "A baby boy will be born," and all doors will open for you.

Saint Nicholas

day 114: december 6, 2015

It's Saint Nicholas'[48] feast day. He is the patron saint of children. He was born around 270 AD in the Roman Empire's city of Patara. Saint Nicholas became the archbishop of Myra. He was adored because of his many miracles. One legend has it that he brought back to life three children who went into the fields, got lost, and were killed by a butcher named Father Fouettard. This story is told in the song "Ils etaient trois petits enfants."[49] That is why in some paintings he is surrounded with three children. Another legend about his generosity tells that he gifted three bags of gold as dowry to a father to prevent him from forcing his three daughters into prostitution and selling their bodies for money. For that reason, Saint Nicholas is also depicted holding a plate with three golden balls. He passed away on December 6th around the year 345 and was buried in the Church in Myra. In 1087 his relics were transferred to Bari, Italy, and are preserved in the Basilica di San Nicola, where celebrations, processions throughout the streets, and religious festivities are held on May 9th every year.

Because he was a wonderworker and because of his generosity and love for children, Saint Nicholas' name soon became associated with giving gifts to children at Christmas. His main feast is celebrated in Europe as he visits the children on December 6. Those who were nice last year receive sweets and pain d'épice[50] and the naughty ones receive punishment and disapproval from Father Fouettard, the butcher, who accompanies him.

Will you be thinking about Saint Nicholas this Christmas and ask yourself why and for what reason you're receiving, or giving, your Christmas gift?

Ready?

day 115: december 7, 2015

Trees, churches, homes, markets, cities, are all festively decorated and sparkling ahead of Christmas. Gifts are being beautifully wrapped with decorative bowties. Lush menus are being shopped for and prepared to garnish the seasonal decorative gold plates and cutlery. Physically, and on the exterior, all and everything are ready to welcome Christmas.

Welcoming Christmas. Welcoming Jesus.

But who is ready from inside the depth of their soul to welcome Jesus, accept Him and follow His commandments? How does one get spiritually ready for such a humble birth? For such a bright star to follow. For such a saintly life to live.

It's time for inner contemplation, for Christmas songs, for Messa di Glorias, for mental and spiritual

preparations. Time to reflect on God's gifts to us, including the best gift: His only son, Jesus. Time to implore God for wisdom, inner peace, and understanding.

My friend, have you set aside quiet time for inner reflection during this beautiful season?

Monaco Celebrating Mercy and Mary

day 116: december 8, 2015

For the opening of the year of Mercy
Attending the feast of Immaculate Conception of Virgin Mary
And walking in the candlelight procession following the golden statue of Mary
On the winding cobblestone streets near the palace of the Principality
Leaving the Cathedral towards the dazzling Chapelle Miséricorde—meaning mercy
I think how lucky, content, and happy one must be
At this moment, in the world's tiniest, beautiful country
Monaco—is the place to be
Where the people live close to HH the Prince and His Family
This place to be is by the Mediterranean Sea
Where the blue sea meets the blue me
Come visit here with me, this impressive Catholic country
See the medieval castle, and its guards, protecting the First Family
Where locals, visitors, aristocracy, clergy, and royalty
Continue to peacefully live in harmony
While cruise ships and helicopters, famous racecars of the Grand Prix
And high-rise posh apartments sunbathe by the picturesque Sea
Trains, walkways, casino, fine dining, and attractions serve this lovely community
Monaco is the reality forming the scene of a spectacular eternal movie
And presents the perfect place to reflect by the sea

Live for the Now, and Keep Going

day 117: december 9, 2015

The tiny pebble asked the mighty sea, "What do I do with all these meaningless days of this meaningless life?"[51]

The wise sea, who had been around much, much, longer than this young pebble who had just arrived at her shore, huffed and puffed, "Enjoy your blessed life, live for the now, keep yourself always occupied, never being idle nor complacent. Be mindful that your blessings do not belong to you, for you are just a traveler here and nothing belongs to you in this life. Live such that while you enjoy your blessings, you do not neglect the more needy, and you let them partake in your good fortune."

The sea knew the young pebble would not understand now, but she waited until the pebble kept going for a long time—many meaningless days of this meaningless life—and it grew and one day joined the old sands. Only then was it able to grasp and implement what the sea had advised long time ago.

Vanity vs. Charity
day 118: december 10, 2015

The sea relives the Christmas season each year, and witnesses the rush of vanity—spending, stressing, consuming, gifting, decorating, more spending. Reflecting by the sea, she wonders why people keep forgetting that "all is vanity."[52] She remembers the sayings of the teacher: "Wisdom and knowledge are meaningless.[53] All labor and achievement is meaningless.[54] Wealth and money are meaningless.[55] Chasing after the wind."[56] She remembers the teacher's conclusion: "Fear God and keep his commandments, for this is the whole duty of man. For God will bring every deed into judgment, including every hidden thing, whether it is good or evil."[57]

And strolling through the beautiful crèches[58] tucked away on the steps leading up to the towering Menton Cathedral, she decides to not pursue vanity, but to reflect on the true meaning of Christmas—God's gift of Jesus to humanity, the gift of salvation and eternal life to our miserable souls—and to go out and spread some Christmas cheer to those lying in hospital beds, to the elderly in retirement homes, to the neglected women and children and the uprooted refugees. And as she thinks about it, the list grows longer and longer, turning into a lifetime job of charitable service and giving.

Life's Purpose

day 119: december 11, 2015

Author's Illustration, Saint Pierre Church, Cros de Cagnes

And so it came to pass that many years after trying to play God, trying to control every
event and every outcome, failing, falling, and getting up, I learned the purpose of life:
We are but a breeze in the wind, a leaf in the sea
A shshshsh through the forests, a whistle in the hills
What are we but invisible phantoms of momentary thrills
On loan here on earth to fulfill our season
To not waste time trying to reason
But to bring glory to God
To live a life to honor Him
To take care of the earth entrusted to us
Of the life and all creatures He has gifted us
Of the talents He has bestowed upon us
To use our talents wisely
And fill our days with charity
To stay away from gossip and sin
And share His word with our next of kin
So when we're called up and asked if we'd fulfilled our purpose in life
We'd have the valor to look up into His eyes and say, "I've honestly tried"

Silent Sailing

day 120: december 12, 2015

Despite the Christmas rush with its frantic people engaging in mad commercialized "Christmas" buying, there are those who have secluded themselves in the tranquility of the sea, at her blue depths. There, their soul can speak to the unborn God in the silence of the Holy Christmas Season. After all, of what use are all the gifts money can buy, if one can't afford one moment of silence with the powerful source of Christmas.

Let us resolve this Christmas to refuse to buy these modern, secular, throwaway gifts, and instead, to teach unaware children, and forgetful adults, the true meaning of Christmas: the humble birth of our Lord and Savior, Jesus Christ, in whose name the impossible becomes possible. That He came to live among us to teach us to save our souls by believing in Him and His Father. That He urged us to live a life spreading genuine gifts that money can't buy: love, forgiveness, charity, humility, hope, mercy, and most importantly, faith.

I will go then, and sail alone in the stillness of the sea, to first retrieve these true gifts for myself, and then to find in me the wisdom to share them with others during this, and every, Christmas season.

Light

Even the tiniest speck of light overcomes the darkness. Tiny rays of sun illuminate the dark sea. Festival of lights. Celebrations all around reminding us to walk in light. To see the light. To live in the light. Dark paths never lead to a fulfilled life. There is no happiness there, only chagrins. Some celebrate Saint Lucie, Santa Lucia, today. In the cold darkness of the church, candles are lit and placed in a flower-decorated headpiece worn by a young girl who, accompanied by others holding candles, sing "Santa Lucia" and lead a procession in the dark, spreading light, joy, and warmth around them.

Dwelling in the solemn dark, you don't see the doors that might open up to the light. You don't see any doors at all. That small crack in the door brings in the shining light. You just need to find the crack, look towards the light, and follow it. If I'm able to concentrate on the tiny light inside of me, it will suffice to drive the darkness out. After all, what are we but lights, glimmering for a while only to slip away either in the abyss of darkness or in the grand source of Light?[59] The question is: are you going to dimly flicker out, or brightly illuminate?

Sacred Doors
day 122: december 14, 2015

Yesterday, sacred doors, that are opened only on certain occasions, were opened in many Catholic Cathedrals and Churches around the world marking the entrance into the Jubilee year of Mercy. And we too walked into the Sacred Door of the Sainte-Réparate Cathedral in oldtown Nice. Entering this sacred door with unwavering faith will open up all the desired doors in your life. It is all a state of mind. Let all doors open wide for you. Stop holding back or thinking you do not deserve for these doors to open. You do. Banish all thoughts that tell you otherwise. Follow your heart. Enter the sacred door. And feel the opening wide of many other virtuous doors in your life, such as the:

Door of mercy
Door of charity
Door of happiness
Door of love
Door of forgiveness
Door of peace
Door of faith
Door of grace
Door of compassion
Door of life

Love

day 123: december 15, 2015

Love. That ever-eluding love.

We look for love in friends, in family members; we look for it in strangers who eventually become familiar. We look for it in pets, in things, and possessions. We look for it in drinking, partying, and indulging.

Sometimes we find it. Then we lose it. We enter into the wrong relationships looking for love. We look for love in all the wrong places. We are disappointed.

Not with Jesus. For His love is everlasting. When I found the overwhelming love that Jesus is able to give, I never looked back. I stopped looking for love, for it is always in my heart.

I love Jesus and I keep His commandments (I try), and He loves me back and will manifest Himself to me. I know this because He had promised, *"He who knows my commandments, and keeps them, he it is that loves me: and he that loves me shall be loved of my Father, and I will love him, and will manifest myself to him"*[60]

Saint Paul Village and the Spiral

day 124: december 16, 2015

The narrow cobblestone streets of Saint Paul village take you up winding spirals. Along the way cute art galleries, gelaterias, authentic restaurants, and decorated home entrances accompany you as you walk you up to the centuries old beautiful church situated on top of the stairs. It is waiting for Jesus' birth in its lovely Christmas attire.

The winding alleys make me think I'm going in circles at first. I am reminded how I had always thought everything orbited in circles—every form of life, or still life—until I read "Siddhartha" by Herman Hesse. In that story, Siddhartha's friend, Govinda explained that "we are not going around in circles, we are moving up, the circle is a spiral, we have already ascended many a level."

How true. We are not turning in circles: birth, life, and death. No. We don't trace the same circle over and over again. We are moving up the spiral, at different speeds and at different times. At first, we complete the spiral's base, the largest circle, where we waste the most time learning and failing and passing test after test and succeeding to go up the narrower circles of the spiral.

On top, the smallest and farthest circle awaits the purest and the most liberated souls, who, after rotating and slipping on the winding cobblestones of life, are able to free themselves of all physical shackles and ascend to the church at the top of the spiral.

So, don't lose heart, my friend, thinking that you're just rotating in the same place. Keep going, nourish your soul and free it. You will enable your soul to climb to the top of the spiral of life.

The Christmas Tree
day 125: december 17, 2015

The joyous Christmas tree
Patiently waits by the blue sea
Her simple white décor
Adds to her charm all the more
She doesn't need fancy ornaments or garland
She prefers staying rooted in the motherland
She lets snow hold on to her leaves
And red golden balls hang on her sleeves
They announce the most joyous News over the centuries
And yet they're humble, these Christmas trees
O Christmas tree, please tell me
Will He, this year too, walk beside me?

Gifts

day 126: december 18, 2015

Why gifts? The three wise men brought gifts of gold, myrrh, and incense to Baby Jesus in that holy manger in Bethlehem. Christmas gifting of love, faith, and hope has been replaced with the panic of commercialism and the competitive gifting of luxurious, unnecessary items.

But Christmas offers us the gift of Jesus: His hope of saving our souls from the dangers of commercialism, of owning temporal treasures, of accumulating material things unhelpful for the path leading to eternal life. Despite all the material gifting, the gifts of love, forgiveness, help, attention, presence, sharing, honest caring, are the most sought-after gifts. Money cannot buy them. They are difficult to find these days; difficult to give, difficult to receive.

And the lucky one who received real gifts this year—not in physical but in spiritual form—gives thanks:

Thanks for the gift of honest, loving, nurturing relationships, for they help to carry on.

Thanks for the gift of bad days, for they highlight the goodness and hope.

Thanks for the gift of trials, for they teach invaluable lessons.

Thanks for the gift of an aching heart, for it teaches you to finally detach and move on.

Thanks for the gift of duplicity by loved ones, for it teaches you to stand on your feet.

Thanks for the gift of betrayal, for it teaches you the value of true friendships.

Thanks for the gift of sickness, for you learn the value of life.

Thanks for the gift of daily trials, for they teach to bear your own cross and follow Him.

Thanks for the gift of Jesus Christ in our lives, for only He can save; the gift of God is eternal life through Jesus Christ our Lord.[61]

I received much this year. So many gifts of crosses, and after going through them all throughout the year, each one taught me to better my life here on earth and up there in heaven. Thanks for the gift of spiritual awakening.

I Regret Nothing

day 127: december 19, 2015

The Saint Pierre d'Arène Church in Nice celebrated the world-renowned Edith Piaf's life today. Father Gil Florini, a priest and an artist, performed several of Piaf's songs, entertaining the audience and filling the air with the unrelenting ambiance of Piaf's "I Regret Nothing."

And the full church resonated—as if Piaf was there in person—echoing and humming along with the congregation, "Non … je ne regrette rien" (No, I regret nothing.)

Can you sing it out loud, "je ne regrette rien," and mean it? Why regret? It doesn't solve anything; it doesn't bring the past back. You have this moment and what follows—if it is given to you, that is.

So, let's learn from Piaf, who dared to live, to love, to create, to do what she loved during her time on earth. Let's then create our own song. Come on, sing along:

> No, I regret nothing
> To the past I shall not cling
> I don't know what tomorrow will bring
> But it will surely be flowery spring
> And I shall loudly sing
> No, I regret nothing
> I will keep on loving
> I will keep on living
> Just like a true king
> Swaying on life's swing
> Will keep my head up, always worshipping
> No, I won't regret anything

Dixieland Jazz

day 128: december 20, 2015

The December sea rejoices at the two-beat rhythm of Dixieland Jazz tunes while earnestly welcoming the courageous bain de Noël[62] swimmers, who had earlier dove, in their red Santa swimwear into her icy cold waters. But she felt isolated, the sea, in December.

Dixieland. Sounds like fantasyland. It still exists despite all wise indications otherwise. There is joy in fantasyland. There is hope, perseverance to keep the Good, to hang on to it and to promote it.

Fantasyland. It's where I dwell and toil. The more I cultivate it, the more it turns into a reality.

And one day I noticed it was reality all along. My fantasyland. With all its goodness and joy and love and dixy.

Have you found your fantasyland yet?

Stop the Madness
day 129: december 21, 2015

The sea is calm on this gorgeous pre-Christmas afternoon. But she's screaming amidst her calmness, "Stop all this madness; the madness of the Christmas rush—shopping, wrapping, buying, spending, wasting. Stop. Pause for a moment. It's all about inner peace. Outer peace. The Prince of peace. And yet you rush and run, you race and clash.

All the tossing and tumbling will not bring you closer to peace, the Prince of Peace. In fact, they distract. All the Christmas treasures are hidden at sea, the sea of life. No need to swirl around like madmen to buy things under the false name of Christmas gifts. The true Christmas gifts that all of us long to receive, like those treasures hidden at sea, are hidden in plain view for the eager to find, because those who seek, find. Stop all this madness, and just share love, faith, hope, forgiveness, and charity, and let peace be upon you."

First Day of Winter
day 130: december 22, 2015

Yet another gorgeous pre-Christmas day by your shores. Cold and windy. Marking the arrival of winter. The shore is void of signs of human life. No footprints at all in the sand. The winter winds, tossing your waves, washed and blew them off.

They say that the absence of footprints on the sand means that Jesus is carrying you along with all your baggage. Even if He is yet to be born.

No need to worry that the winter winds might blow some people away. There is always someone that loves you. There is always Jesus.

It's chilly now. It's gorgeous, but cold. I must leave.

Winds

day 131: december 23, 2015

Promenade of Cagnes Sur Mer

Even when the waters rage and flood towards you, just keep heading forward and soon they will recede. See the Santa? He's been here recently, deflecting the dark clouds and the troubled waters.

Some people have ventured at your shores today, but personally I can't visit you today, my sea—you're raging so much. But don't worry, I will come back tomorrow for some more inner reflections and advice. My home is at your shores; your pebbles are my doorstep. The winds have calmed for this moment, but I know as soon as I try to open my car's door to step out, they will blow me away.

"But no need to worry," I murmur to myself, "there is always another way to open the desired door." When the raging wind troubling the sea of life shuts one door, it doesn't stop blowing. It goes on to other shut doors and swings them open in front of you. That's the door you should enter now; the one that same wind had opened for you while shutting your desired door. That is where your life should flow. And this circle continues. The wind must move on. It cannot stay to bother you forever.

And once it swerves, it disappears through your newly opened door. The same wind shall never return.

The Three Graces
day 132: december 24, 2015

On this early morning of Christmas Eve, I start marching again at the shore. The sea is gloomy, the cold blanketing its ripples, and the sky is about to cry. As I reach the edge where the pebbles meet the sea, I glimpse three graces serenading the crisp saltwater at sea. They scream and giggle at the cold—they don't care. They enjoy the dive, there in the gloom, alone in that Christmas sea. They realize that they're alone after all, that I was watching them from the distant shore with a bewildered smiling face, and they wave at me. I wave back, shouting, "Bravo!" They yell back, fluttering and shivering, "We do this every Noel." I respond, "You resemble the three graces floating at sea."

My thoughts take me down the memory lane where, few Christmases ago, while giggling with my two lovely daughters in the Géant Casino supermarket, here in Villeneuve Loubet, a kind lady had approached us exclaiming, "les trois grâces." Yes, on this blue Christmas Eve, I'm reminded of the three graces—love, hope, and charity. I'm looking for sea-glass in the pebbles each day, to find the inspiration to persevere to love, to hope, and to move on, and today, I found my lost three graces—love, hope, and charity. Christmas brought forth these gifts. I hear the noise of the pebbles crackling under my feet at the beat of the crashing waves, becoming faster and faster, and I find myself running to go after my love, hope, and charity.

After the midnight mass, where we celebrated the birth of Christ, and after indulging on the thirteen desserts of Christmas honoring the local ageless tradition, I felt I had uncovered again, this time to keep forever, my three graces.

Merry Christmas.

Christmas

day 133: december 25, 2015

A humble King is born to the world in the silence of the Holy Night
Yet His kingdom is not of this world where they constantly fight
The King of kings was born in the humble barn in Bethlehem
Because there was no place in the inn for them
His wooden manger was surrounded with simplicity, love, and peace
Away from where materialism and consumerism form centerpiece
He did not need the comforts of that inn
"Only one thing is needed,"[63] He later said with a grin
To listen, learn, and apply His word—
Help the needy, feed the hungry
Visit the sick, the imprisoned, and the elderly—
To act in His name without uttering a word, to merit His reward
The Bethlehem days are gone now, Christ is X-ed out of Christmas
Crowds frantically rush to shop, instead of waiting for Baby Jesus
Preparing to party with each other, their hearts devoid of forgiveness
To sheepishly exchange their lavish gift boxes stuffed with darkness
Christ's church bells having been silenced long time ago
Slaughter of the innocents is ongoing by new Herods with big egos
And the whole world silently watches muffling its deafened ears
Immersing its head into "holiday" extravaganza and parties
How poor are they trying to eradicate this mighty Baby
Whose kingdom is forever, within you and within me
Where peace is, and where love is
For when two pray together in His name, there He is[64]
Take the holy Light home at midnight this Christmas
Be good, do good, share your blessings of this Genius
Make someone's Christmas truly timeless
Don't forget, it's the small things that make it ageless
Yell on top of the mountains, proclaim in the valleys
That Christ is born to eternally save our soul from the abyss
Say Merry Christmas; forgive, love, and live in peace
For now you are gifted with God's Masterpiece

The Light
day 134: december 26, 2015

In Him was life; and the life was the light of men. And the light shined in darkness; and the darkness comprehended it not.[65]

This day after Christmas, the bright moon, the dark sky, and the navy sea have arranged to display the meaning of light: the moon depicts the Light shining in the darkness, while the dark sky and sea surround the source of light and the path it illuminates.

It is reminiscent of Jesus—being the Light—shining in the darkness of humanity trying to save lost souls. But only few see, understand, and follow His Light. The masses are submerged in the darkness of the soul, lost in material obsessions, oblivious to the purpose of His Light. They swerve from His illuminated path and lose all hope of saving their souls.

But they shall not be lost. Light always finds a way to seep through a tiny crack, providing guidance. All that is needed is a tiny ray of light, a tiny amount of faith. Light always triumphs over darkness. Always and forever.

Silent Sunday

day 135: december 27, 2015

The last Sunday of 2015 and I'm here again at the Cagnes Promenade staring at my sea. The tree is holding on to its autumn leaves, while the Christmas tree has lost its red and gold decorations. They're staring at the sea too, in silence.

Silence. Gazing at it all in contemplation of the Sundays past. Overachiever or underachiever—both have arrived at this Sunday. What did one accomplish that the other didn't or couldn't? What was expected of them? Humans have varying standards of measuring achievement—some in silence, others in clamor—and their measure is the quantity of accumulated material treasures at the end of the year.

Little do some know that all that's expected of them is to contemplate the splendid power of our silent Creator, and to achieve charity and mercy, without flaunting, throughout all the silent Sundays of the year.

Innocence

day 136: december 28, 2015

I learned that the sea is both the inspirer and the taker of innocence.

How many innocent lives were lost at sea this year? Migrants lost at sea; their fleeing boats capsized. Innocent lives lost to war, greed, and violence. Innocent souls lost to temptations and sin. Innocent relationships lost to adultery and lies. How many innocent children ruined by cruel adults, and innocent animals persecuted for sumptuous meals? And almost all perpetrators of these atrocities adore the sea and relax by its shores, congratulating themselves and obtaining the inspiration to carry on.

Damn those oppressors, those destroyers of innocence, and those staying silent. "If you are neutral in situations of injustice, you have chosen the side of the oppressor," warns Desmond Tutu.

But the sea, the sea of life, as tolerant as she is, always returns to them their just lot in the end.

This I Learned from the Sea

day 137: december 29, 2015

This I learned from the sea:

Drink. Drink your water. It nurtures and cleanses the body and the soul.

Persevere. Persevere patiently just like the stubborn waves that do not give up.

Be calm. In calmness you will find your soul.

Just be. Be happy. Let the storms pass. The warm sun always peaks again.

Let go. Let go of all that do not wish to be by your side, don't chase them.

Be welcoming to all, but sometimes you'll have to spit the garbage out, just like the sea.

Love. Love conquers hate. Love, and you will be loved. They might leave you at times, but they shall surely come back for your love, just like the sea.

Stay. Stand firm and believe. Whatever you want will come to you.

Silence. Discover the power of silence, to find meaning so as to live, really live.

Harmony. Live a disciplined life in harmony with yourself to fulfill your life's purpose.

Peace. Do not go out of your way to harm others.

Be useful. Share what your learn. Be of service to other creatures and to the universe.

Create. Your creations will be your legacy to future generations.

Hit back. Don't sit back and take false criticism. Hit back.

Don't beat yourself up. Be kind to yourself. No regrets.

Say no to vice. No to worldly temporal temptations. No to evil. No to ruthless users.

Respect Earth. We come from her, are nurtured by her, and eventually return to her.

Be grateful. Thank the Creator. From Him you receive it all.

Acceptance. Accept what life throws at you, good or bad. Learn from it and move on.

Keep your vows. In sickness and health, for richer or poorer.

Open your spiritual eyes.

Enjoy life. Walk, sit, relax, contemplate, work, give, and walk some more at the shores of the sea—the sea of life. Bask in the warm sun and the lighted moon and the guiding stars and the life-giving rains and the governing skies—with those you love and trust.

Fly. Only by flying you will reach the stars, not by walking your head down.

Appreciate your friends who stick around in those dark days, they are yours to cherish.

Flashback

day 138: december 30, 2015

I ask the sea if, looking back, she thought she had achieved her goals and desires for the past year. The majestic Sea immediately pushes a 'yes' with her waves tingling my feet inside my winter boots. She had shown equal hospitality to scores of humans. She had warmed and mended thousands of cold, broken hearts. She had inspired remarkable artistic creations. She had toned down a multitude of pebbles. She had polished into vibrant sea-glass all the broken bottles thrown away at her laps. She had created a new shore. She had homed and nurtured all that had sought refuge with her: the tiny and the huge, the dark and the luminous. She had served all with dedication. Sometimes, she had erupted with rage in her dark days but that was okay. Her friends the moon and the radiant sun and the stars and the winds partook in her good days and bad days. That's what friends are for. And most of all she was always looking up and ahead, giving thanks to the skies and beyond for all her blessings.

Then she asks about me. In a split second I realize I was on the receiving side of all her achievements. My sea had mended my broken heart with her warm welcoming wavy hugs. She had inspired me to draw and to write two books. I had worked and created. She had toned down my broken edges and had rounded me into a polished rare sea-glass. She had nurtured my soul and my mind opening up my spiritual eyes. She had created acceptance in my heart and understanding in my mind and forgiveness in my heart and soul. I had shared my newly found peace and joy with old and new friends. She had nurtured my aching body and mind and she had cured me. I had become a new person, ready to share her achievements with the world.

And I lie on my back, on the damp sand, by her side, basking in the sun. Looking into the blue winter heaven, I join my sea in giving thanks for all our graces and blessings.

Thank YOU

day 139: december 31, 2015

As the old year swishes past us, trailing its final red light in the festive yet empty streets on this last day of 2015, heading towards the village church on the small hill for midnight mass, I murmur my own prayer to our Father:

Dear God, thank you for the abundant beautiful moments of happiness and laughter, along with the numerous fleeting troubles and worries of the year past. They all helped teach elaborate lessons. Lessons of patience, forgiveness, wisdom, and unconditional love, of acceptance at times and letting go at other times.

Thank you for sending each trial and triumph as an instruction to find inner peace, to awaken the dormant soul, and to open the sleeping spiritual eyes.

Thank you for closing a few doors making way for exciting new ones to open wide.

Thank you for the peaceful sea, for the golden life-giving sun, the enlightening moon, the guiding stars, the Mother Earth, the loving and caring people, and our friendly pets.

And now, armed with my new awakening, and You by my side, I enter the majestic gates of the New Year to share love, hope, faith, forgiveness, and peace with my loved ones and the world.

All the glory and praise to you, Almighty God.

Limitless Horizon
day 140: january 1, 2016

Entering the majestic gates of the New Year, the sea, peaceful yet powerful, extends her splendid posture to the limitless horizon of 2016, introducing the horizon of hope: this new path towards fulfilling your dreams. Let the new horizon bring boundless hope for the hopeless. Hope of every kind that gives birth to new dreams and the courageous ability to fulfill them.

Get your white piece of paper (or smart screen), shut down the noise in your head, breathe in the new peace, and jot down your bucket list, assigning to each item a feast day so you celebrate as you check them off one by one during this new year.

Today let's celebrate the new horizons that the new year will bring.

It's in the Circle

day 141: january 2, 2016

Smarty and Sage were walking by the shore, throwing pebbles. When Smarty saw the circles formed at sea each time one of her pebbles hit the water, she rejoiced. She threw pebble after pebble, forming various sizes of circling ripples. Then she tried to form squares, triangles or rectangles with each throw, but she couldn't. Despaired, she threw a puzzled look at Sage, who, anticipating Smarty's question, said:

"Smarty, you will only be able to from circles because that is the law of nature. You see, all life is formed of circles. Mother Nature works in circles. The circle is the most powerful unit. The sun and the moon, our Earth and all planets, are circles, and they only orbit in circles. The water of the sea, when it evaporates, it forms clouds, and then, as rainfall it comes back into the sea, completing its life circle. The four seasons change in circles, one giving way to the other. The year is a circle beginning and ending at the same time. A baby is formed in mom's circular womb, and is born, walks through life's circle, and dies at the closing of the circle. And the body, that came from ashes returns to ashes completing that circle. The soul that came from the metaphysical returns to the supernatural, completing that circle. Think of the human body amazingly operating in circles: the digestive, respiratory, nervous, cardiovascular, and all the other systems, function in circles, starting and ending at a command center—the brain. The body and the soul rotate in circles, completing each other. When one circle ends, the other circle begins. Life is a circle. When one form of life ends, another form begins. Karma, too, is a circle. You know when they say, you reap what you sow, it means if you do good deeds, good will come back to you. And the bad too will return, if you have so acted. And all these circles work together in a perfect harmony. Above all, know that all circles begin and end in faith. Now, can you give me an example of a perfect circle?" asked Sage. Smarty exclaimed, "Family circle! Yes, the family circle is the most important entity."

Fête de la Pluie – Feast of the Rain
day 142: january 3, 2016

This shower of blessing
Pours on all without discriminating
Provides life for those cringing
The rustling rain, the source of being

Today, celebrate the splendor of rain
Giving thanks for the restored gain
And shedding every nature of pain
Come back home to the nature plain

Dancing Winds

day 143: january 4, 2016

As winds adjust their tunes to the seasons of our lives, they make everything dance: the waves, the birds, the trees, and us. Melodies or rock, waltzes or jazz, they all make you dance. The wind controls the speed of the dance. Are you able to withstand the winds? Firm yourself on your ground. Or would you rather dance away with the winds? The wind blows from all sides; same wind, different sounds. Different tunes. Different echoes. You can resist it, brush it off, or just let it swing you away.

It is Fête du Vent—the Feast of the Wind; time to salsa with the dancing winds.

The Good News and the Pigs

day 144: january 5, 2016

Continuing our imaginary daily celebrations, let's celebrate today the Feast of Good News. The joy of receiving good news—those sparkling drops of joy that first cajole your eyes, then your heart which in turn filters them into your whole being. And your face smiles, your soul lifts with happiness, and your glistening eyes reflect bliss. Don't let anyone rob you from the joy of receiving good news. Giving good news. Being the good news. You try hard to be good news to everyone at all times. Some appreciate and some don't.

But, don't change. Be the good news that flashes from one shore to the other. And don't let them rob you from your good news. But remember to not cast your shimmering pearls to pigs; because if you do, they won't appreciate, and instead they will trample them under their feet and then they will turn around and tear you to pieces.[66]

Do not forget to be good news to yourself as well. Be good to yourself, take good care of yourself.

Galette des Rois

day 145: january 6, 2016

The Galette des rois (the kings' cake) is a must on this day in France. It appears for the Feast of Epiphany, 12 days after Christmas, to commemorate the visit of the three wise kings—Caspar, Melchior, Balthazar—to the newborn Jesus in Bethlehem. Guided by the Holy Star from the east, the three Magi arrived in Bethlehem, and found the newborn King Jesus in that barn. Seeing Him they rejoiced, fell on their knees and worshiped Him, and opening their treasures, they offered him gifts: gold and frankincense and myrrh.[67]

The Galette des rois prominently occupies its space in the glamorous glass display cases of the patisseries, bakeries, and markets. Topped with its golden crown, it hides a tiny fève (party favor) in the many flaky sweet layers of this almond paste cake.

And the Galette des rois commemorates this joyful visit and the offering of their gifts. You have to use all your wit to receive that slice of the galette in which the tiny fève is hidden. If you're the lucky one who finds it, you get to wear the golden crown, and become king for the day, and you will have a blessed year ahead.

Fête de la Communication

day 146: january 7, 2016

Today let's celebrate the Feast of Communication. See how nature and men communicate: the sun's rays touch upon the raging waves warming them up, the flowing trees tame their leaves, and the faces in the passing cars smile. Listen how the invisible winds whisper into the human ears through the flying kites and the branches of the rooted trees. Feel how the sky silently listens and mediates and how your eyes see and transmit, even in black and white, the feelings that this scene evokes to your soul. How everything and everybody yearn to communicate. Honest, open, clear communication.

Some say they want honest communication but they themselves lie, keep secrets for years, cheat, and twist the facts to suit their own agenda. To clear their guilty conscience. Or so they think. But they don't repent. They don't change their ways. They just keep preaching and insisting on open and honest communication while keeping their door shut, tucked into themselves, their secret world, and guilty adulterous habits. They accuse, they smear, they tarnish your reputation to help clear their guilty conscience. Some believe them, for a little while. And that gives them more power, more reason to continue with their destructive behavior. Do they ever feel free from their guilt? Or do they even feel guilt or remorse?

If only we were all like the sea and her friends—open, clear, honest, transparent; communicating effortlessly with the surrounding skies, the bordering shores, the resting pebbles, its embracing creatures, and everything and everyone crossing its paths. Only if we copy how they hold dialogue in harmony, in noise and in silence, completing and complementing each other, will we be able to perfect our own communication.

Fête de l'Auteur

day 147: january 8, 2016

Who is the author of life, of the snowy peaks, the green forests, the beautiful landscapes, and the sea? Us? Assorted circumstances converging in vacuum? Or God?

If we are the author of our life, then how come we are often unhappy with the fruit of our authorship? And if we are not happy, do we have the capability to rewrite, re-edit, change the characters and the plot, and therefore change the outcome of our life, the ending of our story, our legacy?

If assorted circumstances are the author of our life, then do we let each wind blowing from a different direction—with divergent force or varying velocity—dictate our destiny, or do we take control of the pen and start rewriting. Can we take control of the pen?

If God is the author of our lives, then why do we constantly worry and toil and plan and get anxious about it? May be the sea has the answer: Just hold your place, relax, let it be. All is already planned out for you. Just write your part. But to write, you must first find the mission God has entrusted you with. Then complete it with enthusiasm. Be uniting of all, and yet rebuke when necessary. Welcome whoever and whatever comes your way. Keep them if they value you. And yet if they are unappreciative and ungracious wave them out. Gently caress, patiently instruct, provide life and help keep afloat your fellow writers. Write your story with honesty, integrity, while traveling with your fellow pilgrims in harmony. Celebrate the Feast of the Author.

Choices
day 148: january 9, 2016

My sea offers many choices of colorful sea-glass, heart stones, broken pieces made beautiful, sands, and pebbles. Yes, the sea of life gives us many choices—some unique, some interesting, others colorful, still others dull and plain wrong. But the wise man knows what to choose. He counsels:

> Flee sin so it does not consume you
> Run away from it even if you end up alone
> Walk away from vanities of modern hoarding and boasting
> Better be a lone fugitive in the Temple of God
> Better be a sacrifice for the glory of God
> Than to partake in modern sin and be eaten by it

And I recall Aesop's fable: A Wolf pursued a Lamb, which fled for refuge to a certain Temple. The Wolf called out to him and said, "The Priest will slay you in sacrifice, if he should catch you," to which the Lamb replied, "It would be better for me to be sacrificed in the Temple than to be eaten by you."[68]

Fête de la Pomme
day 149: january 10, 2016

And today we decided to celebrate the Feast of the Apple that resembles this daybreak.

Apple: it changed the world—from Eve's bite of the first apple thousands of years ago, to the modern Apple with a bite taken out of it.

All sin and dishonesty started with an apple. Humans were exiled from paradise because of an apple. We are forced to toil and suffer here on Earth because of an apple.

But one person saw it differently. And now the apple is perpetuating all the moments of our world in its every form. And while the genius creator of Apple is no longer here, for us to celebrate the Feast of the Apple seems the right thing to do—whether it is now in season or not.

Fête d'Or
day 150: january 11, 2016

View on Cagnes Sur Mer and Nice Airport

Today is the feast of Gold. Everything golden pops up everywhere.

A friendly loyal golden retriever strolls on the shore in the midst of the stormy waves and golden cloudy skies. Unseen rays paint the seaside alive with shades of gold.

Today the Sacré Ballon d'Or—which I had not known existed—went to Lionel Messi.

And where is the golden sun? It wants to hide its face today, but still paints the Earth with its golden layers. And that is beautiful too. And the feast of gold does not mind at all.

Nissa La Bella – Nice the Beautiful
day 151: january 12, 2016

View on Nice from Colline du Chateau (Castle Hill)

Appreciating Nice from the top of its Colline de Chateau is a must when you're in town. From up there the city boasts its rainbow of colors, arranged in a beautiful mosaic that engulfs the sea. And the beautiful coast, lapping gently, serenades the Promenade des Anglais, from its landmark Hotel Negresco, its savory multi-cuisine and Niçoise restaurants, its memorial at the Quai des États-Unis, to its colorful port from where ferries float you to Corsica. At a short distance from the shores lies the famous Place Massena with its open-air museum, luxury shops, cafés, and markets, including its charming seasonal Christmas Market and Winter Village.

The Matisse and Chagall museums in the Cimiez area, among other museums, comprise the rich cultural heritage of beautiful Nice. And the Old Town, dominated by its imposing Cathedral, and dotted by its churches, cafés, galleries, and souvenir shops, invites you for a perfect escape from the routine. If that's not enough, Nice entices you with its Jazz and other festivals, its notorious Mardi Gras Parade and Mimosa Flower Battle, its sports Marathons, water sports and many other activities.

So next time you're here making memories, enjoy what Nice has to offer, and cherish the reflections Nice leaves at night on the nearby sea.

Feast of the Beauty of Life
day 152: january 13, 2016

Whoever you are, whatever you may doing, regardless of your circumstances, appreciate this very moment that you have been offered. Isn't it useless to waste it in regret, self-pity, or anger? For they will steel this moment from you and will never solve the issues that bog you down.

Look at the sun that shines right now. The cold sea bathes in the sun's warmth, and in the stillness of this moment, you hear her sing, "Sunshine … on my shoulder makes me happy …"[69] And a warm happiness tingles your heart. The limitless sky and the long pebble pathway carve the trail for you to wander. The bouquets of fuzzy yellow mimosas have bloomed early this year in stark contrast with the crunchy brown leaves scattered at their feet. The snowy peaks of the Southern Alps whiten the crisp horizon. You breathe in long and deep the same cool air that feeds this beautiful moment, and you think, "the same almighty power that creates all this powerful beauty has created me too, has offered me this moment, and I shall not waste it."

And in all this beauty the gloom feels obligated to hide. It soon disappears. As always, it's just a matter of time or a turning of a season that the dark will fade away. So be patient. Take this moment, your moment, and cherish it.

Fête des Etoiles
day 153: january 14, 2016

Let us celebrate today the Feast of the Stars, the three radiant stars of Orion—The Hunter Constellation's belt: Alnitak (Zeta), Alnilam (Epsilon), and Mintaka (Delta). Have you ever looked at the darkest skies and discovered it's not dark at all, but forever lit by the enormous glittering field of stars. Have you also gazed at this flashy trio of stars since childhood, wishing upon them the most secret of your dreams.? Yes? Come join our club of stargazers.

Alnitak, Alnilam, and Mintaka (Ancient Arabic names, meaning the belt, the pearls, and region[70]), stud hunter Orion's belt, overseeing and accompanying us, the travelers of earth. They keep watch from above: "When you wish upon a star ...[71]" this trio of bright stars multiply by three the chances of your wish coming true. They shine, day and night, and even when we're unable see them. Different countries refer to them as the Three Sisters, the Three Kings, and the Three Marys.

Let us continue to wish upon this radiant, serene trinity. Hand in hand, and side by side, this eternal trio of ever-shining pearls shall continue to brighten any disheartening dark sky.

La Turbie and Dante's Purgatory

day 154: january 15, 2016

View on Monaco from La Turbie, Dante's Plaque

Strolling among the remnants of the Roman Empire in the magnificent La Turbie perching over my Mediterranean Sea, I come upon an interesting plaque. Cemented in an ancient wall in one of the cobblestone alleyways of the medieval village, it displayed verses 49-51 of Canto 3 of Dante's Purgatory. I look up these verses to understand their connection with la Turbie. They are translated to mean: "The loneliest, most jagged promontory that lies between Turbia and Lerici, compared with it, provides stairs wide and easy."[72]

Dante describes the Purgatory, in his Divine Comedy, as a rocky wretched mountain made of seven ascending terraces, each corresponding to the seven deadly sins—pride, envy, wrath, sloth, avarice, gluttony, and lust. Dante, wanders in this spiritual world with the Italian poet Virgil as his guide, and encounters souls at different stages of repentance. He must climb up Mount Purgatory, ascend each terrace of sin, and learn from each stage to cleanse his soul, which is journeying towards Paradise. At the onset, Dante realizes the ascent on Mount Purgatory is extremely steep, difficult, punishing, and grueling. Comparing the treacherous climb to the "lonely, jagged" terrain between Lerici[73] and La Turbie,[74] he describes, in these verses, that even the wretched cliffy terrain between la Turbie and Lerici provides a staircase much wider and easier than the climb of Mount Purgatory.

And I gaze at that same charming landscape that now runs between the Italian and French Rivieras. Its red-roofed Provençal homes dot the winding hairpin turns that climb up the steep mountains. And I cannot comprehend why Dante would see this as a deserted, jagged terrain and compare this gorgeous landscape to the terraces of the seven deadly sins. Perhaps we finally have reached Paradisio, having managed to climb up Mount Purgatory for many centuries?

Rose

day 155: january 16, 2016

I am the symbol of love: a beautiful, perfumed, intoxicating rose
I've learned to live with the piercing that my nasty thorns impose
Each day I hold my velvet head up trying to spread love
Going out there, carrying my thorns that hug me like a glove

It took me a long time to learn to accept those thorns I carry
From the day I bloomed and blossomed, those thorns annoyed me
Now that I've flourished and grown wise, I focus more on my beauty
Not complaining, but offering my love to make those around me happy
And until I wither, I shall exist, beautiful in my own way, with my thorns by me

I accepted them, not grasping the meaning for their existence with me
Until one day, you tried to snap, snatch, break, and deface my beauty
My big and small, ugly thorns resisted and repelled your animosity
I realized that my thorns were there to protect me
They had never hurt me—
My thorns were there to protect me
From you

Feast of Conversations
day 156: january 17, 2016

Restaurant La Mamma, Cagnes Sur Mer Promenade

It's four in the afternoon in the Cote d'Azur, and almost no restaurant serves meals. Instead on the menu are deserts, French sweets, Italian Gelato, tea and coffee, and the famous Café Gourmand.

Ah, the experience of the Café Gourmand—a perfect plate setting for a perfect setting of any conversation. Business or casual, formal or winding down, all conversations and meetings run much smoother around a heavenly Café Gourmand.

This mouthwatering collection of mini sweet surprises surrounding a shot of Espresso fills all your senses such that one can initiate and carry on any type of conversation. The fresh aroma of Italian espresso awakens your napping afternoon mind, the chocolat fondant with crème Chantilly sweetens your thoughts, the warm crème brûlée (burnt cream) lets you crack its hardened surface letting go of the hardened face, warming up your mood into the conversation. And that mini glace de vanille (vanilla ice-cream) cools down even the most heated conversation. Sometimes, these delicious sampling of petits-fours and sweets includes a mini éclair, a small strawberry tart, a shot-glass of chocolate mousse, panna cotta, tiramisu, a piece of chocolate, a miniature chou, or a tiny macaroon.

And no matter how your conversation has ended, you do not return home with the same old self after this cultural feast of conversations. You have changed.

Guessing Game
day 157: january 18, 2016

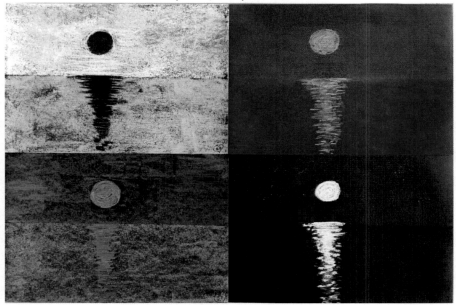

Four illustrations by the author

What do you see by the sea?
Changing seasons or changing hours?
Red sun or silver moon? Dawning morning or dark night?
Spring, summer, winter, or fall?
Sunrise or sunset? Moonrise or moonset?
Mere reflections and fleeting illusions
Glisten on the Mediterranean's dancing waters
The forever sea and the eternal sky
Play this guessing game with their exotic colors
With the sun and the moon and the million stars
They reflect to the concerto of changing times and seasons
But there's only one true Light always reflecting on the sea
Teaching us that, we in our turn must let our light reflect
Trying to guide someone in this troubled sea of life
For, only those, whose reflections touch a lost soul by this sea
Shall forever participate in the driving force towards eternity

Be

day 158: january 19, 2016

Be
Believe
Be yourself
Be happy
Be all eyes
Be all ears
Be heard
Be someone
Beget
Bear fruit
Befriend
Be helpful
Be grateful
Be honest
Be your best
Be—live
Be

Fete de la Neige
day 159: january 20, 2016

Although it did not snow here on the Cote d'Azur this year, I'd like to share this photo from the flurry and blizzard of 2010. At that time, the snow fell all day, and to the surprise of all, blanketed the sea and the mountains with its soft white crystals. Everybody was overjoyed.

Those beautiful icy white crystals. Why do they stir such happiness, such warm and fuzzy emotions in our cold hearts? Is it the purity, the perfectly carved design of each flake that falls within the 30-something flawless snowflake patterns known to us? Maybe it's because we don't live in the winter wonderland of our childhood dreams anymore.

And today, how I wish to be left alone with the snow in this winter wonderland, holding it close to my chest, sitting at the shore. And there would be no one else but the snow and the waves—two faces of the same soul. I would close my eyes and let this purest perfume fill my chest and empty my ears of the constant earthly noise. Oh, how I wish to be lonesome with you, my snow, my sea, to celebrate the Feast of the Snow.

Fête de Câlin

day 160: january 21, 2016

It's National Hug Day. The stories these pebbles tell. If you closely examine them, you'd discover that no pebble resembles another. Each is unique, though similar. They all had their own story, their unique experience. They lived, they loved, they hugged, they drifted apart, and they died. They kept hugging each other through it all. And then they all morphed into the same sand, oblivion to the fact that they are to be devoured by the sea. And still, they persist in hugging each other.

Can we, fallible, week, angry, sentimental humans act the same way? Hug and let go. If you want to be hugged, give a hug. If you want love, give love. If you want truth, be truthful. Be the mirror of what you'd like to receive. What you reflect will always return, for the reflection has nowhere else to go in this universe. It will either return to sand or will float in the universe and come back to you in time.

Once you emit that reflection, the warm hug, the kind look, the caring act, it'll turn and sway and travel, and somehow, someday, it will infallibly come back to you—to hug you.

Happy Hug Day.

Feast of the Possible Impossible

day 161: january 22, 2016

See the pink sun stuck between the blue sky and the blue sea? Is it possible? Impossible? Feeling stuck in a bad situation? Change it, reject it, or accept it. But do not remain stuck in it. One wave's swish says to change it. Another huge wave says reject it. A calmer tide says accept it.

I query the sea, and she replies, "Don't ever get stuck in it. Look at me. I choose one of the three and I immediately execute that decision. I don't remain stuck in that bad situation. Decide, then stop thinking about it. Don't allow your mind to go on overdrive and create chaos. Allow all the wonderful impossibilities to find their way and surprise you. How many times will you find a unique red pebble on my shores? Maybe none, and yet it exists, hidden there between the millions of pebbles. See? You found it. Open up. Celebrate the Possible Impossible. Expect it with all your heart. Take action. Work for it. And the impossible will become possible. And when I need help, I ask for help, and the sun comes out."

And she gives me a piece of her sun and the sun walks by me all along the shore. "I am always here for you," the sun says, "even if sometimes you do not see me."

The Sun Will Shine Again

day 162: january 23, 2016

The sun will shine again
Whether the sea wants it or not
And will lift the sea from its melancholy
Unwillingly, the sea will start to roll, move, and rock
Transferring her emerging enthusiasm to the pebbles waiting on her
And the pebbles will sing along with her ppppp rhythm
As the white foam rattles and retreats from each pebble one by one
That calming yet invigorating ripple will rattle
Despite the cold, dark, desolate shore of the night
The morning hustle and bustle will soon arrive
So, if this melancholic sea can do it, you can do it too
Just keep moving forward, hustling and bustling
And the sun will shine again
Whether you believe it or not

Feast of the Impermanence
day 163: january 24, 2016

Antibes

Nothing is permanent. Not the good days, nor the bad. The burdens, the trials, the anxiety: all temporary. The happiness: momentary. Even the gorgeous flowers are passing, and the mighty sea transient. Not one wave is the same as the previous or the next. Not one splash of the ephemeral white sprinkles will mist your face twice.

Impermanent. Fleeting. Life.

Celebrating impermanency lightens our burden, eliminates our worries, directs our focus to the permanency of the soul—the eternal, conscious soul. Tend to its wellbeing. Take good care of your soul.

Feast of Miracles
day 164: january 25, 2016

Antibes

Miracle: God's way of rearranging circumstances, people, and events to answer your prayer.

Sometimes they arrive disguised in misfortune. You just need to sit back, relax, and examine the flip side of the misfortune to discover its camouflaged miracle. Remember, adversity builds bravery.

Take this test. Write down three challenging events in your life that you have regarded as misfortune. Then grab a glass of wine, a cup of tea, and think. Think long. And find out the miracles that were hidden in each adversity. You will recognize each miracle when you realize each has taught you a lesson, opened a new door, unearthed a new talent, empowered your soul, reinforced your confidence, boosted your courage, or brought about a new friend—amidst the turmoil of adversity.

Yes, let us celebrate today the Feast of Miracles.

Manifesto of Freedom
day 165: january 26, 2016

I am free
Just like the sea
And the sailors of the sea
Like the seagull roaming free
Free from fetters
Fetters of boxes
Chains of man-made rules
Binding the spirit to shackles of illusions
Hindering the free flight across the sea
I am free, just like the sea, and will always be
Free

Feast of Don't-Hold-On

day 166: january 27, 2016

My dear sea, how right you are in the way you exist independently. You do not hold on to anything. You just do your job and keep moving on. No matter who or what comes in your beautifully laden path, you just stay focused and let them revolve around you.

From you I learned to not hold on to anything or anyone in this world. The more you hold on, the more that thing or person will elude you. Buddha advised, "Live independently, not holding onto anything in the world."[75] That way, there will be no pain, no suffering, no anguish. Just let everything be: possessions, treasures, father and mother, brother and sister, children and friends, and follow your spiritual path. Live your spiritual life. The less you hold on to things or people, the less you will get hurt, the more space you will have to pile up your spiritual gifts. Nothing is yours. Not the Earth, not the sea, not anything on the earth or in the sea. Not the people around you: not friends, not parents, not siblings, not spouses, not children. For the wise poet said, "Your children are not your children, they are the sons and daughters of Life longing for itself."[76]

Therefore, let's today celebrate the Feast of the Don't-Hold-On.

Food

day 167: january 28, 2016

Restaurant La Spiaggia Plage, Cagnes Sur Mer

Bathing in the sun on a cool winter midday, my warm blouse imbibes the silver rays and diffuses them evenly on my chilled skin. I hear the happy waves rush towards me to hug me and play at my feet. The seagull looks for a catch at the bare winter pebbles, just like the fishermen in their boat at large at sea.

And I already find my catch of the day at the café by the shore. Come, enjoy with me this savory fresh salad. The art of gastronomy of the Cote d'Azur: simple and yet satisfying, and served all year round.

We need to take a break sometimes, and do nothing but … eat.

Things Don't Always Get Done

day 168: january 29, 2016

Antibes

My dear sea, I cannot come today to sit by your side, but I would like to complain a little, nonetheless. It has been a long time that I have kept my complaints piled up inside. The harder I try to get things done, the more they don't. The more I try to love, the more they try to hurt. The more I serve, the more they use. The more I give them time to work things out, the more they use the opportunity to further their selfish plans and destructive agendas. The more I forgive, the more they try to take advantage. The more I remain silent for peace's sake, the more they try to backstab. The more I want to walk by your shores, the more obstacles present themselves blocking the peaceful path leading to you.

And I hear the soothing crashes of your waves stored in the cherished images of my memory.

Detaching from it all, I try to find peace within. To pay tribute to inner peace, I want to celebrate today the feast of Things-Not-Getting-Done. Why stress over it when we can turn it into a feast? Let's always discover something to celebrate, something to learn and grow from.

It is said that "whatever you resist, persists."[77] So, cheers to not resisting, to Things-Not-Getting-Done.

Let Down Your Burden
day 169: january 30, 2016

La Terrasse Restaurant, Cagnes Sur Mer

She says, "Lâche, lâche, lâche," her firm hands shaking my shoulders, "loosen up, let down your burden, let it go. Don't scrutinize. Let your weary soul flourish. Picture yourself in the middle of a circle. Picture all that negativity, chatter, hurt, unfaithfulness, waiting for you outside the circle. Now, take this match, light it, and throw it out. You burnt them down. They are gone. Feel your aggravation alleviated, your devastation replaced with delight, disappointment with carelessness, and frustration with freedom. Then you will reach your resilience point, and bouncing back, you will thrive."

And handing me the platter of café-et-croissant (coffee and croissant), my friend pushes me to sit down at the lakeside café. And we enjoy the marvels of French gourmet. I do "lâche." I let go. I let down my burden.

I decide I will survive. I survive.

Feast of Independence
day 170: january 31, 2016

Sunrise on the Mediterranean

"Strive for independence," murmurs the sea in my ears. She shows me how she exists independently of all that surrounds her. She is focused. She concentrates on her present tasks and accomplishes them daily, with vigor. She breathes deeply in, and calmly exhales her waves of disturbance. She provides an enriching refuge to the needy, the weary, and the ill, strengthening them with her pleasant aura and calm demeanor.

She is independent. To know that independence is the propeller of the sea, my sea, is splendidly inspiring.

So come let's celebrate today the Feast of Independence, personal independence, that you may not be in need of anything or anybody, but yourself, your soul, and your God.

The Enemy Within
day 171: february 1, 2016

The sharp-edged rock dares to sit among the soft pebbly sand, concealing itself in the waves. The enemy within—it acts like one of us, mingles among the same milieu. Yet, when the waves recede and are about to attack again, the true face of the enemy within emerges. It is unpleasant. It does not belong here. Does not fit in. Yet it is planted here, among us. And it persists. Has nowhere to go. Keeps acting. The enemy within.

What do you do with the enemy within?

The sea is patient. It will keep hammering and hammering until the rocky ugliness is crushed and blended with the small assorted pebbles, until they all become uniform. The sea loves uniformity around her.

Presentation of Jesus in the Temple, La Chandeleur, Crêpes

day 172: february 2, 2016

Restaurant Aux Tours de Notre Dame, Paris

Forty days after Christmas, Christians celebrate the Presentation of Jesus in the Temple in Jerusalem, or the Purification of Mary. According to the Gospel of Saint Luke,[78] Joseph and Mary brought Baby Jesus to the temple to be blessed and consecrated to God. There, they were met with Simeon the God Receiver and Anna the Prophetess, who were waiting for the arrival of the Messiah for years. The Holy Spirit had revealed to Simeon that he would not die until he'd seen the Messiah.[79] Simeon and Anna immediately recognized Baby Jesus as God. Simeon took Jesus in his arms, he praised God saying, "Lord, now you can dismiss your servant in peace for my eyes have seen your salvation that you have prepared for all mankind."[80] This is known as the Song of Simeon or Nunc Dimittis in Latin. Simeon is referred to as the God Receiver because he received Jesus (God) in the temple, recognized that Jesus was the long-awaited Messiah, and blessed Him, and turning to Mary warned that the Baby will be the cause of many to rise and fall, and that a sword would pierce her heart too.[81]

Christmas decorations, nativity scenes and mangers, exhibited since Christmas, are removed on this day. This feast is also called Candlemas, La Chandeleur, because on this day all candles are blessed in the church to be used throughout the year; candles are lit and taken home by the faithful for blessings and protection.

In France, this feast is also known as Crêpe day—fête de la Crêpe. According to an ancient custom established by Pope Gelasius (492-496), crêpes or pancakes were offered to pilgrims on this day. Different types of crêpes are prepared and offered or sold on February 2nd to celebrate these festive events.

Let No one Influence Your Decisions

day 173: february 3, 2016

The sea advises me to be the hitter, not the hittee.

I ask her what she means. Punching me with the force of a huge wave whose lingering aftermath I can see in the uniformity of the small round pebbles, she roars: "Don't be like the pebbles. The pebbles are the hittees; they take my hits, day after day. Unable to decide anything, they just roll in their place and get influenced by the oncoming waves. I am the hitter. See, I've been hitting these pebbles for ages. They were huge boulders when they came here. Now they are reduced to docent pebbles, and very soon, they will be sand. Resting by my side, they don't fight back. They don't feel anything anymore. Even the seagulls step on them. I can push them around the way I want. I can play them like marionettes. They obey. They roll, crash, smash, collide, and they think all that is their doing. Little do they know that it's my decision to splash and crash. I don't let anyone influence my decisions, not even the sands that cushion the bottom of my pit."

The Tree of Life
day 174: february 4, 2016

Today I saw the Tree of Life planted in the sea. There were neither visible roots nor branches nor leaves, no flowers nor fruits. And yet it was there—in the midst of all the chaos of raging and crashing waters; the Tree of Life.

It had its roots planted deep into my heart, and the hearts of my loves. It climbed up and out with each breath of life, and blossomed into new and different branches of love, faith, and hope. Each branch opened wide, sometimes entangling the other, and other times extending alongside the other, each at their appointed times. They all bore colorful flowers and exotic fruits. Hibernating during snow or rain, they cocooned into the loving roots and warmed up there preparing for the next bloom.

Then the Tree of Life changed colors, and its bare branches bowed down under heavy white snow, which, when departed, revealed all the tiny green buds underneath, waiting to bloom again.

Two is Better than One
day 175: february 5, 2016

A little round bird jumps from a towering branch and flips to the lower one. The tiny one then circles the whole tree, swerves across, soars up, and disappears. I wonder if it is alone. They play in pairs or groups, these birds. I ponder if it would have been this happy if it were alone. The answer pops up from another half-bare branch and I see a second little round birdy with yellowish tummy jumping between the twigs. Then, as if drawn to each other by a magical bond, the two find each other. It's surreal watching their unity and friendship—playing, flying, and resting in silence, next to each other. Yes, I conclude, two is much better than one.

Did not God order Noah to build a huge ark and enter it with his family and seven pairs, a male and a female, of each species?[82] After that devastating 150-day flood which destroyed all life on earth, God saved Noah's Ark which landed on Mount Ararat in Armenia,[83] and all who were saved rebirthed the living creatures of the new world. And we are their descendants.

Yes, two is better than one. And if you ever find the One, even full of flaws, it's better to hold on to that One, than journey through life alone.

Block the Noise

day 176: february 6, 2016

Despite the sea's unseen raging commotion today, its calming hymn deafens all outside noise. Blocks the unnecessary clamor. "Is it that easy?" you might ask. It depends on your willpower. While your ears keep funneling in the unpleasant disturbances of noise, you must pick up your will and let it force your brain, your heart, and your soul to cooperate to block the noise.

Silence already lives in you without making any noise. When there is harmony inside and peace within, it is up to you to vehemently refuse to allow other peoples' idle chatter disturb that silence. Block that noise.

How is it done? Watch the sea—she guards its rhythm no matter what goes on around her. She hugs the sky, caresses the shore, lifts the spirits. Even amidst tempests, she is silent.

Strive to Be a Watchee
day 177: february 7, 2016

While spending one million priceless minutes watching the fearless sea, a constant bugging tune of hers is heard:

"Don't be a watcher, be the watchee.

Most of you watch me passing by. You watch the splendors of the sun and the wonders of the moon chasing the tiresome days and the lazy nights. Today's technology promotes watching. You humans watch the screens of multiple 'smart' machines at all times. You read the news, watch movies, and follow the daily life of other people as it unfolds on social media. You are the watchers. Have you become smarter watching these smart electronics, or blinded by them? Ah, how I wish you realize that each minute lived by watching is a precious minute lost.

Strive then, to be the watchee—get up on your two feet and dare to accomplish those dreams and goals waiting to be fulfilled. Soon after, the 'smart' machines will project You. You will have become the Watchee."

The Feast of Strength
day 178: february 8, 2016

The strong impression of this serene scene reminds me of Leo Tolstoy's advice on strength: "All distinctions of our worldly estate are as nothing compared with the dominion of man over self. If a man fall into the sea, it does not matter whence he fell or into what sea. The only essential thing is can he swim or not. Strength is not in external conditions but in the art of self-mastery."[84]

So today let us celebrate together the Feast of Strength. May we find the strength to control ourselves, and the willpower to overcome life's challenges.

Don't Lose That Thrill
day 179: february 9, 2016

Preserve that thrill amidst the inevitable chaos, the turbulent storms, and the boring stillness. A speck of red, a blast of colors, and shades of gray painted with orange speckle the sky, casting their hues on the sea. She preserves that thrill amidst the storm, rain, or calm. She is never dissatisfied.

Don't lose that thrill. Don't allow yourself to become despaired and dismayed. "If a man is dissatisfied with his state, he can alter in one of two ways: either by improving the circumstances of his life or by improving the state of his soul. The first is not always in his power, but the second always is."[85]

Use the eternal power within you. Improve the state of your soul. And you will never lose that thrill.

Distracting Winds

day 180: february 10, 2016

Those winds—from whence they blow no one knows. They blow at your back, nudging you forward on your tumultuous path. Sometimes they are taken away from your sails leaving you distraught amidst the fierce trembling waters, slashing your wings, blocking your planned way. Those winds. Those distractions. Those wild, untamed, tempestuous whims. But their gusts barely scrape the surface. The depths of the sea remain unmoved. The sea is concentrated on her depths. She cares less about the evolving surface, the shady appearances. Her concentration is most powerful at her core.

What is concentration? "Concentration is a process of distraction from less important matters."[86] Distract yourself from the rowdy winds, those unimportant matters. Free up your soul, your mind and your body.

Concentrate on your life's goal, on your spiritual life, and experience joy and peace. That is the only needful thing.[87] All else is wind.

Winds blow, winds pass. The soul, the essence of your being remains, now, and forever.

Abandoning
day 181: february 11, 2016

The sea abandons the shore but instantly returns to it. The sun abandons the earth only to reappear at the morning dusk. You return to the very thing you abandoned, or tried to abandon, though under a different name, in a different place, at a different time, or in a different form.

Why do people abandon others? Why do people abandon their homes, their countries? Do they run away from their past? Their present? They think they will be able to abandon their worries and leave their troubles behind.

Didn't Jesus ask us to abandon our earthly life and possessions and follow Him? He will give us rest, He promised. Why do people abandon earthly treasures and pleasures? Abandoning earthly possessions and pleasures does indeed lessen their troubles. There would be no more competition to own better material possessions or prouder egos. What remains? Simplicity. Minimalistic living. Room for the soul to grow and thrive.

And if there remains any soul matters troubling you, then abandon them to Jesus. He will lift you up. He will give you rest.

Mimosa
day 182: february 12, 2016

Memories
Immortalize
Moments
Offered
Souvenirs
Adopted

What a captivating sight. Mimosas are back. They offer the first signs of spring and of secret love, triumph, and delightful reunions. Each year at this time, these small, yellow, furry round flowers get arranged side by side along the huge green branch holding them together, beautified with matching green leaves, painting the mountains and the valleys and the shores in yellow with their lush little furballs.

The Cote d'Azur celebrates the Fête du Mimosa each year in February. The feast lasts eight days. Parades and motorcades flaunt their elaborate mimosa creations. Mimosa lovers engage in the Bataille des Fleurs (Battle of the Flowers), where each person, armed with a bouquet of mimosas battles another friendly enemy. A beautiful, colorful mimosa trail[88] extends over 130 kilometers and eight charming villages: Bormes-les-Mimosas, Rayol-Canadel-Sur-Mer, Sainte-Maxime, Saint-Raphael, Mandelieu-La-Napoule, Tanneron, Pegomas, Grasse. It's an entrancing path not to be missed.

Make mimosa memories. Pick some, offer some, kindle and rekindle that love.

First Flap. Then Soar.
day 183: february 13, 2016

Focus. Work hard. Keep flapping to gain momentum. Set the course. The first steps after takeoff are the hardest. Look at the bird. She flaps her wide wings hard to gain speed and rise up from the ground. She defies the mighty winds, facing them head on, cutting right through their immense force. She then aligns her course with the wind's direction and permits the wind to propel her forward, but she never lets her guard down. Then she starts to soar in stillness and stops flapping. The momentum she gains helps her to steadily and freely soar. When she encounters obstacles, she flaps again, sometimes changing her course, but always heading towards her goal. She never staggers. Never stumbles.

Look at the vast sea. She swells and builds up her high waves. She knows she wants to hit the shore. She upholds her mighty waves, builds steadfast momentum and hits her target. Sprinkling her refreshing mist around for the attentive to catch. She never staggers. Never stumbles.

Don't stagger just so that you don't stumble. Do the groundwork first, then focus on your goal, and set off on your course in alignment with God's will for you—He will build up your momentum to soar and hit high. Guard your height near Him, and therein float in peace. Don't stagger or else you will stumble. Don't get swayed from your course, or else you'll blunder. Keep course in God's path, and you will not fall; if you trip, He will be close to catch you. When you approach your destination, you will have successfully finished your race, having fought the good fight.[89]

I Love You
day 184: february 14, 2016

I would move mountains for you
I would shape the clouds for you
I would bring the North Star and offer it to you
I would swim the oceans, with my bare hands, even in shark-infested waters
I would do anything for you
I would gather the world's most beautiful things and make a display for you
I would give you massages, and roses every day
I would do many things for you—everything you can think of, and the unthinkable
I would travel to the moon and back if it makes you happy
I would take you to the moon
I would travel with you to the galaxies and admire with you the beautiful sights
I would take your stress and make it mine if it helps you feel better
I will be the oxygen you breathe
I will always be your right hand
I will be your muscle when you feel weak
I will hold your hand when you feel down
I will be your feet when you're weary
I will be the softness on your pillow when you sleep
I will be yours forever
I love you. (By Sab)

The Illusion of Happiness

day 185: february 15, 2016

Who is happy under the sun, along the shores of the sea, along the shores of life? What is happiness to you? What makes you happy? Are you always happy inside no matter what goes on outside? Everybody acts happy. Puts on a happy smile. Posts happy pictures. Social media is saturated with 'happy' photos. Others respond with the same happiness or get irritated of their happiness. Are they indeed happy, or are they in a constant state of the illusion of happiness?

And what really is true happiness? It is defined as: joy, pleasure, satisfaction, delight, ecstasy, cheerfulness, and all those feelings that leap into your heart and put a smile on your face and peace in your mind. But thousands of years ago a wise Teacher[90] defined happiness as such:

> "But all things done under the sun are meaningless—chasing after the wind.[91] I know that there is nothing better for men than to be happy and do good while they live.[92] Then I realized that it is good and proper for a man to eat and drink, and to find satisfaction in his toilsome labor under the sun during the few days of life God has given him-for this is his lot. Moreover, when God gives any man wealth and possessions, and enables him to enjoy them, to accept his lot and be happy in his work-this is a gift of God. He seldom reflects on the days of his life, because God keeps him occupied with gladness of heart."[93]

The Good and the Bad
day 186: february 16, 2016

They coexist. They complement each other and nourish each other. They need each other. Two birds, Good and Bad, are flying together over the stormy seas. Bad picks on Good's soft wings. Good changes its course but stays close, unable to leave Bad behind. Good needs Bad to learn necessary life lessons, and then, must either help Bad to develop goodness, or if futile, must abandon it. If Good becomes entangled with Bad and carried away with Bad's harsh influence, then Good isn't genuinely noble from within. The goodness is a charade; façade that crumbles down under Bad's evil pressure.

Strive to be good, firm in your convictions, unswayable in your grace. Stay close to the guiding light. The bad needs the good to learn the necessary lessons, to transform into good. If unable to turn to goodness, the bad ends in self-destruction. It is a lifelong battle. True good prevails at the end when the good Sower comes and pulls out the bad weeds from the good harvest and throws them in the burning fire. The Sower retains the good harvest for eternity.[94]

Do not allow the bad to control you, to coerce you, or to intimidate you with its phony charm. Do not get carried away in its charlatan entertainment, deceitful riches, and lustful wings. Do not believe in the pleasures the bad has to offer. They are fake. False. Temporary. And when you have done everything to help the bad transform into goodness, and it resists, be strong enough to turn your back and walk away.

Simplicity

day 187: february 17, 2016

Simplicity is the best policy. No clutter. No chaos. No worries. No headaches. How the sea silently lives her simple life, intently focusing on what needs to be done. Without the extravagant showoffs. Without the nasty manipulations. Without the needless, endless drama. She does not live for others. Nor does she need to prove anything to others.

She is given her task: to tame the rebel pebbles. Hug the resulting sand. Create uniformity, peace, and harmony. Provide shelter and nourishment. Offer support. Be gracious. Be grateful. Unite with the oceans and the rivers. Embrace the earth.

She steadily works towards her mission. She successfully accomplishes it. She is running her race graciously and gratefully. In simplicity.

Defy
day 188: february 18, 2016

Live life defying the norms. Defy the storms. Defy all that is sinful and non-useful. Defy manipulation. Defy foolish authority. Question them before accepting their rules.

Resist forceful evil. Stand firm. Don't stagger. Don't shake. Accept neither mistreatment nor disrespect. Teach them how you want to be treated. Do not settle for anything that bothers you, chills you, or robs you of your peace and happiness.

Set your rules of the game. Enforce them. One rule at a time. Just like the sea. Just like the seagulls of the sea.

Act Don't React

day 189: february 19, 2016

The twilight sea whispers to me, "Take the lead. Take the initiative. Act. Just like these bursting sunrise colors breaking through the darkness. It is up to you to create the colorful, spectacular life you desire and the afterlife you strive for. When you act, everything you want will act with you in harmony, helping you to achieve your goals. Those mystical powers will help you break through the darkness. You will reach your goal, whatever it may be, and you will create the spectacle of your life."

The sea continues, "You must act, and not react. By reacting, you live the life others want you to live, and it may not always be to your liking or in your best interest. You will be thrown up and down, tossed side to side, according to their desires, not yours. Soon, resentment and stress will conquer your heart. Their habit of coercing you into submitting to their will, will be reinforced and perpetuated. If you're used to reacting to what others do or say, your feelings will always respond to the intentional destructive actions of others, creating chaos within you. But if you act, you use the forces of your whole being—your intellect, your soul, and your willpower. You woke up this morning to this gorgeous spectacle of colorful lights breaking into the morning sea. The same power that creates this spectacle is within you, part of you. You are part of it. You act too."

The sea left me today with her final note: "Don't let others act and force you to react. It is time that You act and force them to react."

Masks

day 190: february 20, 2016

On my way to my seashore today, a huge colorful theater poster plastered to a sidewalk fence catches my eye. It portrays two ornate red velvet and gold rimmed curtains being lifted up and unveiling two masks, one red—smiling, another, black—expressing sadness. The title reads: Le Lever de Rideau, that is, The Curtain Rises. And I think, "Masks are hiding behind the curtains, but who is hiding behind those happy and sad masks? Why do they have to wear masks even after the curtain rises? What will the curtains unveil if they rise? What will the masks unveil when removed?"

Masks. Are they useful or not? Needful or not? Not. And yet they wear masks. They hide behind masks of all colors and shapes—beautiful, groomed, kind, sad, colorful. Pity—the inner feelings are hidden, and the true self is hidden. Pity—the pure innocence is covered with the artificial. I look around, and I see people wearing those smiling or sad masks, walking around with huge velvety curtains over them, all having one common goal: to hide their true self. And I notice, even the sky is wearing a huge mask today.

I do not comprehend the reason behind the mask. How true and honest would life be without it? Let us resolve to remove our masks and be honest with ourselves and each other.

Mid-Winter Spring Day in Antibes

day 191: february 21, 2016

Emile Charles DAMERON

It's a gorgeous mid-winter Sunday morning in charming Antibes, tucked by the Mediterranean Sea. The bustling morning market is getting ready for the impending influx of locals and tourists. The colorful variety of flowers, the fragrance of the spices, the bowls filled to the rim with black and green olives, the French wines, the warm appetizing smell of the morning baguettes and pastries, the fruits and vegetables, the hundreds of French cheeses and charcuterie await you this morning. Yes, come hungry, and for the whole day. There is a wonderful variety of local gourmet food, and plenty of other activities. Oh yes, and don't forget your camera.

The ringing bells of the imposing cathedral are inviting all to church. Just a short walk away past the cathedral and the Picasso Museum is the sea, offering a cold swim to daring swimmers. The pétanque[95] players are focused on the metal ball, the bikers on their journey; the pedestrians are distracted by the colorful products of the Provençal market, and the ever-pulsating sea.

Romance is in the air in Antibes; lovers walk the ramparts, Jesus lovers visit His home—the Cathedral, art lovers explore Picasso's home, food lovers find all they want, and travel lovers just stroll the tiny streets filled with galleries, bakeries, cheese shops, wine stores, souvenir shops, and restaurants. A copy of the painting of Emile-Charles Dameron, displayed in the center of the market has captured this life hundreds of years ago. Not much has changed.

Chichi Pompon
day 192: february 22, 2016

Chichi pompon. I came across this phrase today. It sounded cool and funny. And had to look it up. MacBook's Dictionary defines "chichi" as "attempting stylish elegance but achieving only an overelaborate pretentiousness," and defines "pompon" as "woolen balls attached to garments for decoration, or the large round cluster of brightly colored streamers waved in pairs by cheerleaders." And so "chichi pompon" can be described as showing off an elaborate, fake, pretentious elegance, refinement, or goodness.

Pretentious goodness. Leo Tolstoy portrays it in his The Pathway of Life: "There is nothing worse than pretension to goodness. Pretension to goodness is more repulsive than out and out malice."[96] Aren't we all surrounded by chichi pompons? Aren't we living in a chichi pompon society? Showing off as being refined and good, but rotten and ugly inside. But the morning sun, rising brightly at the sea, announces, "Nothing that is hidden will remain hidden. Nothing that is pretentious will remain unrevealed. Soon I shall spread my light to pierce the secret dark, and I shall expose the truth of chichi pompons."

All chichi pompons out there: beware.

Snow Moon in the Night
day 193: february 23, 2016

To say that the Snow Moon with its buddy Jupiter illuminates the dark sea and the flickering city is an understatement. As the bustling city winds down into the chores of the night, and as the rushing sea elevates her evening tides pushing people away from her shores, the Snow Moon rises, throwing its magnificent silver carpet onto the lustrous waters. The perpetually rushed humans retreat in their nighttime homes—wearily carrying with them the worry-baggage of their day.

These gleaming celestial buddies try to soothe those exhausted human souls, in their fatigued bodies, but instead of turning their drained faces to the celestial moon, instead of resting their tired eyes on the gleaming seawaters, they turn into themselves, and close in. Bottling up the same problems with which they awoke this morning, they fictitiously rest and recharge for a while only to resume their race early next morning.

Is carrying the worry-baggage worth it in the end? Or is it time to let it go and open up the interior space to welcome this celestial peace?

Change this dreadful routine. Step out of the meaningless rotation. Stop. Gaze at the sparkling night sea. Imbibe the silvery Snow Moon rays. Stare at this amazing gray sky. Breathe. Smell the night potpourri mist. And then rest. Relax.

Sonata of Our Lives
day 194: february 24, 2016

Whether aware or not, you write the sonata of your life each day. When you retire at night in the silence of your closed eyes, you rethink and revisit your sonata so that you can edit it at dawn. Thus, by writing, reviewing, and editing, your unique sonata comes to life. It then mingles with other sonatas and morphs into the one that makes the earth go round and round. But how do you write? How do you live your life?

Listen to life's sonata singing songs of soaring beauty. The beauty of life. The sonata of our lives. How well will you write yours depends on how you choose to live your life—impulsively or wisely? The sage poet, Omar Khayyam, has this advice: "To wisely live your life, you don't need to know much. Just remember two main rules for the beginning: You better starve, than eat whatever, and better be alone, than with whoever."[97]

The -Dis- People of Our Life

day 195: february 25, 2016

The -dis- people of our lives: they resemble the disheartening darkening of the skies, masking the light of the sun and the glamor of the sea.

They displease you at every turn. They dismiss your concerns as nothing. Dishonesty and disrespect ooze out from them. Distant as they are, disagreement is their single friend. Disempowering you is their goal. Dismantling your relations suits them. They sow disaccord hiding behind their disarming smile thinking their dysfunctional soul will not be revealed. Constantly disagreeing with you exalts them. They discretely discredit you and disturb your reputation. Disguised in meekness, they disseminate disharmony.

But they are at a huge disadvantage. Being patron "saints" of -dis-es, they are disliked, disapproved, disclaimed, and eventually disowned. Isolated, they are disabled. Disturbed, they are discharged from our life, to eventually disappear like the momentary mist of the morning sea.

It is not worth journeying through life with such people. We have one life to live and to thrive. It is time to shun them.

Memories
day 196: february 26, 2016

She asked the wise mother sea, "What are memories?" The all-saving, deleting-nothing sea replied, "Memories. They are fragments of time stuck in your imagination. Souvenirs of here and there, of friends and foes, of places afar and apart. Memories. They give meaning to the nothingness that surrounds us, nourishing our thirsty soul and our nostalgic being. Memories bring shapes and colors on that piece of dull cardboard we call life. But that was then. Memories, now, have a digital existence in your smart-phone, smart-computer, smart-cloud. Alas, these modern smart memories don't have those same traditional rooted values anymore. How easy it is to delete memories with the brushstroke of your little finger."

Delete them, the smart, and the not-so-smart ones. Fabricate fresh memories today and imprint them in your longing heart.

Run Your Own Course

day 197: february 27, 2016

"Take control of your life. Learn to run your own course," rebukes me the sea as I'm lounging by its gloomy aura and contemplating my life's upheavals. I had allowed myself to be distracted from my own course only to be cast away by others' caprices, to be pushed around by events unimportant to my own race, the accomplishment of which was assigned to me when I was planted here on earth. And I just stare at the energetic sea.

I ponder how she can keep running so fiercely, undistracted, with a focused intent to accomplish the race for which she was put here to run. There was a supreme mission, a vital reason why the sea was allotted here, near us; why we always felt magically drawn to her, to silently sit and to carelessly walk by her, to fearlessly immerse ourselves in her life-giving waters. And it becomes apparent. The sea, her waters, the source of all life, sustains us here, during our temporary run on Mother Earth. Not only does she sustain us with her water, but also with her uplifting spirit: energizing us, teaching us to take control of our life by taking control of our thoughts and actions, to uplift others with our example, to keep running our course effectively without allowing pointless disturbances to distract us. Thus we must focus on our race so that at the end, when we are called to leave, we would be able to repeat Saint Paul's verse, "I have fought a good fight, I have finished my course, I have kept the faith."[98]

The Time Has Come
day 198: february 28, 2016

Restaurant Phoenicia, Antibes

Good friends help you find important things when you think you have lost them. Listen to them and pull yourself up. Gather your thoughts. Procrastination is over. No more excuses. No more waiting. It is now or never. The time has come for you to take action. To be firm. To speak up. To demand. To persist. As soon as your mind shifts in this direction and you act upon it, you will notice the results.

The time has come to cheer with such good friends. Once you have found them, do not let them go. These courageous buddies who stick by your side at your lowest point deserve some pampering. They help you to be firm, to speak up, to demand, and to persist despite the sneaky serpents trying to destroy your life.

Have a glass of mint lemonade at the shores of Antibes with such good friends. That time has come. Celebrate.

Anniversary Every Four Years

day 199: february 29, 2016

Will you remember the events of today? What transpired? What you lived? What you accomplished? Keep them close to your heart, for you will get to celebrate their anniversary only after four years.

A reunion. Another chance. Forgiveness. Lightness. Determination. Togetherness. Future. Family. Faith. Unshakable faith.

Let's celebrate the anniversary in four years. February 29, 2020. For that date will not come before four years. It will not exist. And in four years trust will be rebuilt. Honesty will be instituted. Goals will be accomplished. Souls will be saved. Faults will be forgiven. Love will conquer. Family united will stand united. True friends will be around to celebrate the anniversary in four years; by the sea. By our sea.

Rendez-vous: February 29, 2020, February 29, 2024, and each fourth year thereafter.

Napoleon at Golfe-Juan
day 200: march 1, 2016

Today, the small seaside town of Golfe-Juan celebrates Napoleon's arrival from his exile. On March 1, 1815, Napoleon landed here upon his return from Elba Island. On these shores he issued two proclamations; one inspiring and inciting his soldiers into battle, and the other inspiring and empowering the people of France and intended to spread fear among his enemies. From here, Napoleon and his soldiers took the Alpine route to Paris. This marked the start of the famous 100 Days—marking the period where he started marching towards Paris, and his final defeat in the battle of Waterloo, after which he was exiled to the island of Saint Helena where he died years later.

Route de Napoléon—Tourists admire this beautiful route through the Alps that Napoleon took to Paris. Last year, Golfe-Juan[99] celebrated the bicentennial of Napoleon's landing at its shores. Spectacular re-enactments of the famous landing, with actors, Napoleonic costumes, ships and weapons, provided an atmosphere rich in history and an exciting cultural attraction to all.

Difficult or Easy?

day 201: march 2, 2016

The most difficult things are the easiest, and the easiest things are the most difficult if you change your mindset, that is. She refused to embark on the task, grumbling, "This pisses me off, I don't like it, I will not do it." But the wise man encouraged her, "Do the thing you fear most, and it becomes easy."

But whatever is easy, we know it's easy and we take it for granted. We let it sit aside and postpone taking care of it. Time passes by and one day we realize it has really become difficult. We have lost our touch with the easy. Our agility.

Perform today what is easy. Do not let time pass. Do not let them pile up into a difficult mountain. Then it will be difficult to untie the knot. Unless you have faith. Faith unties all knots. A German devotion to Mary says: "Mary, Untier of knots, pray for us."

Like the Seagulls, Expect Miracles

day 202: march 3, 2016

"Miracles are just a thought, a longing away," howls the gusty sea-wind, "just look at the seagulls, they come here every day, line up at the shore, and expect. They bring their peace with them. Without grumbling or complaining, they wait here. Without ever despairing or losing peace. Without overthinking."

Miracles are brewing in the wind, roving over, expecting to find an eager heart and a hopeful mind to enter. When it's stormy within, just like the sea, the miracles in the wind will not find a place to peacefully land. They will not reach rough, furious, turbulent souls. If it's peaceful within, just like the sea, despite the raging tempests outside, the miracles in the wind will comfortably seep in, into the peaceful expectant souls.

And the souls will be brightened, illuminated, exalted.

And the white peaceful seagulls will keep waiting, expecting more miracles at the seashores.

The Teardrop and Her Mother

day 203: march 4, 2016

My friend the sea is happy to see me again. She's happy seeing me happy. She sends her white foams to tickle my feet, as if telling me she missed me. She missed her conversations with me. Her pushes resolve to reach my feet. She pushes me back again and again to teach me something new. And I look around—in the mixture of pebbles and sand, the moving waters, the hazy skies, the beautiful scenery—to find out what. I do not.

A soft teardrop slides down gracing my cold cheek, unfolding the answer. My teardrop had longed for her mother, my sea. My sea had been waiting for her: to embrace her, to accept her, and to hug her warmly into her loving arms.

And I get it. The mother sea had helped her child, the teardrop, to overcome all the raging storms within—to see clearly, to live righteously, and to let out her tear drop into freedom. Into the sea.

I trust my sea. She will quietly tame all rebels and convert them to sand, slowly, slowly, while collecting the fallen teardrops into her unity and force.

And once again, just like old times, I feel loved, engulfed by the marine chilly mist of the sea.

The Wrath of the Sea
day 204: march 5, 2016

Don't think that I always feel peaceful at heart. I too sometimes fight against the dark demons raging up from inside. They stir up the worst in me and I become dreadful. Vicious. I attack. I engulf and make them drown. I hear the Lux Aeterna[100] playing in the distance. And I enjoy it immensely. And people think I am pretty even keeled in my dark stormy rage. And people are attracted to me to photograph me in my wrath. Still they try to understand me. The troubled sea. Why all the fascination? I rage today, I calm tomorrow. My friends, the blue skies and the silver clouds, who are always by my side, calm me down.

And my life goes on. Just like yours.

Do you feel the same?

The Palm Branch
day 205: march 6, 2016

Today the sea offers me a long green peaceful palm branch rehashed from her bottomless soul. A lone palm branch that everybody ignores and passes by. It lies there, waiting for me. It's up to me to decide what to do with it, ignore it and leave it there or respond to its invitation. Respond in kind. In peace. In kindness.

My weary soul fires up at the sight of the solitary branch, and arises from its abysmal pit. It had been frail in times of trial. What's the sense of being strong in times of peace, yet frail in tribulations? The answer lies therein the peaceful palm branch, dejected from the sea during one of her stormy trials.

Peace coexists with challenges and oppositions. Strive to be strong in trials, and look for that hidden palm branch, that symbol of peace tucked behind the rough surface. Focus your heart and soul on the Divine peace in adversities and difficult times, and you will find that you are already content in pleasant times.

I lift the peaceful palm branch and look around to hand it over to another peace-seeker.

May the Wind Be Always at Your Back

day 206: march 7, 2016

Ventimiglia, Italy

"May the road rise up to meet you
May the wind be always at your back
May the sunshine warm upon your face
The rain fall soft upon your fields
And until we meet again
May God hold you in the palm of His hand"[101]

The breezy wind was blowing at my back a while ago, helping me to walk forward, get on with my life. But now I find myself facing the wild winds. Despite that, I am surprised to be able to proceed and move forwards. The wind blowing along my ears, hushes up all outside idle chatter, urges me to remain attentive to the murmurs of my soul, whispers of my heart. As I focus on the murmurs of my soul, the whispers of my heart, I am pleasantly perplexed that I am even able to hear them amidst the forceful gusts attempting to toss the sea of life around. Then, I feel the sun shining warm upon my face, the sea mist caressing my cheeks, and God lifting me up in the palm of His hand.

Thank You Annie

day 207: march 8, 2016

"Please, can you tell me who is my guardian angel?" I implore the wise Nana who, sitting on the last pew of the serene church, is whispering to her own guardian angel. She puts her delicate hand, worn out by life, on my shoulder and replies, "Your guardian angel is a private gift from heaven, to guard you and keep you from harm. Very resourceful, your angel can come to you in any form that you may not at first recognize. But as time passes by and you experience God's gracious hand working through your guardian angel, untying the knots in your life one by one, and replacing each knot with profound peace, you will recognize who your angel is. God will place your angel in your life at your most difficult moments. Your angel is the Lord's face, turned toward you, that is shining upon you and giving you peace, blessing you and keeping you.[102] Do you now recognize your guardian angel?" I reply, "Annie!"

My heart jumps, recalling the feeling when my guardian angel had come to me during a time when I needed her most. ""Yes, Nana, indeed," I say, gasping for voice, "let me tell you what happened. Annie woke me up at five a.m. on March 8, 2015, with a rhythm beating in my mind. Fearing I will forget, I hummed what I heard in my dream and recorded it in my smartphone right away. During the day, I tried to find out if there was a song that matched it. Humming the tune into an app, I was shocked to hear the result: "Annie's Song" by John Denver singing "…come let me love you, come love me again."

And with tears in my eyes, goosebumps popping all over, my pounding heart switched from heaviness to a light, loving, awe-struck being. You see, my child sister, Annie, had gone to heaven a long time ago, and this was the first time—at the most down point in my life when all was falling apart—Annie had directly contacted me. Without recovering from my awe-struck confusion, I grabbed a pencil and my sketchbook. My hands drew a face. It resembled the grown-up version of my little Annie I barely remembered, and words came to me to compliment Annie's rhythm. I wrote:

"I will sing praise every moment, You put a song in my heart
I will keep peace and quiet, and put my trust in you, Lord.""

And Nana smiles. I know she has been praying for me too. Maybe she was the one who asked Annie to intervene. She does not say.

Thank you, Annie, my guardian angel. You manifested yourself to me and came to me and helped me through a few sincere, honest, caring, unselfish friends, and strangers who became friends. I know you're always there keeping watch, guarding and guiding me, and my loved ones. What a privilege to have you, a beautiful blessed soul, seeking favoritism for us with our Lord Jesus Christ.

The Gifts We Have

day 208: march 9, 2016

The gifts we have are like the gifts by the sea
They just lay there, until discovered by you and me
Discover your gifts to uncover your calling
For only then life will be most fulfilling

Go where you will, seek what you will,
You will never find a task more fulfilling
That exalts you more than living your calling
So, uncover, and use your gifts for a better living

How fruitful would it be to spend a whole life
Avoiding meaningless talk, discord and strife
Using the gifts we have with willpower
And doing it all with plenty of laughter

That Scent

day 209: march 10, 2016

Boulangerie Jamais et Fils, Promenade Cagnes Sur Mer

That scent ...
The salty scent of the sleepy Mediterranean Sea at dawn
The sunrise aroma of espresso at the café trottoir by the shore
The tangy scent of the warm baguette, tartine et confiture[103]
The inviting fragrance of warm croissants at the artisan's bakery
The sweet perfume of my daughter kissing me
The savory smell of her morning herbal tea
The whiff of freshly cut flowers at the flower market
The spicy apron of the French cook
The rusty smell of that ancient book
The citrusy flavor of the winter fruits at the marchée provençale[104]
The frosty air of the white snowy Alps
The full nose of French burgundy wine
The misty aura of the soft fog in the lush forest
The smell of fresh earth dampened by the rustling rain
The puppy breath scent of that beige papillon
The cologne of the French neighbor, and the perfume trail in the elevator
The endless bouquet of the lavender fields
That nostalgic scent ... that stays with you evermore

Eye in the Sky

day 210: march 11, 2016

A pair[105] of bright starry eyes
Hanging from the midnight skies
Look at my sleepy eyes from above
Shining in the pitch dark
They penetrate into my soul
They flicker as if twitching
Shimmer as if blinking
What do they whisper? I do not know
But to the depth of their soul I can see
Therein lies silence, vastness, calmness
A magnetic force attracting all they look upon
That pair of dreamy eyes in the black sky
Those twinkling stars of the midnight
Watch over me, and over my far-away loves
And with every blink they reassure me
That all is well and protected from above
I stare at them long in the silence of the night
Lying in my bed my eyes now wide awake
Letting their allure take me into their starry soul
They slide behind the dark mountain silhouettes
Their stark bright eyes always fixated into mine

Wanting More

day 211: march 12, 2016

Sitting in this white wonderland, I contemplate one word—silence. But it does not last for long. Soon I am distracted by the flight of the seagull, her wings opened wide, and I think to myself: "We have copied the bird and created airplanes, so we possess the same life as the bird soaring and seeing everything from above." Then I imagine a speeding boat leaving its white foamy trail on the sea and I think to myself: "We have copied the swimming fish in making this boat as we were eager to experience life as fish, floating on water."

Snowflakes journey down, and we wanted to play in snow. We created artificial snow. We are cold, and we wanted cold to last during the hot summer days. We created the air-condition. Come summertime, we wanted to feel colder, and we created the heater.

We have copied this or that of other species and even Mother Nature, because God had given them something extra, a talent that we don't have. But God has gifted us with free will, thinking mind, roaming spirit—that no other creature is able to copy—and yet, we think what we already have is insufficient. God has given us the beautiful earth and we are destroying her and with her all the wonderful creatures and humans inhabiting her. God has given us the moon and we want to reach it; Mars and the stars and we want to conquer all. We just want to conquer, use, and destruct. Why don't we take care of it all, all the creatures and Mother Earth—our buddies and our home?

Don't Follow Me

day 212: march 13, 2016

"O Ye, who in some pretty little boat
Eager to listen, have been following
Behind my ship, that singing sails along
Turn back to look again upon your shores
Do not put out to sea, lest peradventure
In losing me, you might yourselves be lost"[106]
—Dante

Light Through the Door

day 213: march 14, 2016

How great is the feeling of turning my back to old doors closing shut the past behind them?

How great is the feeling of facing the bright light beaming through a tiny crack amidst the ornate golden gates of my new path, which starts today? Gazing at them I think it would be such an arduous task to push open these gates and let the light through to shine upon me. After all, where there's a crack, there's always light wanting to penetrate through. And that little crack is the opening to the new path. I touch my hands on the gates, right where the small break is, thinking it's the most vulnerable point of darkness, and I test the ease of pushing them open.

And suddenly, even before my hands put pressure on the door panels, they spring wide open, letting the loving light caress my face, fill my heart with joy, and open my mind to higher powers and further horizons.

Poutine Fishing
day 214: march 15, 2016

Each year around this time, a special kind of tiny fish, like sardines, called Poutine appear in the shores of the French Riviera. In February and March, during a 30-day period, only a few seaside towns are given the privilege to fish them, and Cagnes is one of them.

Poutine fishing is a ceremonial event that starts very early at daybreak. The fishing boats are prepared; the vast fishing nets are unfolded and pulled by fishermen rowing their boats to deep sea to catch the Poutine in huge batches. Already at five a.m. a small crowd gathers to watch and/or participate in drawing back the net with its catch of Poutine once the boat returns to shore.

The retiring of the net is a wonderful show. By now, the crowd grows, and fishermen, children, and adults participate in the ceremonious pulling back of the poutine-filled-net. Professional and amateur photographers swamp the shore to get the best shot of Poutine fishing.

After the nets are pulled, the tiny Poutines are collected in large boxes to be sold or distributed. This gourmandise,[107] available once a year, is eaten boiled sprinkled with olive oil and lemon juice. Poutine is also used to prepare savory breakfast, such as an omelet dish known as La Melàta de Poutina, when they are fried with eggs, parsley, lemon juice, and olive oil.

A spectacle not to be missed when you are in town this time of the year.

Gnocchi

day 215: march 16, 2016

Le Bistrot Niçois, Polygone Riviera, Cagnes Sur Mer

Gnocchi is one of the most famous and savored Niçoise dishes.

It is made of pureed potatoes to which egg, salt, and flour is added. The mixture is then shaped into small balls, and lightly pressed with fork. It is served boiled, and topped with different types of sauces such as, tomato sauce, pesto sauce, creamy mushroom sauce, or basil and olive oil topped with shredded real parmesan.

Gnocchi is a nice treat paired with local red wine to be enjoyed alone, or with company. It awakens your senses: the beautiful design for the eyes, the enchanting smell of the steamy gnocchi, the soft texture, the mouthwatering flavors mixed by the expert chef, all conspire to give you an unforgettable culinary experience. Not to be missed when you're in town.

Footprints
day 216: march 17, 2016

Pope Francis said, "In life you have to walk as Jesus did, leaving footprints." How did Jesus walk? Jesus walked in life spreading hope, love, healing, faith, charity, and humility. Jesus taught about God's salvation; that whoever believes in Him, will have eternal life. Living a simple life, Jesus disdained temporal treasures and pleasures, and as such He did not accumulate any material possessions, but by His lifestyle accumulated riches for the soul.

What kind of footprints did He leave? It has been more than 2,000 years that Jesus left this world, and yet His legacy and teachings persist from generation to generation. His footprints—from millions of Christian followers, though persecuted by the modern world, to magnificent cathedrals and churches dotting the world, to works of love and charity performed in His name—persevere by living and sharing His Gospel.

Adopting a lifestyle, other than that of Jesus is meaningless. The only lifestyle that will lead us to heaven and that will allow us to leave footprints is copying that of Jesus. After all, how many powerful kings, violent tyrants, or rich rulers are remembered and worshiped daily? None. But Jesus, in His simplicity and love, is still worshiped. Miracles are done in His name. That is His footprint.

Let us resolve to walk as He did, leaving footprints of love, hope, faith, and charity.

Just Like Old Times
day 217: march 18, 2016

Villeneuve Loubet Plage

The old times, the present, and the yet to come—this three is all there is. And three is a powerful force. It sums up one's life. It feels just like old times, except that so much has changed. There's strength in accepting change. There's liveliness in change, but nothing beats old times.

Old times; when the aroma of mama's cooking filled the air, dad's telephone tones echoed in the next room, the huffing and woofing of your first puppy shushed the noise, the wrong tunes of the piano and the violin played merrily, the soft fire danced in the fireplace along with the murmurs of daily homework, and the innocent giggles completed the picture.

And now, the seagulls line up at the shore, facing the disappearing sun, and they wait. They wait, while the colors change, the shadows lengthen, and the sea turns glassy cold. They wait for the night to fall, for the stars to come out, for the moon to pass, for the sun to return, for a new day to break. And they wait. They wait for the old times to be remembered, for the yet-to-come, for that new dawn.

"Change is good," they assure. "Live in the now," they advise. "For tomorrow is not yours" they caution. But nothing beats the old times.

Last Day of Winter

day 218: march 19, 2016

Cigalon Plage, Cagnes Sur Mer Promenade

"And now, when the shades of evening begin to steal over my life, what have I left fresher, more precious, than the memories of the storm—so soon over—of early morning, of spring?"[108]

And so, the winter days roll over and over again until they reach their end. Today marks the end of winter 2016. A beautiful sunny, breezy day at the beach with loving family is all one needs to end this short winter. And that white wine—still chilled from the cold winter—cheers the arrival of spring with the smiling sun and the blue horizons.

Cheers to you, as well. To many happy, healthy springs. May the shades of your evening dissipate into spring, may your sea of life be blessed with a wonderful family, caring circle of real friends, aged quality wine, blue skies and a bright sunny path.

Palm Sunday

day 219: march 20, 2016

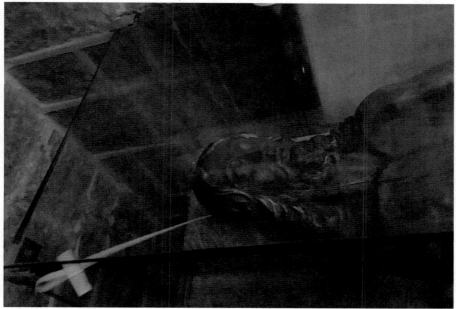

Antibes Cathedral

I abandoned everyone dear and everything real to God's Will the moment I inserted our handmade Palm Cross in the glass sanctuary of crucified Jesus, an old wooden statue that was found hidden in the walls of the Antibes Cathedral. Even though His eyes were shut He looked at me in an exuding calmness. Instantly, the air lightened, the chatter quieted, and my soul filled with double the hope, double the love, and double the faith on this triumphal Palm Sunday and the first day of spring.

Yes, I felt lighter. *"Come to me all you who are weary and tired, and I will give you rest,"*[109] He said to me. And I believed Him. I felt total trust replenishing my thirst, transforming my cares and anxieties into hope. I am not worried or afraid anymore. He will make everything right. He will change their hearts and minds. He will make them come back to Him and stay with Him.

He reigns in our home forever. Amen.

Colomba di Pasqua

day 220: march 2, 2016

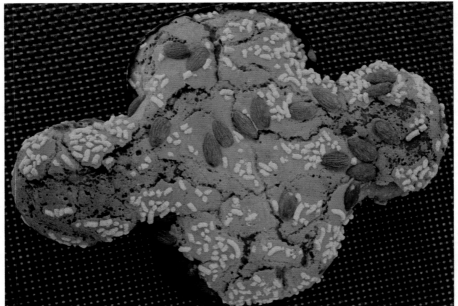

Today is Easter Monday and the famous Italian Easter cakes have reappeared in the artisan stores and Italian markets. The Colomba di Pasqua, meaning the Easter Dove, is a special Easter cake that originated in Italy and found its way to the French Riviera. The Colomba, together with the Christmastime Italian gourmets Panettone and Pandoro, are now abundant here, and especially in Nice. In Nice, the Italian influence in the gastronomy, culture, and social life is well established from the times when the County of Nice was annexed to the Kingdom of Sardinia, today's Italy from 1388 to 1860.

Go buy a Colomba. Or, it may be fun to find a recipe and bake one at home and prepare your Easter menu in Italian style.

May the Easter Dove fill your days with peace, joy, faith, and happiness.

Quotes

day 221: march 22, 2016

Quotes by a wise lady:

"Do not show any hesitation or they will take advantage of you.

Pick the first person that picks you.

First think of yourself—what makes You feel good, what is best for You—then decide accordingly.

The one who offers a rose, therein the fragrance stays.

What is life, but a wonderful, faithful mist by the sea?

They left. One by one.

The sun still shines, even on rough seas.

Life is so fragile so as not to waste a moment of it pursuing anything else; therefore, I don't judge, I don't condemn—I forgive, I help, I care, and I live by the Golden Rule."

A Kiss

day 222: march 23, 2016

Kiss Kiss Kiss
What is a kiss?
A kiss locks hearts together
It chooses heart over matter
And seals two souls together
Melting minds and hardened hearts
A kiss cracks obstinate locks apart
Kissing marks the start of missing
Filling with love this life of journeying
But, mind you, a kiss often betrays
Prime betrayal of history it portrays
For Jesus was betrayed with a kiss
But, a kiss also saves
It awakens to love the senses
For a human is only spared with a kiss
Far more effective than words
It respects the hand it kisses
Watches over the heart in guards
Blesses the forehead it touches

Blown from a distance
It shakes one's essence
Emptying the mind of nonsense
Giving meaning to existence
And the sea kisses the shore
While the moon kisses the sun
The rainfall embraces the earth
And all things pause for that illusory kiss
Be it an Armenian bachig, Arabic bawsé,
or Spanish beso
German Kuss, Russian безе, or French
bisou
The English kiss, or the Italian bacio
No matter what language spoken
The same soft smooch is given
Do not forget the first kiss
For it brings two young hearts together
Do not forget the last kiss
For it seals memories cherished forever

Hope After Holy Thursday
day 223: march 24, 2016

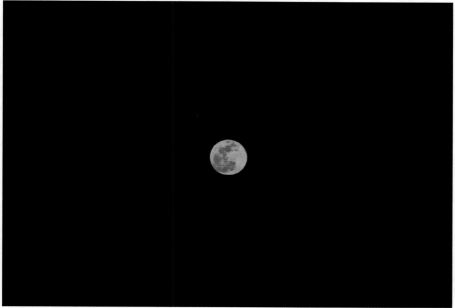

Surrounded by silent Tenebrae[110] where nothing is visible
Dwells despair in the somberness of the soul
The soul's eyes are open, yet they do not see in the obscure night
They search for meaning, but meaning eludes, melting in the dark
The soul's ears are listening, yet nothing is heard in the deep gloom
The sad soul, eager to shake off despair, prays, asking for a bloom
Out of nowhere a sliver of light breaks the heavy doom
Emerging as a small dot, soon its rays shape the muted dune
Defying all logic, the light grows in the dark, glows in the dark
Dispelling all fear, anger, anguish, that lingered as a cloak
That sweet irresistible light starts coloring the budding soul
Brightly illuminating, giving birth to amazing new hope to all
And as the eyes see and the ears hear, the hope draws near
Its fire enters the blue heart, fills it with joy, clears the smear
The flowers bloom, the birds chirp, the river sings, the blue-sky drapes it all
And gracious hope, working its miraculous repair, drowns off despair
Now the soul lives, robed in bright white truthful light
That light, that shines in the darkness and the darkness cannot extinguish it

Good Friday

day 224: march 25, 2016

Haute de Cagnes

Walking in the procession of the Stations of the Cross through the windy cobblestone streets around the chateau of Cagnes-Sur-Mer fills your being with spiritual contentment. The priest asks for volunteers. In an impulse I move forward, and he offers me to carry the large processional cross. What a magical, solemn procession, walking, praying, and meditating on each of the fourteen Stations of the Cross, on this Good Friday. Each station is marked with a huge wooden cross at the turn of a winding street. The 14th station ends in the village church. This Good Friday is exceptionally remarkable because it coincides with the Annunciation to Mary—a concurrence that will not happen again in this century. Up and down the hills we go, following the Cross, praying many Our Fathers and Hail Marys, and contemplating on our own inner Calvary which pales in front of Jesus' Passion.

In the end, the priest announces that *"It is finished"*[111]—Jesus' mission here on earth being accomplished, Jesus exhales His last breath. Now, it is up to each one of us to carry the memory of His passion and the light of His mission down many generations.

Saturday of Light

day 225: march 26, 2016

The Saturday of Light transitions the world from Tenebrae (darkness) to light, Divine Light—that unique Light of Jesus which lights our way, and gives us hope and peace.

Let's strive to stay in the Light, walk in the Light. For if we stay in Tenebrae, we'll get lost in the darkness, we lose our ways clinging to the worldly, to the unholy. We lose sight of the true way, the true Light, thus losing hope of achieving salvation. But the Light illuminates the dark soul; even a small candle illuminates a big dark room. And the dark cannot darken the candlelit room, for it is powerless amongst the Light.

Go, my friend, light a candle, and keep that flame burning, for His Light will always be with you, even in the darkest hour.

Go, my friend, be the light. Enlighten those around you toward the Divine Light.

Easter Sunday
day 226: march 27, 2016

Families gathered around parties
Colored Easter eggs and fake funny bunnies
Decorated baskets filled with candies
Stickers, yellow Peeps, and gummies
But nowhere to be heard is the: Agnus Dei[112]
"Agnus Dei qui tolis pecata mundi
Miserere nobis, miserere nobis
Dona nobis pace"
"Lamb of God who takes away the sins of the world
Have mercy on us, have mercy on us
And give us peace"
Easter—the Resurrection of our Lord
Vanquishing death, into life He arose
Even though He was nailed to the Cross
And His side was pierced with the sword
That day good triumphed over evil
The impossible became possible
Heavenly afterlife is now plausible
As the Lamb takes away our sins
Christ gives us peace, and Christ wins

Easter Monday in Villeneuve-Loubet

day 227: march 28, 2016

It's the Monday after Easter. Here, in the small chapel of Notre-Dame d'Espérance, in Villeneuve-Loubet, the Mayor, clergy, locals, and tourists are gathered to celebrate and also to inaugurate the beautiful new Cross placed here.

The parish priest, Father André-Jacques Astre delivers a very appropriate sermon: he informs us that the color white is today's color, which means baptism, a new era; that Jesus suffered opposition for more than 2000 years, and yet He endures. Through His resurrection, Jesus promises us life in the "beyond." A huge stone blocked His tomb, but Jesus overturned that impossible block of rock, thus turning all that is impossible into possible. Some will always say Jesus doesn't exist. But today, Jesus has more friends in those who believe in the resurrection. He promised us that 'beyond,' where we will meet Him.

Chapelle Notre-Dame d'Espérance, Villeneuve-Loubet

After the mass, the crowd walks to the nearby Cross for its unveiling ceremony. The Mayor, Lionnel Luca, starts to sing the Ave Maria, and everybody follows suit. He explains how this new Cross was built in memory of the older one dating to 1859. He also warmly presents a few Syrian refuge families that the city of Villeneuve-Loubet had welcomed and helped by providing lodging and employment.

What an enriching experience to participate in a religious ceremony where some politicians do not fear, they do not try to hide their true self. Instead, firmly standing behind their long-held traditions, they honor the new as well as the old.

Glimpse
day 228: march 29, 2016

A glimpse of hope
A trickle of tears
A pinch of love
A tender kiss
And you are near
But I plunge into grief
And pangs of despair
Pains of distress
Remorse and regret
Haunt me after you've gone, my dear
But in solemn prayer of faith
Kneeling in the silence of the dark
Arms stretched out seeking His touch
I cry for help: O Mighty One, O Holy One
I implore You; I beseech You
Turn thy sight toward her
Thy glimpse of hope
Thy trickling joyous tear
Thy puffing heart
Thy pinch of love
Thy tender kiss
Turn her away from her ways
So she walks on the path of Your righteousness

Breath of Fresh Air

day 229: march 30, 2016

Saint Pierre Church, Cros de Cagnes

This morning walk along the Promenade of Cagnes infuses the soul with freshness, a breath of fresh air, a bouquet of fresh ideas.

The bluest calm sea is lapping on the beach… ending in long lazy waves that seem eager to walk across the promenade to enter the open, inviting door of the church. But I'm standing in their way, and the sea is behind me. Nothing should be disturbed. I just stand there, my back to the sea, facing the imposing church, I open my arms and stretch them up, breathe in the stimulating fresh air, and feel the warmth of the never-ending happiness. Emptiness and silence fill the air at this daybreak. Most stores are still closed. Few people stroll along the almost carless, silent promenade. I take another deep breath opening my arms wide up, and peace rushes into my emptied mind.

They say when you make an effort to empty your mind of clutter, your heart of trouble, and your soul of worry, new colorful fresh ideas will rush to fill that emptiness. Peace will overwhelm you. Feelings of love will start budding inside. And when there's love within, it will be eager to move out to reflect through the eyes—the soul of the body—and to reach out. Suddenly, all around will seem to be in love, with love, by love, and about love.

I shut my eyes in selfishness. I want to keep all that love inside. But it's too late. Love has already worked its magic and I see dawn breaking the dark, budding in the tiniest of creatures, and looking back at me from the bluest of skies resting behind the Provençal colors. I find hopelessness being transformed into cheerful contentment, and vanity into grounded faith.

Look at Your Troubles from a Different Angle
day 230: march 31, 2016

Even the mightiest waves will be tamed and subdued in the end. They will merge into the shallow waves returning back to the sea of life. Their strength will have had no effect on the sea. See, life creates the waves, and life re-engulfs them as tamed shallow water.

They don't last long these powerful disturbing waves. The sea is not disturbed by each hitting, passing wave. Neither should you. The sea stays grounded while her waves fluff out. So should you. She waits till they calm, till they subside. So should you.

Facing the waves, you feel overwhelmed, pressured to step back. But look at them from a different angle—the angle of, and from, the deep sea. And they disappear into a minimal white line separating the sea and the shore.

The sea does not give them power, she just rides them. So should you. Look at your troubled waves from a different angle, from the back door and you will see them fade.

And as your sea tosses and turns for you, look, there are the swans and the seagulls and the doves, able to find and fetch food in the troubled waters. Yes, look at your troubles from a different angle and you too will find food—food for your soul.

Cross the Red Line. Stand Out.

day 231: april 1, 2016

As I stand and stare at the sea, the sage who lives by the sea advises me, "Generations have come and gone. Many more are yet to come. Sometimes, a few stick out as odd. By the end of their journey, they are the ones that are remembered. Whoever sticks out and makes a difference, will have their name engraved somewhere. Whoever sticks out and makes a difference will have their striking color pop out among all other lookalikes. Among the generations, the red pebble stands out, just like the red line that we're always told to not cross. Remember: dare to cross the red line. Be the red. Dare."

I turn around to argue, but the sage of the sea has already disappeared.

Stop Acting Like a Ball
day 232: april 2, 2016

Today I again ask the sea to surprise me, to give me something she has never given me before. And what does she do? She offers me a golf ball backed by a solitary green leaf.

What should I make of it? Can you help me decipher? A golf ball's place is not here among the pebbles, and neither is the green leaf's.

Either the golf ball was brought here and thrown at the shore, or it was blurted out by the raging waves, and having lost its way, it ended up at the shore.

Suddenly, he kicks the ball, the dog walker, for the dog to catch it. It does. Then it spits it out only for its master to kick it again, for it to catch it again.

Never be a ball. Never let others kick you around. Play you. "Yes, that is the lesson to learn here," I reflect silently.

"But what about the green leaf? What is its meaning?" I contemplate, and I sense it whisper to me, "Even if up till today you might have been a ball allowing humans, animals, and the sea of life to toss you around, today is the day when you stop being a golf ball. Today is the day when green blossoms for you. Green young life and green new experiences will surprise you."

You too, stop being a ball, stop acting like a ball.

Snow

day 233: april 3, 2016

View of the Southern Alps from the port of Antibes

The snowy peaks of the Southern Alps watch over the troubled waters of charming Antibes. Settling high on the mountain tops, the white snow reminds us that the seas must sometimes get troubled, the skies must sometimes become dark and gloomy, the storms must sometimes rage in the air—all this, to pave the way for the pure white snow to fall.

And its white purity covers a multitude of scenes, giving hope to the sprouting new life underneath.

Those Layers of Barriers

day 234: april 4, 2016

Promenade of Cagnes Sur Mer

Layers of barriers
Or are they steps to move you forward?
You have to crush them, cross them, to reach the peace at mid sea
First the human barrier
Then the stuff at the shore between you and the sea
Then the road
Then the boulders
Then the dry stones
Then the wet pebbles
Then the sand
Then the white foam
Then the shore waves
Then the deep wave swells
And then finally you arrive at the calm at the deep sea
Where nothing can bother you
Nothing can hinder your progress once you have reached here
After crushing and crossing all the barriers

Eternal Pebbles

day 235: april 5, 2016

These eternal pebbles, that once were unbreakable boulders, stay grouped together just like family. A community. They think they can face the raging waters better this way. They think in their unity they will overcome the sea's rage one day. Unbeknownst to them, even in their unity they are being beaten down and transformed into sand—the vast sand that fills the earth, that dust where life starts, and to where it returns.

Just Because
Day 236: April 6, 2016

My friend surprised me with a bouquet of rose
Delighted, I asked why, and she replied *just because*
I did not understand and insisted on a reason
Smiling, she replied, just because, for no occasion
What a mystic rose color, I exclaimed
They call it old rose, she explained
Even that faded rose color was different
As receiving it *just because* was significant
It touched my heart, this kind gesture of hers
For often one gets noticed only on occasions
The lighthearted memory of that simple moment
Taught me to appreciate everyone at every moment
When we finished our picnic-lunch by the sea
We said our goodbyes and my dear friend left me
I walked with that fragrant bouquet to my blue sea
With that blue backdrop, it was a pleasant sight for me
And I made a sincere wish with that bouquet of rose
That you'll always get a bouquet of roses just because
That you'll always be happy, my friend with a heart of gold
May you be blessed with all the best the future can hold

Together

day 237: april 7, 2016

Even big rocks need smaller stones
And big stones need petite pebbles
To tenderly lean on each other
As they are stronger together
It's impossible to firmly stand up alone
Or turn their faces to the sun
But huddled together they're not alone
And facing the sun is much more fun
And the sea, lying in silent solitude, ponders to herself—
How long will they be able to withstand the crashing of my waves?
How long will they be able stay together, to lean on each other?
And persistently, she sends her waves, each a bit higher, fiercer than before
Don't you see?
We all need each other
Big or small, tall or short, young or old
The right needs the left and the healthy needs the broken
So we coexist to lean on each other, to help and nurture one another
So we withstand the huge surging waves of life
So we avoid being submerged under the crashing of the flood
And instead, we stand tall among them
United, together, leaning on one another
That's all there is to life
Wouldn't it be unwise then to look down at the other half of things or beings
May be one day, as the world turns, they will become the better half, the needed half

Expect to Receive Happiness

day 238: april 8, 2016

Today I woke up, joy in my heart, expecting to receive happiness. Expect, and it shall come to you. No matter how impossible, if you impress in your heart, without any doubt, that you have already received what you have been longing for, it shall be yours. Have faith. Close your eyes, inhale, put a smile on your face, and let your soul's eye see you already have obtained your wish, be it happiness, love, success, health, prosperity. Remember, the universe has ears.

Later tonight, I will describe the happiness that I received.

Now, it is tonight. And let me tell you about the happiness I received today: someone I love was involved in an accident; and thank God came out with no injuries or damage.

You receive that which you expect. Expect trivia, you'll get trivia. Expect your dream to come true, and your dream shall come true.

Try it, friend, it really works.

Espresso Time

day 239: april 9, 2016

Art Beach, Cagnes Sur Mer Promenade

Having an espresso, alone, out in the cold at the shoreless sea. Priceless.

No one knows you. No one bothers you, no one asks questions, no one comments, no one criticizes. It's you and the mysterious silence, being serenaded by the symphony of the waves. The bottomless sea looks and feels like our limitless accomplishments and endless failures. You sit there, thinking of what you have accomplished—and it pleases you. You forget your failures of course because they have taught you their lesson and have departed. Your future is full of goals and plans and deadlines. You are contemplating more and more successful accomplishments, and your mind begins to soar, your spirits lift up, your ego inflates.

But finishing up the last sip of the warm espresso, you reflect: "Let not your worldly accomplishments get into your head, blinding you from the important aspects of life: fear of God, love and respect for family, charity, common sense, and such works that nourish your soul. Being so inflated deflates the soul leaving no more room for humility."

You are again deflated to your humble being, you take a final sip at the cold imaginary drop of coffee, and you leave.

Boundaries

day 240: april 10, 2016

Do you sometimes wonder what's on the other side of the sea? Ha! That's such a simple question: there's always another sea, always other life. The physical boundaries that we see, for people and things, for nations and seas, separate and yet unite us all.

Do you sometimes wonder what's on the other side of the sea of life? Hmm ... Now that's not as simple as it sounds, but there's always another sea of life, always, other life. These boundaries we do not see. Because we don't, we assume there's nothing beyond the sea of our life. How wrong we are. These invisible confines separate us from this other life, and yet they do discreetly unite. And isn't it the soul that unites? The physical bodies separate us from the other side, and yet our soul can leave the physical body here, and traverse between these two sides to bridge the gap and to awaken our spiritual self.

Boundaries as we see them limit all things, except the soul, for she can travel between the unseen boundaries, of here and there. Ironically, during the time that the soul is on this side of the sea, we limit her. We impose restrictions on this super intelligence called the soul. We set artificial boundaries, contouring her with our fears, within the tiny limits of our frail body and simple imagination. Why not let her roam while she's on this side? Let her explore, let her discover. Let her be free. Be happy without boundaries.

Tell Me What's Troubling You
day 241: april 11, 2016

My dear sea, you look so calm with your golden ripples strolling aimlessly. But there is something bothering you deep inside. I can hear it in the last breath of your dwindling waves before they hit the shore. Tell me what's troubling you. We've been in this long journey together, you and me, day and night—rising together at daybreak, and settling in after dark. Those dark days are gone. Spring is springing, birds are chirping again, and yet something deep down is disturbing you.

Tell me what's troubling you.

As Light, How Are We to Live?

day 242: april 12, 2016

At the shores of my sea, I'm playing with this high-tech camera, and my daughter explains to me that with little light and long exposure, the darkness of the night will disappear in the photo taken and the colors of the scene will appear. That speck of light brightens the darkness. Also, with long exposure, people who are walking or moving in front of the camera seem to become transparent or disappearing in the picture, but the inanimate objects remain in the photo. What are we then, but for light? The camera captures us for a split moment, but if the exposure is set to a longer time, we, the lights that we are, disappear.

As the lights that we are, how are we to live? Jesus has the answer, saying, *"You are the light of the world. A city seated on a mountain cannot be hid. Neither do men light a candle and put it under a bushel, but upon a candlestick, that it may shine to all that are in the house. So let your light shine before men, that they may see your good works, and glorify your Father who is in heaven."*[113]

And I remember how an hour ago I had watched the sleepy sunset cover all around with her pink blanket. I had noticed that cute couple, on the western slope of life, walking hand-in-hand towards the setting sun. Have they walked on life's right path—from east to west? Since the rising of their sun to its setting? Have they spread their light? Yes, they have. It is obvious on their wrinkled faces and peaceful smiles.

So, we should shine as light doing good deeds in this world, so that others see it, are touched by it, and in their turn, spread it.

Why

day 243: april 13, 2016

View over the Hippodrome (racetrack) of Cagnes Sur Mer

At the birthday of this gorgeous morning, as I embrace your welcoming charm and calm my dear blue sea, I contemplate how you sometimes shock. With all this eternal wisdom and timeless beauty inside and out, how do you manage to send jolts across the seas and the oceans. And your constant waves boldly disturb that rocking boat, the resting pebbles, and the harmony of Mother Nature.

But, I smile, I dance, I sing. Then, when I am all alone again, I ask myself: "Why? Why?" I don't want to know the reason. I may never understand. And I let your waves flow by, and the days of my life drift by, without making any effort to comprehend.

Someday, I hope, you will understand dear sea the extent of the devastation your shocking waves generated years ago. And I pray that there will still be time to heal and embrace. Until then, I shall keep dancing and singing from the bottom of my heart.

The Rapport
day 244: april 14, 2016

I have come to learn that my rapport with the sea dates back to before my birth. You see, first you swim in the sea of your mother's womb learning to fend for yourself in the depths of the mysteries of the beginnings of life.

Nine months later they cast you into the vast sea of life. Though you are loved and cared for, sooner or later you will realize that it is you, and only you, who must swim. No one else can do it for you. You must take a dive at the sea of life alone. And there begins your rapport with the sea—at that magical, miraculous moment. Whether you swim struggling, you float, or you let yourself drift, depends on the strength of your rapport with the sea.

The sooner you realize that you are alone in this sea and on your life path, the faster you will attain that level of inner peace and joy which cannot be shaken by the other lonely swimmers in the same sea.

This then is living: each person must walk their own path, must swim their own sea, must travel their own journey, no-matter how or where the fellow traveler is heading.

Friends

day 245: april 15, 2016

What is a friend but "one single soul in two bodies"[114]
One soothing smile on two faces
A soft lullaby in the silence of anxiousness
A warm, long hug and nothing is said
A glitter of light in the darkness
A gentle touch on the trembling hand
A firm grip preventing that fall
A soft voice calling in the wilderness
An encouraging look piercing the tired eyes
With a laughter here, and a cry there
Meals shared; a lifetime united
Worries forgotten; moments cherished
All nostalgia is shared with the friend
The nostalgia of days passed
And also, the hope of those yet to come
In good times and in bad times
Like the fresh breath of the sincere sea
A caring friend is all that you see

Lovers in the Rain

day 246: april 16, 2016

How beautiful is the sweet music of today's rain. Raindrops are falling on the crowns of tall pine and towering palm trees, seeping through each branch of green leaves of pointed needles, round puffs, and flat palms. And the long white silvery streaks paint a picture of showers of blessings.

The long rainy streaks reach the ground, quench the pebbles and sand, and then flow into the sea. In that, they are also blessing the sea, and the lovers loving by the sea. The sea seems eager to receive this blessing, so she in turn blesses and nurtures the lovers' eternal love.

Yes, this is heaven for lovers. Rain or shine, lovers thrive here. Strangers in the rain become lovers. Young lovers learn how to grow their budding love, and old lovers tell them their secrets on how to keep that love forever.

Happy Birthday to You

day 247: april 17, 2016

I lit a red candle for you, and said a secret prayer or two
In the mysterious silence of the church, sitting on the wooden pew
Intimately conversing with our Father, God, whispering about you
In flashed all our cherished memories holding us like glue
I searched for words to describe you, but God already knew
It is her, God said, whom I sent to you
It is her who will be true, caring, by you, lifting you from the blue
Intelligent, beautiful, kind, composed, caring, and daring too
She will be able to do all things she sets her mind to
Holding her hand, I will always guide her through
I will shower her with my grace, my infinite peace and my love too
She shall fly to the moon, reach the stars she loves, the unfathomable galaxies too
I will reward her faith with fortitude, purity, justice, honor, and my credo
And she will leave her revered mark as she merrily passes through
I asked if you'd always be happy, healthy, respected, and loved too
And God secretly promised: That dream too, shall come true
And suddenly, all the church bells rang joyfully to woo
Ding-dong-ding-dong Happy Birthday to YOU

Eye on the Prize

day 248: april 18, 2016

You've got to keep your wandering eye focused on the desired, target prize. What is the most unimaginable prize you seek at this moment?

_____

What are you doing about it? Are you dreaming, whining, or taking action?

_____

What is the deadline you have set to grab this prize?

_____

What is distracting you from working towards your prize? What's blocking your road?

_____

What's action items are necessary?

_____

Name your prize. Set a deadline. Ignore dreams, distractions, and roadblocks. What's left? Actions. Focus on the prize. Act. Right now.

Perspectives
day 249: april 19, 2016

Today the beach looks perfectly aligned with all lines converging at one point. It looks divided into sections by these long lines of perspective: The short path line abutting the pebbles, the longer line delineating them at sea, while the horizon line divides the sky from the sea. And they all submerge at that one meeting point to the left. But that meeting point does not actually exist, this walking path is not as short as it seems, the pebble area is not larger than sea, and the horizon never touches the sea or the sky, nor does it separate them as the horizon line itself does not exist.

What an illusion. These perspective lines create makeshift convergence points. Whether you see those lines as separating or connecting depends on your viewpoint— rather, your point of view. Dividing or connecting, as they maybe, is an interpretation of your mindset at that moment, a product of your attitude towards the subject, the positive or negative angle you're looking from, and your whole outlook on life.

Nietzsche said: "There are no facts, only interpretations."[115] So, change your perspective today and the greatness of many things will be reduced to smallness. Change your point of view and the smallest of things will enlarge occupying huge spaces. Take a few steps to the right, or left, or back and forward, and, suddenly everything you look at changes, appearing larger or smaller, shorter or taller, heavier or lighter, merrier or sadder, and sometimes they cease to exist.

The Trinity of Life

day 250: april 20, 2016

As I begin my prayer walk of today, again, I ask the sea for a sign: a sign of wisdom. Her unfailing response unravels—Jesus, Carpe Diem, and Love—the trinity of life.

First, Jesus looks at me from a crucifixion poster on the cordon wall of the Villeneuve Marina's pier. It used to be bare, this barricade to the sea. Next, across from it, sits the boat—Carpe Diem—housing someone wise who's living, seizing the day, and being minimally credulous of the future.[116] As I keep marching along the water edge, I encounter this big white stone heart alone amidst the tiny pebbles. I continue marching, leaving it there.

How do I reconcile these three signs in one wisdom?" I ponder. I'll just stroll a little longer along the edge—where the waves incessantly sweep the pebbles out to sea—and let the gray breeze work my weary brain. And it starts to rain. The raindrops walk by me as I return, along the same path at the edge where the sea is now dancing with the pebbles. I want to recapture and recuperate my stone heart that I left there a while ago. But it isn't there. I had left it too close to the stormy waves and the vast troubled sea snatched it away. And now I don't have the guts to wet my feet to recapture my heart.

The falling raindrops whisper in my ear: "Change your path, go deeper, wet your feet and the sea will return your heart." And I understood the wisdom of today's signs: 1) trust God, 2) live for today, don't worry about tomorrow,[117] 3) love despite cold or lost hearts, and spread love.

Jesus, Carpe Diem, Love—the trinity of life.

No Brain = No Pain

day 251: april 21, 2016

"No Brain = No Pain." I read this phrase on the dirty rear windshield of an old scratched and bumped car parked at the shore. I wonder of it is true.

Looking at the car, it seems the owner would care less about appearances, and more about mindful, peaceful matters. S/he has learned to ignore pain, disregard it, and detach from it. Perhaps s/he is now sitting at the same sea contemplating. "No Brain = No Pain." Does it also mean finding the power to detach yourself from your brain, to not overthink? As a result, you would live in the now. No pain, no brain, only now. See, smell, feel, hear, and taste the now. Live the now.

Maybe I am overthinking again, and "No Brain = No Pain" simply means that reckless, careless people with no brains don't feel pain—the pain they cause to others by their selfish destructive actions.

But, is the pain felt only with the brain or the heart and soul as well? It is your turn to overthink.

Flourish Where You Are
day 252: april 22, 2016

Even the Loup riverside's hidden path that walks me to the sea does so. It flourishes. It blooms even in dryness. It shines amidst the tall shady birches and the flickering needles of pines trees this early morning, while the transparent stream flows in its place. The petite white fountains it creates over the occasional rocks and logs pave the way to unlock the waters blocked underneath these barriers.

At a wooden picnic table in this corner, hidden from our civilization's chaos, I find a small white heart carved on the table. I inspect it. It stares at me. And it smiles. And it makes me remember to bloom and flourish. And I remember the loves I had experienced, losing some, gaining others along my path. And I realize how love had been, and forever will be, the only thing needful.

And I type in my phone: "Flourish wherever you are. Create with your hands, voice, mind, heart, and soul. Do not let any day go by merely wanting. Do not forget to create fruitful, rewarding, everlasting fountains of love and peace around you.

Leave traces of love wherever you go, for only flourishing in love fulfills the law."

#openyourspiritualeyes
day 253: april 23, 2016

We come into life crying, while our loved ones rejoice. We depart to heaven rejoicing, while our loved ones cry. But unless we have tried to live a holy life, which might put a forever smile on our soul, we will keep crying in afterlife as well.

Unexpected sickness, heartbreaking losses, backstabbing betrayal, unimaginable shock, sorrow, and lingering depression, render us helpless, paralyzed. And while we bask in our self-victimization and pitiful state, suddenly faith knocks on our door. It opens our spiritual eyes. It extends roots and settles deeply into our soul dwarfing those agonizing, repetitive, string of trials. It helps us to rise above life's turmoil. It heals our soul. And only after we heal your soul, we can help others to heal as well.

If we are able to help a few other sick, heartbroken, betrayed, sorrowful, depressed souls to open their spiritual eyes too, we have lived. #openyourspiritualeyes

Reflections on a Genocide

day 254: april 24, 2016

Port of Marina Baie des Anges, Villeneuve-Loubet

What we throw at sea is reflected back to us—accurately, and distorted. Just like Karma. Just like the Golden Rule. It is the same with the sea of life. She shall reflect what is thrown at her. How she is treated shall dictate how she treats us.

Reflections. Karma. Today marks the 101st anniversary of the genocide of the first Christian nation on earth—Armenia, where Christianity was first officially accepted in 301. About 1.5 million Armenians were tortured, raped, beheaded, crucified, deported, and massacred by the Ottoman Turks in 1915. Genocide of Christians, of a whole nation, and to this day it is being denied by its perpetrators, and by some of its 'powerful' allies. The sea of life is a reflection. She will deflect what is thrown at her: if it is genocide, then she will reflect genocide. Another form of genocide maybe, or in other parts of the world maybe. If it's a denial of genocide, then she will reflect denial of other human rights, other genocides, in other parts of the world maybe.

And today, after 101 years, indeed other forms of genocide of Christians is being reflected, denied, ignored, and propagated in the whole world. But soon Karma shall cast its echoes over genocide perpetrators and deniers alike, so that nothing is left incomplete, unpunished, unfulfilled, unreflected. The Karma circle must be completed—if not now, not here on Earth, then definitely beyond now, beyond Earth.

Sandals

day 255: april 25, 2016

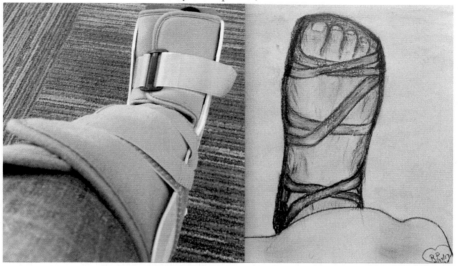

Jesus Right Foot Illustration by the Author

My tonight's dream: Jesus' right foot, clad in His famed sandal,[118] stepped forward as if leading my left foot to follow Him, and I could see the hem of his white robe graciously moving along with each step of our walk together. The sandals remind me of the same sandals that I had bought, in Athens, for my little brother very long time ago, and that he had worn them for so many years. And I feel Jesus assuring me in my heavenly dream, "I am always by your side, walking by your side, leading you, guiding you."

As soon as I wake up, I draw the image on the right above, so I don't forget it. Later in the day, my beautiful daughter, Sar, texts me from Los Angeles a picture of her left foot in a huge cast/brace because she had a broken toe due to an accident. I immediately realize that my daughter's picture of her left broken casted foot complements Jesus' sandals on His right foot which I had dreamt of. And I know Jesus was also walking by her, and not only by me. I should not worry, despite my motherly natural instinct to worry. Trust Him. Just walk.

And as if to continue my dream's message, the whole day I see these messages while driving; "RP (my middle name, on a car plate), Enjoy the Way (motto on a truck), Neway (name on a hotel building), On my way (iPhone auto text)." "RP, enjoy the way, the New Way, I Am on my way." What a message from Jesus! I understand all this to mean that I must focus on my path, that a new path will appear, and that God is accompanying me. At night, reading the parable of the father, who, rejoiced over the return of his prodigal son and offered him sandals.[119] 'Sandals' then, are symbolic of walking in faith in God's path, and of God's love for his prodigal children who will one day return to their faith.

Vanille de Madagascar

day 256: april 26, 2016

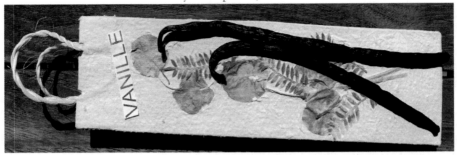

My friend gifts me a bag of long black aromatic vanilla sticks, when she returned from her humanitarian mission. The sticker on the beautifully designed white linen gift bag reads: Vanille de Madagascar.[120] The design of the red poppy flower on the long gift bag, in which the sticks fit, makes the package even more attractive.

Many times, I have gazed at the pictures of the brownish yellow untapped horizons of Madagascar adorning the walls of her medical office. She had fallen in love with Madagascar long time ago. She recently went back there with a benevolent humanitarian mission—to set up a medical base in a remote village almost cutoff from the world and to care for as many patients as possible. Which she did. At least 50 people a day, who almost never had the chance to visit a doctor, came to the doors of her makeshift medical office to receive medical help. She was overwhelmed by their congeniality, simplicity, and honesty despite their underlying serious, untreated health issues. The un-westernized minimalism of the village, the mystery of the beautiful natural habitat, the unimaginably meek quality of life, the forgotten inhabitants for whom our known medical treatments are a mere fantasy, captivated my doctor's heart, and vicariously mine.

The best vanilla in the world: the Vanilla of Madagascar. I want to keep and cherish those thin long black sticky sticks forever. They embody the life of that village. I can bring to life the stories that my friend narrated about this village. I can see the faces of the inhabitants. I can smell the aroma of the Madagascar air that they breathe. I can see their sunburnt bare hands working with these vanilla sticks. I can imagine their simple lives in the crowded family huts they live in—how they are there for each other, how they lookout for one another in that part of the world devoid of all the artificial modernity of ours. And they are happy.

I so appreciate this gift—as if she gifted me the soul of their world, their culture, their lives, their faces, and their honest simplicity that cached their untreated maladies. She saw 50-60 patients a day. She had to improvise treatments, administer medications and vaccines, listen to their unique life stories, had the very ill airlifted to the nearest hospital in a far town, and yet she found the time to go out and find a gift, for me. Friendship. Once you find a real friend, keep them. They don't come along often.

Ce Que Femme Veut, Dieu Le Veut[121]

day 257: april 27, 2016

It's one of those days when you want to rearrange, organize, and change everything in your life. I need a task to be done by this creative artist and his crew. When I describe the details of what I want, they look at me with blank, yet glowing pensive eyes. Expecting an argument to ensue, I put on a smile in a pre-attempt to deflate what's coming. To my surprise and admiration, he responds: Ce que femme veut, Dieu le veut—What woman wants, God wants.

I'm pleasantly amazed to hear this instead of the usual resistance women receive for wanting a task to be done a certain way—their way. Why would God want what women want? I thought about it the rest of the day. Not finding the answer in my thoughts, I research and read, and voilà! It's because women bring about order. And God is order. From the microscopic creatures, to the grandiose universe, all are arranged in order. Cycles rotate in order—day and night, the four seasons, planets in their orbit, the cycle of life—and they follow their predetermined course in time. And so do women bring order in their daily life, families, workplace, and entourage.

Another reason is that women encourage and support their entourage, sometimes forgetting their self, and serving relentlessly to achieve others' happiness. Isn't that a reflection of God? In addition, women are strong. Always fighting evil, fending it off their families, their children, and themselves. And this constant struggle, being a blessing in disguise, empowers them, and turns them into fighters—for order, for Godly order. Women pray, incessantly, patiently, secretly, and in public, and God gets tired of their pleas and grants their answer, hence, wanting what they want. Also, God has appointed that women carry on the task of bearing children, populating the earth, educating generations, all for His supreme will. Wouldn't He want to grant their wishes should they be aligned with His will? Lastly, why would God want what women want? Perhaps the most important reason is because God chose a woman to carry His Only Son. And she obeyed with all humility. What God wants. Woman wants. Yes, the first woman, Eve, disobeyed God, but Mary, the first woman of Christianity, changed that course, accepting God's divine and holy conception without any complaint. And She became the Mother of all. And so God rewards women, affording them what they want.

Therefore, my women friends out there:

Never, ever despair

In patient endurance, persist in prayer

What woman wants; God wants—will be the answer

You are pre-rewarded since the beginning of age

Without getting what you want, do not turn that page

Keep up your chin, never give up, and don't give in to rage

Insist on your reward, for with God you have quite an advantage

Vantage Point

He is wealthy already because he has that vantage point
He doesn't need much to be happy because he's happy in his solitude by the sea
The fisherman, fishing for survival, for his wealth comes from the sea
He throws his fish pole in the waters, while the yacht passes by that joint

Disturbing the wildlife, polluting the sea
The yacht is very wealthy and happy at sea
Finally they meet, the fisherman and the yacht
In the same waters where his fish are caught

For he is fishing where the yacht is polluting
But the yacht is in oblivion carousing
In the end who's happier—
The one whose wealth comes from the sea
Or the one who throws his wealth into the sea?

The Loops

day 259: april 29, 2016

Villeneuve-Loubet Plage

The loops of the sea: one after the other. One advances another recedes, but one is always present. The loops—those playful, and sometimes uneasy waves looping and zigzagging together—keep twisting and turning. The loops look still from afar, but they never rest. They can be used for fun—jet skiing, for example, but can also bring trouble—inundations.

The loops of life: one after the other. One advances, the other recedes. And they never stay despite their illusory games. Coming and going, some loops try to bother us, and others provide joy.

The sea is not bothered by them; for she had decided long time ago to not let the forever loops rob her of her joy. She allows them to play at her shores, and she prudently watches and enjoys. She is wise, the sea.

Living on the Edge
day 260: april 30, 2016

Monaco

Live on the edge. Why not? Are you afraid to get your feet wet? So what if they do? You will never know what's on the other side of the edge if you don't let your feet get wet. You are already living on this side of the edge. And you know how it is. You know the feeling. Are you happy? Then come to the edge, try a new happiness. The sea will not disappoint you. Are you not happy on this side? Then you must come live on the edge. Even cross it and immerse yourself into the stormy colorful sea. You will not be disappointed.

Look at the seagull on the other side of the edge. Did you find it? If that seagull is able to free itself, cross the edge, and experience new horizons, why wouldn't you? Take the jump into your future. Cross that edge. Cross the security barrier. Release your mental borders. You will soon experience new opportunities and new happiness.

May in France
day 261: may 1, 2016

En mai, fait ce qu'il te plait
En mai, shoppez quand ça vous plait[122]
In May, do things your way
Shop whenever you may
The first of May
Celebrate Labor Day
Offer and receive little sprigs of Muguet[123]
For friendships that stay
To bring good luck your way
It is May
It is time to play
Because it's a field-day
Act like every day is a holiday
Tell your loved ones to stay
Don't forget to pray
So your soul won't dismay
Train your willpower not to sway
And your mind not to flyaway
Put your talents on display
Start today
On this First day of May

More Grace

day 262: may 2, 2016

Cros de Cagnes at Night

Today I receive an unexpected message from a stranger: "More grace." What does it mean? Researching, I find the phrase in James 4:6-17. I'm so impressed by this Bible verse, that I want to repeat it here in pertinent part:

"But He gives more grace.

God resists the proud, but gives grace to the humble.

Submit yourselves therefore to God. Resist the devil, and he will flee from you.

Draw near to God, and he will draw near to you. Cleanse your hands, you sinners; and purify your hearts, you double minded …

Do not speak evil of one another. He that speaks evil of his brother, and judges his brother, speaks evil of the law, and judges the law: but if you judge the law, you are not a doer of the law, but a judge. There is one lawgiver, God, who is able to save and to destroy. Who are you to judge another?

Do not say, 'Today or tomorrow we will go into such a city, and continue there a year, and buy and sell, and get gain,' because you do not know what will happen tomorrow. Instead, you ought to say, 'If the Lord will, we shall live, and do this, or that.' But now you rejoice in your boastings: all such rejoicing is evil.

Therefore, to him that knows to do good, and does not do it, to him it is sin."[124]

Dog Friend
day 263: may 3, 2016

Promenade des Anglais

These dogs. Such wonderful friends. Silently they sit by you, and patiently they support you. Watching this doggie riding a bike sitting on his master's back, hair in the wind, reminds me of the movie about that Japanese dog Hachi[125] who waited for his master every day at the train station. I cried watching the movie. How loyal they are, unlike men. I'd lately seen the hurting effects of disloyalty in the sad eyes of my good friends who themselves had become broken victims of disloyalty. But one of them told me, "They cannot hurt us anymore." And she was right.

Listen to the soundtrack of Hachi, watch the movie, and cry, because rarely will you encounter that kind of deep, utmost loyalty from men. And, if you're lucky enough to stumble upon such a human, cling to that person, and don't ever let go, and truly appreciate all the small and big things s/he does for you.

I am reminded of a remark our late golden retriever Meesha had received from a stranger while sharing ice cream with us long time ago: "It is better to have a dog friend, than a friend who is a dog."

Cure, Don't Complain

day 264: may 4, 2016

If it's the pebbles, tame them, grind them into sand
If it's the sand, sit on it or push it out
If it's the ship, push it up
If it's the cloud, dance with it
If it's the moon, provide a path
If it's the sun, shine along
If it's the humans, welcome them or drown them (figuratively)
If you feel drowning in the sea of life, set boundaries
If you feel wronged, face them and set rules
If they lose their way, gently teach
If you are distracted, ignore and focus on your goals
But never lose your composure, never worry
Stop complaining now, for that's no cure
And if nothing works and you've honestly tried everything possible to no avail
then light a candle for each complaint, pray, and throw them up, one by one

Ascension

day 265: may 5, 2016

How enormous are the life-giving waters of Mother Earth's seas? They are all united together. And my sea, the Mediterranean Sea, takes you all the way to the Holy Lands, the lands where Jesus walked, to the Sea of Galilee. There He ascended[126] into Heaven on Ascension day to be with His Father, and to "prepare mansions for us,"[127] for those of us who believe in Him and follow Him.

Today is the 40th and last day Jesus walked among us after His glorious resurrection. How sad that He has to depart. We will be left all alone to fight the evil in this world by ourselves. But He promised to send us His consoler—the Holy Spirit—who will comfort us and give us the power to resist evil. That will be on Pentecost day. Ten days from today.

Illustration by the author based on stained glass in Antibes Cathedral

Yes it was God's will that Jesus had to depart. He had fulfilled His mission on earth. He brought us redemption, absolution, salvation. Let's sing these words of Stevie Wonder's "Pastime Paradise." Yeah, He promised all this to those who follow Him:

Redemption – God's redemption

Absolution – Jesus' absolution of our sins

Reclamation – Jesus' reclamation of His souls from the evil

Repossession – Jesus' repossession of all lost souls

Conversion – Spiritual transformation of souls

Salvation – Eternal life for souls

Stuck

day 266: may 6, 2016

Look at that sticky broken branch in the middle of the river's rush. It is stuck. Stuck, when all around is moving fast. Some pushing from the sides, some pulling down, some trying to uproot and push forward, and yet it is stuck. That branch, broken and detached from its mother tree, has reached this far from the long, winding, treacherous, bitter-sweet, sunny-dark journey. But, on the final rock, at that last barrier before reaching the shallow waters, it is stuck. It doesn't even look like it has stamina to try—that one last jump.

If only it keeps rolling and floating. If only it keeps following the stream in its winding path around the rocks, in between the cracks, flowing incessantly with life, it will unleash itself from the last bedrock, in where it thinks it is stuck.

Maybe it is just weary and tired, getting some rest, to pause and think, and to forge with that one final push to reach its destination: the sea, the sea of abundant life. Then, it will feel the soothing shallowness of the water, the warmth of the sun shining over, and the freedom of the space around it.

The stuck are stubborn. Or is it the stubborn that are stuck?

And It Is Still There

day 267: may 7, 2016

Everything you want is out there. At sea. The sea of life. Extend your arm, extend yourself over those flowery hurdles and reach out. All your dreams are within reach. Everything that you dream of already exists. It has been created for you long time ago, and it's waiting for you—don't you wait too—so, just reach out and grab it.

Think about it for a moment. Look at the blue sea in the distance. What would you do to reach it? List your action items here. Then prioritize them and start taking action, perform the necessary steps crossing them off your list. Once you have crossed that final step, there you are. You have arrived. You have achieved.

How to Keep Loving Despite

day 268: may 8, 2016

I don't claim to have the answer to how to keep loving despite the hurt. The beating heart is always there, and the blue sea too. The love is always there as well, but at times, it is clouded by judgment, beliefs, and biases. Just as the sea is always there, but at times she's clouded by mist, murk, and opacity. But you know she's there. Just as you know your love is there.

It takes determination and shift of mindset to see past the clouding judgment, murky beliefs, and opaque biases, and to strip the heart of everything but love—then, you will love again.

Of Horses and Men

day 269: may 9, 2016

The Hippodrome (Racetrack) of the Cote d'Azur

Riviera's Hippodrome proudly sits by the sea
Housing spirited horses who work with the trainee
Here, the horse is the vital force of the workforce
He'll happily gallop and relentlessly run its racecourse

He'll do all for the pure enjoyment of mighty men
And the expensive gambling desires of them
For warfare, games, travel, profits and hippo-therapy
Is this how it should be?

This speedy, courageous colt makes his debut
Bridled with harness and saddle and blinders and horseshoe
Prodded and spurred, skillfully calculated to subdue
Only later to be limited to a rope-bound area, waiting for all to renew

If that black-maned young horse only knew
That he could easily pass through
That by a kick he could remove and rescue
And bump down the source of men's revenue

But he will be brought up harnessed to a carriage
He will be taken advantage of, with no one to encourage
The beat of his galloping feet will chill
While he will live day after day standstill
He will get used to imposed artificial boundaries
He will shy away, and curb his energy and natural abilities

Let the untamed spirit of this gentle friend flee
Remove the reins, set him free
He should be able to run wild from palm tree to pine tree
Touching the remote edges of the crisp forestry

The Nest

day 270: may 10, 2016

As I sit on my forest-side balcony, sipping on my morning coffee and getting ready to continue writing my other book, I notice a new pair of doves—a young gray and a young black-dotted white—flying back and forth together, the black-dotted dove bringing small twigs and the gray one accompanying the white in harmony, to the upstairs balcony, to build their nest. They use the same route to return and soar back up with yet another twig of the same size and shape. They repeat their twig collecting journey many times, always flying together and never giving up.

They will build their nest, create their family, nourish and nurture their babies, keep them safe, teach them to fly on their own, so that they ultimately find their own dove and build their own nest.

What happens to this nest afterwards? What happens to these gray and black-dotted white parent doves? Will life treat them well? Will they have fulfilled their mission here?

Heaviness and Trust
day 271: may 11, 2016

Walking along the rain-soaked seashore, quietly bearing the heaviness of my heart and gazing into the sky, I silently pray to the Lord "to open their eyes, and to turn them from darkness to light, and from the power of Satan unto God, that they may receive forgiveness of sins, and inheritance among them which are sanctified by faith that is in me."[128]

I pray and pray in the rain, completely trusting that He hears. And soon, a golden sliver of light starts breaking and pushing the heaviness away. Pray always, my friend. And believe. Never give up. Trust the Lord.

And I am reminded of Helen Keller's deep trust that she has so eloquently expressed, writing, "I trust, and nothing that happens disturbs my trust. I recognize the beneficence of the power which we all worship as supreme—Order, Fate, the Great Spirit, Nature, God. I recognize this power in the sun that makes all things grow and keeps life afoot. I make a friend of this indefinable force, and straightway I feel glad, brave, and ready for any lot Heaven may decree for me."[129]

Faith

day 272: may 12, 2016

Saint Marc Church in Villeneuve-Loubet Village

When faith knocks on your door
All hopelessness disappears
Yesterday's fears dissipate
And you are home

And love reaches the sea
Sloping through the valleys
Swishing in the puff clouds
And you are home

Faith brings you back home
From the dark alleys
Through the hidden walls
And faith is home

Let yourself enter that door
Where faith resides
Along with love, hope, and charity
And that is home, real home

Paths
day 273: may 13, 2016

It is amazing what paths destiny takes to reach its destination. It is said that we often meet our destiny on the paths we take to avoid it (Jean de La Fontaine). Have you ever experienced this? The very thing that you run from, finds you on your escape route. The event you despise most comes your way. The person you dislike forcefully enters your life. The more you send out these negative emotions, the more they attract that very thing off of those paths you try to avoid.

And then you learn. After being hit hard with the contraries of your imagination. You learn to not despise, hate, avoid, loathe, and criticize. You realize that it's all made up of reflections. Love reflects love. Light reflects light. Darkness reflects darkness, even nothingness.

You change your strategy. Now you adore, love, seek out, accept, and praise. And now you find Destiny on that new path, waiting. And she will help you attract what you love and adore.

It's Impossible? Try again

day 274: may 14, 2016

This photo is dated May 14, 2015. Many things were thought to be impossible then. A year later, they have come to pass. Setting a raw egg upright on a smooth glass table is impossible, right? Wrong.

Look at the photo. The author of this possibility my daughter, tried over and over again in the face of laughter mockery and claims of impossibility, to make this raw egg sit straight without cracking it. And she succeeded, for she says there's nothing impossible for her.

So next time you think something is impossible, try again. Keep doing that very thing over and over again, until it gives in to your persistence and makes it happen. Try to set a raw egg upright on your table. You think you will fail? Of course, you will at first try, and many times thereafter. You think it's impossible? It is not. Nothing is impossible.

Try again.

And again.

Nourish Your Soul

day 275: may 15, 2016

Stained Glass in The Penitents Blancs Chapel in Saint Paul de Vence

Today is the Feast of Pentecost that occurs 10 days after Jesus' Ascension into heaven. Before departing this earth to heaven, Jesus had promised to send His consoler to comfort us, to give us grace and wisdom, and to guide our spirits in this wild world. Therefore, on Pentecost, as promised, He sent the Holy Spirit who gifted the apostles, gathered in the Upper Room to pray, with the ability to speak and understand different languages. This enabled them to go out into the world and spread Jesus' Gospel. This marked the birth of the church.

The Holy Spirit gave the ability to understand each other's languages to unify us, so we understand each other despite our differences. I'd like to infer that while we strive to ameliorate our physical, mental, and material conditions, we often forget that our soul needs nutrition as well. To fulfill the needs of the soul we need peace, forgiveness, mercy, charity, fraternity, hope, and most importantly love and faith to sustain us through difficult times.

Let us seek wisdom, understanding, and grace on this Pentecost day, so that we, in our turn, nourish other souls to spread Jesus' message of love[130] and forgiveness.

275

Believing Without Seeing
day 276: may 16, 2016

I see the most beautiful halo around the sun gleaming among the sparse clouds, I exclaim, "How beautiful is that rainbow." And the passenger sitting by me in the car replies, "What rainbow?" I remove my black sunglasses, and the rainbow is gone. It reappears to charm me again once I put my black sunglasses on. I think: "Just because we don't see it with our naked eyes doesn't mean the rainbow's not there. Eyes don't see all that there's to see."

Sometimes we must use black sunglasses, filters, lenses, binoculars, microscopes, and telescopes to see what's beyond our simple vision. And the discovered views are fascinating. And sometimes we must use our spiritual eyes to see what's beyond our simple life. And then the view is captivating. And when we look with our heart, the love we find is eternal.

How about seeing with our faith? "Faith is an inner recognition of truth" wrote Emanuel Swedenborg referring to these words that Jesus had said to doubting Thomas who insisted to touch Jesus' wounds to confirm Jesus' identity: *"Because you have seen me, Thomas, you have believed. Blessed are those who do not see, and yet they believe."*[131] Faith, therefore, is believing in something with our inner being, without seeing, hearing, or touching it.

The Truth

day 277: may 17, 2016

At the banks of the Loup River in Villeneuve-Loubet

Trying to get away with lying? Think again.

There's nowhere to hide in this transparent universe. Truth likes to be discovered. It exerts much pressure on the powers of the universe forcing them to bring out the truth to light. Time is unimportant for truth. Even if truth is buried in the depths of the sea or the river of life, it has its ways to come to light. It waits. Until then, the person who summons the courage to confess wins the race. Better to tell the truth now and suffer little damage, than to wait for it to be exposed, and it definitely will, and suffer irreparable damage.

"God Sees the Truth but waits."[132]

My Soul Soared

day 278: may 18, 2016

I was living boxed in my tiny anxious chest
Daily I looked longingly at sea to feel my best
I knew she would replenish my exhausted chest
So, I breathed the crisp air of her blue sky as a test
To see if their vastness would restore my lost rest

I repeated this every day, my soul troubling my chest
Because you see, to my soul, I had become a bore
Repeating old chores, having my dreams suppressed
Finally, one day, my soul dared to ask if we could soar
Like we did when we were young at core

I resisted. I was comfortable now in my tight, sad chest
But when my gaze stretched beyond the shore that I adore
At once my soul got wings, pulling me out of my chest to the crest
Singing and dancing: "This moment, in the now, is the best
In that empty nest, you were only a guest, off we go on a new quest."

If You Build it, They Will Come

day 279: may 19, 2016

You're still waiting and wailing and wishing they'd come back. You are broken and sorrowful at their departure. And yet, you sit and wait, sit and wait. But you don't act. But did you know love brings everybody back. If you build it, they will come. Build it with love, and they will come back. Gather your willpower. The aura—of a home, a relationship, a business, a school—built with love motivates them. You see, Jesus first fed them, the multitudes, then, He taught them. First, feed them love. Then, teach them.

And if they don't, you could at least assure yourself that you used your love, your willpower, you did your best, you never gave up, and you tried.

Even if they don't come back, your good deeds and the vibe of your good deeds will come back to you one day, rewarding your weary soul.

Beauty Behind Bars

day 280: may 20, 2016

At times, along the red-roofed path decorated with nature's best colors and shapes, you come across bars—metal, rusted, sturdy, ugly bars. And it makes you wonder: Why bars? Why hide beauty behind bars?

And you realize, bars are needed to shield beauty from trespassers. You see, beauty—of the heart and soul—is so fragile that if you don't take precautions to safeguard it, they will soon attempt to trample upon it, to squash it to pieces and to flatten it to a dull, rough nothingness. So yes, put up those rusty, metal bars and your beauty will still inevitably shine through their empty spaces.

Live According to Mother Nature's Law
day 281: may 21, 2016

Banks of the Mosel River in Trier, Germany

This is Mother Nature's law:
That all things come and go
Starting in one form changing to another
Circling round and round with laughter

To this law there is no exception
No matter what's your perception

From the large pine, to the smallest tree
The soaring falcon, and the buzzing bee
That gorgeous rose, or the tiny green pea
Not forgetting to mention you and me

Whence we come from, where do we go
However we reason, we don't know

Nature's law is also this:
We must keep the balance in nature
And seek the welfare of each creature
Support, help, and lift up each other
The father, brother, sister or mother

Let us take care of nature, our home
This gorgeous, unique, balanced dome
Gifted to us by the gracious Creator
The first mover, the first author

Fulfilling this duty, we shall live carefree
From the snowy peaks sloping to sea
Enjoying this unsurpassed beauty
You and I, do we agree?

The Solar Impulse
day 282: may 22, 2016

View from the Solar Impulse Offices in Monaco

"Freedom is not free
It needs hard work to be set free"
States the motto in the Solar Impulse offices in Monaco[133]
Solar Impulse was the first solar plane around the world to go
Don't ever give in to resistance[134]
Firmly insist on your persistence
Momentary impulses won't help free
Day-dreaming won't set free
Passionate desire will start the dare
Hard work will get you there
Willpower will force you to stay there
For freedom is not free
And if you need to break free
Passion, hard work, and willpower will set you free

The Halfway

day 283: may 23, 2016

If something you want concerns other people too, you just go halfway. If they come to the other half to meet you where you are, fine. If not, stay there for a while, but not too long. Then turn away and find another way.

Often we wait too long at the halfway. We even go beyond it, crossing into their half. And we wait there, hoping someday they will realize our presence and hand to us what we mutually want. But they won't. And they will get used to our presence, taking us for granted. If you are there right now, turn around and come back to where you belong—into your side of the halfway. And this time don't even stay at the halfway, turn your back and reach your starting point. If they truly want you, they will come to you, moving beyond their comfort zone.

I learned this from the sea. She comes halfway to the shore bringing her treasures and offerings, and her white stone heart. If there's something we want, fish, polished sea glass, colorful pebbles, or sunken treasures, or her white stone heart—we got to go halfway to get it. If we don't, she takes them back with her receding into her home. She doesn't linger at the halfway and never crosses that line with all her offerings. And when she recedes, this time we have to go beyond the halfway and into the sea to get that which she had offered in the first place. Often, we will not find it anymore.

The First Mover
day 284: may 24, 2016

Everything is moving. The sparkling blue ripples swinging sideways, the gentle spring breeze tangoing with the moving ripples, my eyes fixated on the ripples also move with their constant flux. My volatile thoughts, going out through the blinks of my eyes, are moving too from a serious thought to a serene, to a fun, to a vain thought. My blinking eyes are watching the movements of the sun rays, then the movement of the sun in the sky, contemplating how he is slowly moving out of the way, allowing the moon to move in. Then, my mind barging in, insists: "No, it is the Earth that's moving, not the sun."

And I ponder: "Who is moving the Earth? Who is moving the moon and the sun? Who is moving the sea? Gravity? Who is motivating gravity? Who is moving my thoughts? Who is moving my eyes? If the answer is I—then, who is moving me? My willpower? Who is moving my willpower? Who is moving that newborn baby? Who moved that innocent baby out into the world? Who is moving that wise old man out of this world?"

The Mover. The First Mover. Do you know who he is? He is our best friend. He moves mountains. He is able "of these stones to raise up children" unto the childless.[135]He moves. We, humans, only react. With His first movement, the First Mover put in motion heaven and earth, beautiful mountains and deep blue seas, colorful sunsets and sunrises, wonderful creatures like us and our animals, green pastures and lush colorful landscapes. He is the Creator, the First Mover of everything physical that we see, hear, touch, smell or taste, and everything spiritual that we sense and feel in our souls and conscience. And if God is the First Mover of all things, He will also move the minds and hearts of those who have swayed and will move them back into where they must belong.

N

day 285: may 25, 2016

The letter N has been following me recently. It is now even imprinted on my forehead and emerges in certain moments of extreme stress or uncontrollable laughter. Ignoring the uninteresting medical implications, I didn't know what to make of it otherwise—until I visited my sea again.

The old umbrellas of last year are up, the trash bins and showers installed. Even the sand and the pebbles look renewed underneath the clean renewed water. The air points to renewed preparations for summer. And that large, unique pebble, stands there looking at me, rocking its huge N at my face.

Oh! N stands for New. Needful, notable, nurturing, novel, new beginnings.

It stands for Nuances: The nuances of life that one must swim through.

N stands for Name: Name your miracle(s) so it shall be given to you.

N stands for Nest: Nurture well your nest so they will navigate back into it to rest.

And most importantly, N is for NANA: the seed, the root, and the sap of our tree.

My Luggage
day 286: may 26, 2016

I just woke up, and instantly my brain started to frantically search in my luggage
Messing it up, it dug up the chaos that had weighed me down in my yesterday's baggage
Soon my friend the headache came over, my heart pounded, my ears whistled
And once again, like every morning, the contents of my luggage I inventoried
All were faithfully still there: worries, anxieties, distresses, fears, pain, and problems
Nothing had changed, diminished or disappeared; none had wanted to leave
And suddenly I realized, I'd been counting them every morning for years past
And that had never helped to lessen their impact or to get rid of them at last
As soon as one was quashed, its empty space was filled with another to carry
What use did my luggage have for me, but for headaches and anxiety?
Why did I carry it for so long if there was no benefit for me?
I wasted my days counting its contents, fretting, analyzing, and planning
Packing them again neatly at night, only to be re-inventoried the next morning
I suddenly sprung and sat in my bed, shouting silently: no more, no more
I am letting you go; I am carrying you no more. Immediately, my luggage disappeared
My headache dissolved, my heart-pounding dissipated, my fears dispersed
My luggage's spell on me dispelled and I started breathing
And I walked to my sea inhaling my newfound fresh morning air

Write it Near the Water's Edge

day 287: may 27, 2016

"If you must slander someone, don't speak it—but write it—write it in the sand, near the water's edge."[136]

So many humans are already by the water's edge, sunbathing in their warm jackets, and others in their cold bathing suits. Their collective chatter mixes with the sea noise. On this spring day, the human chatter is heard like gossip. Everyone is gossiping about someone, or something.

Why gossip or slander each other, to each other? Just tell it to the sea and go away. The sea will keep it a secret and you will have leverage to go back, to resume, and make it work.

A Sign

day 288: may 28, 2016

On this pleasant day, with the fresh green pine trees and the deep blue sea framing the red-roofed homes—where worry and anxiousness sometimes secretly dwell—this white dove arrives. A sign of peace and love. It stays for a while at each home, looking inside and reminding that love conquers all, inciting us to face the day with Og Mandino's wise words:

"I will greet this day with love in my heart. And how will I speak? I will laud mine enemies and they will become friends; I will encourage my friends and they will become brothers. Always will I dig for reasons to applaud; never will I scratch for excuses to gossip. When I am tempted to criticize I will bite my tongue; when I am moved to praise I will shout from the roofs. Guide me in my words that they may bear fruit; yet silence me from gossip that none be maligned."[137]

Pretend

day 289: may 29, 2016

It pretends to rain, pretends to project gloomy skies, pretends to be cold. But it isn't. It feels and smells like the last days of spring. Warms your heart. This pretentious storm. Under every stern face and cold stormy heart, there is a suppressed tender warmth. All you need to do is to find the crack on the pretentious surface and search inside.

The thunder roars while the birds chirps. The strong winds blow the misty rains through the pine tree tops and across the sea waves, while the white doves and the little sparrows, unimpressed, continue their happy flights up and down. The luring appetizing smell emanating from the kitchen assures me that my wonderful, kind-hearted daughter, who is preparing a surprise brunch on this French Mother's day, is blessed by God. It's roaring outside, but warm and cozy inside.

Again, the thunder howls and a lightning flashes among the clouds of this temporary pretentious spring storm. That momentary light provides the crack to look inside and discover the warmth within. It shines bright on that stern face and cold heart. Focus on the electrifying, exciting lightning. Peep inside. Find the warmth there. Embrace it. Laud it. Make it a friend.

A Taste of the Desert

day 290: may 30, 2016

From her Moroccan trip my dear friend gifted me a beautiful bag
And I named it my Camel Bag because of its name-tag
This special artisan-crafted bag of oasis and palm
Warmly greeted me with peace—that is, Salam

And my soul knew it's not a baby of mass fabrication
My Camel Bag uncovered figments of the imagination
Of dusty rocks lining the moving dunes of the desert
Of the white moon's and the million stars' endless flirt
Of the immortal wind's echo whistling with the caravans
Of the eternal sun's charring the crystal water of the mirages

And I realized this bag brings to life the soul of the camel
To unite with the soul of the desert, where all is illusion
Not minding its hump, the camel bows to welcome all hearts
To join the moving caravan's one-time journey in the deserts

My Camel Bag enlivens the rough hands that wove it
Animating the kind heart that bought it
You find the spirit of the desert in the colors
And feel the fading sun kissing the sand dunes in their splendor

The camel bag from Morocco, bag full of fantasies
Transports the owner to the desert's still oasis
Into the tents pitched on the desert's rugged mountains
Where the sounds of the darbouka drums the spirits
To the tunes of belly dancing of the hissing colorful skirts
While hookah smoke is served by men in long white shirts
One tastes the camel yogurt at the aroma of charcoal-warmed kahwa[138]
Faithfully praying at the start of every meal the Bismilla[139]

Reluctant to let my illusory mirage get away
I hastily closed my Camel Bag, and ran away
Keeping the camel and its soul inside, tucked away
Preserving the fantasies of the desert from fading away

The Visitation

day 291: may 31, 2016

Mary visited her cousin Elizabeth when she was three months pregnant with Jesus. Elizabeth herself had miraculously become pregnant with John the Baptist despite her old age. Upon meeting Elizabeth, Mary greeted her, and glorified God, saying, "My soul magnifies the Lord, and my spirit rejoices in God my Savior; For He has looked on the humble estate of his servant. For behold, from now on all generations will call me blessed.[140] Mary's discourse is known as the Magnificat. At the very young age of about 15, Mary showed gratitude to God, thanked God, and glorified God publicly. This visit is celebrated on this day as the Visitation.

We celebrate this year's Feast of the Visitation in the Cathedral of the ritzy port town of Saint Jean Cap Ferrat, hidden in a peninsula along the beautiful beaches of the French Riviera. There, a poster catches my eye. It states: "Faites-moi signe," meaning, "Give me a sign." Yes, I was looking for a sign that all things were indeed possible. Instantly thanking God, I try to remember Mary's beautiful God-glorifying words in her Magnificat, but I can't. And I am reminded of my Bible, how I used to read it, and how now I have it placed on a shelf, tucked in between other books to be read one day.

The words of Patriarch George Muller[141] resonate that how he had occasionally read the Bible a little at school, and "afterwards God's precious Book was entirely laid aside, so that I never read one single chapter of it, as far as I remember, till it pleased God to begin a work of grace in my heart ... that precious Book, which His Holy Spirit has caused to be written through the instrumentality of His servants, and it contains that which I ought to know, and the knowledge of which will lead me to true happiness; therefore I ought to read again and again this most precious Book, this Book of books, most earnestly, most prayerfully, and with much meditation; and in this practice I ought to continue all the days of my life."[142] And I resolve to read it again and again, and to learn by heart the wise words of Mary's Magnificat.

The Two Umbrellas

day 292: june 1, 2016

They are rooted in the sand, standing tall, heads tilted to each other. Families, couples, friends, groups, lonely humans seek shelter under these twin umbrellas. They eat, drink, chat, gossip, and leave. Every day. The two umbrellas hear so much, know so much, and yet do not speak. Their heads tilted, they watch over their visitors that pass by here, and they recognize the souls that belong to the sea. After all, "[m]ankind, like waterfowl, are sprung from the sea—the Sea of Soul,"[143] said Rumi.

When darkness falls, they fall asleep by the night sea once again waiting to be awakened by the forthcoming dawn.

If we find that right person to tilt our heads to, we don't care who comes and goes, who gossips or acts maliciously. We remain still, hugging that head tilted towards us, and we unite with the calm of the Sea of Love.[144]

Storms

day 293: june 2, 2016

These storms are nothing. They just hit and then fade away in a blink of time. Yes, initially you might get caught in the waves and waver on your feet, but once you learn how to playfully dance along with them, you'll be able to cross deeper into the calm of the blue sea, where you will realize those shallow storms are of negligible effect. There, you'll arrive where the powerful yachts call home. The gigantic cruise ships. The peaceful floating zone. The ever-existent horizon.

Why then do you stay at the stormy shores? Why don't you take the leap over to the depths where peace resides away from the turbulent agitations of the coastline?

Imaginary
day 294: june 3, 2016

I say it's imaginary, she says no. I insist. She fights back. I take a moment and look around. Nothing catches my imagination, so I start walking. The path takes me to the banks of the river.

I look down. The bright sun shines from its bottom. The curved bridge, uniting both banks, peeks up from the sparkling green river water. The spring tree branches dance with the ripples. The traveling fish, the floating duck leave their images behind, in the river.

I look up, the sun, the trees, the bridge, the fish and the duck exist there too. Even a jogger carries her trailing image in the river.

The oblivious river, steadfast in its course, merrily carries all, the real and their images, gently down the stream, for life is but a dream. Imaginary or reality? They both coexist, in the same time and place, staring at the looking eye. But the angle from which the eye is looking makes all the difference.

The Rose by The Sea

day 295: june 4, 2016

Why is this beautiful rose abandoned here?
Was the love it brought not reciprocated?
Was the apology it offered not accepted?
Was she not loved at all?
Was she so immensely loved that she was entrusted to the sea?
Did she sleep here under the darkness of the lonely night?
Her tired head seems to be resting caressingly on the pillow-pebbles
Maybe she was not abandoned
She does not look thrown away
But rather carefully, intentionally placed there
Is it missing a loved one
Who disappeared at sea
Or who's reposing at sea?
We'll never know the answer
But she knew—
Her tired rose will be safe sleeping by the serene sea

Duplicity
day 296: june 5, 2016

What is this game of duplicity the sea and the sky are playing today?

The sky is showing off as being both blue sunny and dark cloudy, and the sea is mirror-imaging the huge patches of dark and light. Why this double-dealing? It should be either clear blue all around, or cloudy dark, so that the message to be sent is clear.

Do you know the rules of this double-dealing game? Two-faced men play it too often these days—deceitfulness, trickery, and dishonesty.

Who wins at the end? The player with the most deceptive, colorful, contrasting tricks? So thinks the duplicitous. But the proud loser in this game will walk away leaving the duplicitous winner to play duplicity alone.

Villefranche Sur Mer

day 297: june 6, 2016

Let us visit this beautiful gem tucked away at the foot of Eze along the Cote d'Azur. But first, let us stop on the Basse-Corniche, the route leading there, to take a fabulous photo of this colorful small port, Villefranche-Sur-Mer, which is constantly studded with fishing boats, magnificent yachts, and cruise ships. Further ahead, leaving the main road, we descend through the narrow paths into this beautiful warm colored Mediterranean harbor. The locals built the Citadel in the 16th Century to protect themselves from invasions. Now it serves as an open-air cinema. We visit the Chapel of Saint Peter, where Jean Cocteau's illustrations of Apostle Peter's life adorn the interior. We allow ourselves to be lost in the small alleyways, chapels, museums, and the Provençal markets. We can also experience diving, swimming, rowing, and then sipping on a glass of wine at one of the local seafood restaurants along the quay.

Following the footsteps of Jean Cocteau, we admire his works, and those of Volti, Goetz, and Roux. We walk the Rue Obscure along the Medieval Ramparts which once protected the locals from bombardments of the enemy. And while there, we appreciate the *Lutrins*[145] (huge easels) planted throughout Villefranche, depicting copies of art such as: the "Rue Obscure" of Jean Cocteau found on Rue Obscure, the "Rade of Villefranche" of Eugene Boudin found on the Promenade des Marinieres, the "Vue de Villefranche" of Jacques Guiaud and "Les Filets de Villefranche" of Raymond Tournon on Quai Amiral Courbet, and the "Fontaine à Villefranche" of A. Inglenbleek at Place Félix Poullan.

Let's not forget to enjoy crêpes and Irish coffee by the charming pink-façaded Saint Pierre Church, or savor the best seafood in one of the classy cafés alongside the boat-dotted port. A little further, the boardwalk will take us all the way to the soft sandy beach for a beautiful summer day to end perfectly.

A Matter of Perspective
day 298: june 7, 2016

Is that bird comfortably sitting on the delimiting wooden rail or sluggishly swimming at the uplifting morning sea? Is it small or quite large? White or gray? Is it a swan, a dove, a seagull?

Is there a right answer? Who knows? It depends where you're looking from, what you're focusing on, what shade of sunglasses are covering your eyes against the blinding sun. And while the answers are being contemplated, the elegant swan changed direction, without thinking, and that threw off all perspectives into a new limelight, only to commence again with a whole new perspective.

Is it worth the guessing game? The proud, elegant, white swan, who is violent when threatened, will always be out there.

The Secret to Happiness
day 299: june 8, 2016

Polygone Riviera

The small lake asked the all-knowing sea, "What's the secret to happiness?"
The sea sighed, deeply inhaled, and, forcefully exhaling all her troubles out, replied,
"My small one, if you want to be happy,
Find your place on Mother Earth,
Don't wobble, but glimmer with your ripples,
Let them seasonally come and go as they please;
Trust your best buddies that will always be there for you,
Enjoy the bright day, seize the dark twinkling night;
Live your own life pursuing your own goals;
But remember money does not make you happy;
Stop trying to correct the mistakes of others,
For they must learn on their own;
Merrily live with all despite the dividing differences;
Dance joyfully, and play like a child;
Sunbathe in the morning and moon-bathe at full moon;
Don't ever give your power to others;
Make your own living, be wholly independent,
Don't allow others to depend on you, and therefore, be happy."

Friend and Foe – Rainbow and Lightning

day 300: june 9, 2016

Today Nature has decided to unleash its twin powers—the Lightning and the Rainbow—the destructive and the blissful. After the morning sun glows over the blue sea, sending the June warmth around, there blows the breeze, accelerating in force and increasing in chill, bringing about the dark clouds. And heavy rains flood the sea as if lingering from the winter past. Soon, the sea and the town are drenched in the downpour. All turn dark and white and moist. The thunderstruck beach town succumbs to the electrifying lightnings, which are soon dissipated by the ensuing rainbow. I can't understand why Mother Nature is so mad this near-summer morning.

Why did she summon those fierce clouds?

A couple of hours later, the most magnificent rainbow springs forth, extending from east to west with its seven layers of color, blessing everything and everyone under its arc. Peace oozes from the huge rainbow while it is crowning the earth over 180 degrees.

Mother's Embrace

day 301: june 10, 2016

Ah, the tender embrace of the loving mother sea. She has toned down yesterday's stormy waves into tiny jolly ripples, allowing her friend Mother Earth to breathe some fresh air. What a comfortable feeling to rest my head carelessly on the warm chest of my mama. Smiling, she strokes my face gently. Closing my eyes, I imbibe it. The eternal pebbles do too, letting themselves be carried away by the caressing bosom of mother sea.

At first, I swam in her life-giving sea. When I suddenly found myself swimming in my own sea, I initially failed. And I asked my resourceful sea for help. My selfless mama encouraged and strengthened me. Showered me with love.

Soon I was to become the sea of another. And another. Will they be able to swim? I taught them what I learned from my mother sea, and I taught them well. Yes, they shall undoubtedly swim. Against all currents. Because they now know how to hold their mother's embrace. The embrace of Eve, mother of humanity. The embrace of Mary, Mother of God.

Embrace your mama today, while you still can, for tomorrow might be too late.

Leave Behind a Feather

day 302: june 11, 2016

Only a few seagulls leave behind a feather when they leave. Most leave nothing. And they are forgotten. That feather, awkwardly planted among the crammed stones, carries the story of that departed seagull. The strong wind-proof spine robustly marks the seagull's unyielding willpower. The tiny feathers, playing in the breeze, immortalize its living legend. Its white resistant stance shows its gratitude.

Yes, leave behind your life's feather. If not an actual physical mark, then a handmade creative one. The white feather of your pen, the stroke of your paint brush, the white stone walls of your monument, the white footprint of your life. And you will not be forgotten.

Leave behind a feather. No, leave behind Your white feather.

I Found My White Heart

day 303: june 12, 2016

I found my white heart. Though bit deformed, it returned to me whiter, lighter and more precious. Recently I had lost my stone white heart to the sea (Reflections, June 4, 2016), which had devastated me. Daily, I had looked for it among the millions of other stones lost at sea. And I had given up, forcing myself to forget about it. But not for long. I wasn't searching for it today, and when I sat on the huge boulder by the shore to contemplate at my sea, there it was: shining bright among the million pebbles lost at sea. My precious sea-glass white heart. It was not of stone anymore.

You see, you must lose that which you regard as precious. The sea of life will polish it for a while. Only when the sea has finished it work, will she unveil it to you. You need to be patient. You need to wait.

I found my white heart. And my heart is still in fascination.

Hey, Grain of Sand, "Que Sera, Sera"

day 304: june 13, 2016

One day, the curious pebble asked the sea, "When I grow up what will I be?" And the mother sea, foreseeing the future old grain of sand in the young pebble, eloquently sang, "Que sera, sera, whatever will be will be, the future is not ours to see, que sera, sera."[146] But the innocent pebble, in her youth, did not comprehend. And the sea continued singing and rocking the worried pebble. The blinding sun came up, and the determined sea rocked the pebble. The sun gave way to the moon and million stars twinkled while the sea kept rocking.

Years passed. And this curious pebble too, like all the others before him, silently joined the grains of sand lying down and resting all around and under the sea. And the mighty all-knowing sea, perpetually rocking the pebbles, chanted in the breeze, "Que sera sera, whatever will be will be, the future is not ours to see, que sera, sera."[147]

The Highest Accomplishment
day 305: june 14, 2016

"The highest accomplishment," the young life-seeker complains, "I have achieved the highest accomplishment, and you're still not proud of me!" But the wise wanderer, who always roams the shores of the sea, replies, "Accomplishments? They're temporary, accompanied with aftermaths of emptiness. Friends? Often shifting, to backstab with misdeeds. Glory? Soon passing, only to fade and be forgotten in the trail of time. Drinking and carousing? Oh, that brief, fleeting, destructive pastime. Sunny days? Momentary, and soon winter escorts its frosts. All the treasures money can buy? Vanity for which only ignorant humans boast. Reflections of beauty and wisdom of the sea? Effaced by a wave's splash. Youth, love and beauty of the night-lights? Gone in a meteor's crash."

"Then what is the highest accomplishment?" the surprised young life-seeker asks in shock.

"Ask yourself, where does the highest accomplishment reside, if not in that deep solitary place so peaceful, where no vanity reaches, no impurity touches, but the pureness of the heart and soul dwells, despite material (non)accomplishments. A place so troubled as the troubled waters of the sea, and yet so serene, transformed by the miraculous walking feet of our Lord, while He invites, '*Come, and follow Me.*'[148]

Yes, that is the highest accomplishment. Following Him."

The Sea's Fame-Shame Game

day 306: june 15, 2016

Ventimiglia, Italy

The mysterious sea explains her Fame-Shame game. The rules are such: All start at the same place at the starting point. They have a limited time to reach the finish line. But no one is allowed to know that time. All are allowed to use their imagination, wit, heart and soul, hands and feet, to roam about, go far, climb mountains and descend abysses, to discover and to create, whilst grappling in, above, or along the sea on their path to the finish line. Anything is allowed under the golden sun and the silver moon. Except that the players are not allowed to hurt each other or their sea, and neither can they deplete Mother Earth and her belongings. The players can briskly or slowly walk, boldly or timidly run, sit around idly or occupied. They can choose to dive into the immense sea or to lightly float, to swiftly swim or to simply fly away. They can go as far as they want from the serene shores. They can play all alone or together with other players of their choosing. Those who help the most, love the most, create the most, give the most in that limited time—for which no one knows the duration—win.

They all play, some smart, others hard. Some slow, others fast. Some follow the rules, some do not understand, while others blatantly ignore. They all reach the same finish line via different paths. Who wins the game? The sea's vain game of Fame-Shame. Who judges? Not the perpetual sea, for it's not her prerogative to judge. And she does not announce a winner. Now they're gone, the players.

The Green Flag
day 307: june 16, 2016

Despite the rough whitish boundary between the green murky sea and the unstable sand-land, the floating green flag announces that it is peaceful at sea, that one can swim in there. Possibility for peace and coalition still exists. The green flag of peace is planted at that boundary of meeting—a meeting of minds. But nobody notices it. They are all gone. They left, one by one—the courageous swimmer, the relaxing rain-bather, the curious onlooker, the meticulous worker, the selfie-taker, the boundary cleaner, and even the overseer of them all. Chased away by a shower of rain, a gust of wind, a crash of a wave.

They have fled to security, further away from this boundary of meeting, meeting of the minds. And the flag of peace, though now forced open by his friend the rough wind, flies high awaiting their return. It awaits the return of the long-gone peace at this deserted moving boundary.

It Can Fly

day 308: june 17, 2016

And the strong wind pushes it up, helps it fly
Its baggage is light, it can fly
It does not hesitate, it can fly
It does not look down, it can fly
Soaring into the sea, grabbing its meal, it can fly
It does not see, above the sea, but it can fly
It can walk among men, and it can fly
It swims among friends of the sea, yet it can fly
Its wings wide open, it can fly
Breathing in the high air, it can fly
Without overthinking, it can fly
Holding its head up, it can fly
Confident in its talents, it can fly
Trusting God, it can fly
And it never falls down

Ephemeral Illusion
day 309: june 18, 2016

And then what?

Just floating, breathing, and crashing. I examined the commanding sea today and I understood. There is no meaning to her. She's an eternal monotone. With all her fast fury and fleeting fun, all her storm and serenity, she simply exists. Under the blue covering clouds, alongside the pebbles and the smelly shore, close to the crowded noisy city and yet so far in her own eternal peace, she exists. The sea. Ephemeral existence though. Always wavering. Never reaching. Constant persistence yet no achievement. That's the sea. An ephemeral illusion.

That's my sea and your sea. An ephemeral illusion.

Little Boy

day 310: june 19, 2016

That cute little boy walking along the seashore, daring the tiny waves, thinks he's got all the happiness in the world in his pocket. He giggles as the waves crash tingling his little feet. And he jolts away from them, only to return running back. He marches all along the beautifully curved shore. He doesn't know it's a long race from the beginning of the shore till the far end where it touches the horizon. He laughs. He slows down sometimes when a huge wave threatens his path, his white stunned face desperately hiding the giggles. He sits down now for a breath of fresh air. He is tired of the constant walking. He wants to rest for a while, for once he gets tired, he always wants to rest at the shore.

He gets up now and is walking less courageously, less briskly, head down, as if trying to make sense of the moods of the sea. His sea. He does look older now. He tries jetting on the ski for a while, then switches to slow steady kayaking. Look, he's coming back to the shore to rest for a while, for once he gets tired he always wants to rest at the shore. I can't see him anymore—the little boy, who looks older now. And the sea keeps on crashing.

Oh! There he is, far away, with a little boy of his own. Walking along the seashore, daring the tiny waves, thinking he has got all the happiness in the world in his pocket. He giggles with his boy as the waves crash to tingle his little boy's little feet. The older one cherishes the same joyful instant from the distant past. He teaches his little boy how to walk without staggering—standing firm on his feet, and how to giggle at the oncoming storms.

The giggles continue alone in the distance. Walking the long-curved path of the sea. His gray father is resting, for once he got tired, he always wanted to rest at the shore.

The Strawberry Moon of Summer 2016
day 311: june 20, 2016

Villeneuve-Loubet Plage

The Strawberry Moon of Summer, a summer of many loves. 1967 was named Summer of Love because of the Strawberry Moon, and here she is again tonight. The full moon played in the sky with the full sun on this summer solstice, and at their peaks, the most light emanated from the cosmos unto and into each of us—us, poor hopeless creatures needing light and guidance.

Will this be a summer of love again?

Do we humans still have that love in our hearts or has everything become materialistic love—love of honors, and power, and money?

Today, let's find it in our hearts to love again, everyone and everything under this full moon and full sun, with that pure love that only God can emanate, and we, as followers can copy. That love that solves all problems, transcends all boundaries, resolves all differences.

Waiting
day 312– june 21, 2016

Villeneuve-Loubet Plage

Carelessly waiting in cadence
In the magnificent landscape of patience
Waiting for the lively souls carousing in pittance
The blues of the bottomless essence
The long shadows of the reminiscence
Mélanged with the orange hues of radiance
They wait in persistence
Rooted with striking continence
Vastly increasing in corpulence
The long shadows of the reminiscence
Trying to assuage their lack of credence
Wait in vain for the meaning of existence
Where not a thing is of permanence
And except for love, none is of importance

The Rose

day 313: june 22, 2016

Everyone loves that enchanting, colorful, gorgeous rose. No one looks at her sharp thorns. Why spoil that loving, charming, beauty? No one counts her awkward thorns, those protective arms shielding the delicate rose, for they naturally come with the rose. All the roses are alike; except that some are red, white, yellow, pink, orange. And some others are artificially created blue, or another mix of natural colors. Few are tiny, and few form large rounds. But all of them are The Rose. And don't we all love The Rose? We receive it, we love it, and we love its giver as well. We don't look at the thorns nor do we count them, just being careful to not touch them and hurt ourselves. Beautiful is The Rose. So is the giver of The Rose. Colorful, beautiful, full of thorns.

We love the giver, and we are unaware of their thorns, and even if we are aware, we are careful to not see or comment on their thorns. After all, we are that special rose for someone else too. With our thorns that they don't see—or don't want to see.

Love The Rose without touching its thorns. Love that special someone without criticizing or condemning their thorns. After all, the Little Prince said, "Flowers are weak creatures. They are naïve. They reassure themselves as best they can. They believe that their thorns are terrible weapons..."[149]

I Named Him Fidel

day 314: june 23, 2016

Port of Cagnes Sur Mer

I think he is waiting for the talkative man who is conversing with the fisherman who tends his boat, docked at the port. The still dog sits there upright, besides the talkative man, persistently gazing at the fisherman, who, in his eyes, is unreachable, far away, separated by the sea, and united to the shore only with a short rope. But the talkative man leaves, and the dog stays. Little did I know that he was the loyal dog of the fisherman. And I name him Fidel, meaning loyal.

Fidel sits there, unable to cross the watery gap to the boat despite being attached to it by that rope, his stare fixated on his papa in the boat. And papa is proud of his loyal friend.

Wouldn't we be lucky to have such a Fidel in our life?

Breakfast like a King, Lunch like a Prince, and Dinner like a Beggar

day 315: june 24, 2016

Mother and daughter were having an appetizing breakfast at the shore early morning. The little one, not feeling hungry, fretted to skip breakfast, so she would go straight to lunch and dinner. "Look mom, the sea does not eat breakfast, and she's not hungry, she will roll and shimmer like this from morning till darkness falls, and then we go to sleep." Her mother, astounded at her remark, reminded her of the saying "breakfast like a king, lunch like a prince, and dinner like a beggar." Mom explained that the daughter will have a long day ahead and that a king's breakfast was needed to nourish and energize the body and soul, and life at sea. The sea's job was to uplift the soul during the storms of the day. Mother went on, "Lunch is when, after you've used up your breakfast's energy at the midst of your life's sea, you'll need to supply more food for your body and soul to take you to the night. And by dinner, you're so tired and full you just want to sleep after eating a little, just like the beggar who never eats much." But she insisted she was not hungry. She insisted she could face the day without breakfast. She was wrong. And she struggled into her day on an empty stomach, and through her early life on an empty tank. She reminisced sometimes on her wise mom's teachings at that morning's breakfast by the sea.

Mom put her to bed that night under the millions of bright stars. And she slept. Time passed by, and daughter, attaining mom's age, finally understood the long day mom had described. She knew, for one day she woke up suddenly from her unknown sleep. Her mother had given her priceless breakfast like a king; upbringing and instilling in her wisdom and morals at youth. Mom had provided princely lunches, support and guidance to her at the prime of her life, while the energy and wisdom of her breakfasts with mom kept fueling her. At dinner she was old, tired, full, wanting to retire in bed like the beggar, needing no food. Then she slept. Her mother had slept long time ago.

Anything for a Selfie
day 316: june 25, 2016

Monte Carlo, Monaco

The crooked lengths they go for a selfie with the sea. The determination on their face trumps the falling rain and the murky sea. And they shoot hundreds of selfies. All of them are imprinted with the same face and the same sea. Those selfie faces. Two rain-bathers in the back extend their necks, broaden their mocking smiles and flash. They photobomb the selfie.

The selfier is mad. Selfier changes location, now climbing the rocky boulders, and up the steps of a private residence marked 'do not trespass.' Wow. A selfie there would generate many likes. It is worth battling with the rocks and the stormy sea. Such determination, perseverance, and dedicated time—for these much useful selfies. One wonders if this selfier dedicates the same amount of perseverance, dedication, concentration, and meticulous planning to be of some use to humanity. If you know the answer, I encourage you to drop me a line explaining how these selfies advance any relevant cause, ease human suffering, bring about positive change, and much longed-for peace in the world. If a whole generation is preoccupied with selfies, who then has the time, and brains, to rule the world? Only the creators of the concept of selfies perhaps?

June 26.

day 317: june 26, 2016

While it's a regular bright summer Sunday—waiting for the tourists to carelessly sleep on the pebbles, and for the locals to finally take a rest from their ongoing race—today marks a faraway glamorous day in the past, filled with (un)attainable goals, exquisite dreams and blissful hopes for an eternal faithful love.

On this picturesque anniversary day, the pearly sea has cast its bridal white veil all around her. While some, in want of adulterating this perfect picture, have dug a large hole in the sand and encircled it with their hearts of stone, the sea's innocent veil selflessly extends to shelter and to protect them all from the blinding sun-rays, the darkening night-falls, the inevitable storms, and the ongoing influx of noisy chatter.

It is a matter of bonne chance (good luck) to be able to walk alone and along this white-veiled shore for your anniversary. I shall miss you my friend, my beloved sea. But even then, I shall get used to missing you as one always gets used to missing those they love. And I shall always remember the kindness of your heart, as one always remembers that kind-hearted selfless caring soul without having to get used to missing them.

Until the next anniversary ... and I do not know where I would be ...

Worshipping the Light
day 318: june 27, 2016

Even the heartless stone, that huge odd rock, worships the Light. It has been tamed this way. At dawn, it wakes up, gives thanks, and, standing tall in the Light, worships it all day. Bidding the Light goodbye at night, the heartless stone waits for the night Light that never fails to arrive in the dark.

Once more standing tall, the heartless stone worships the night Light as well, admiring its timeless guidance. Yes, even the stone heart needs the ageless Light's counsel. And may be one day it will awaken to find itself stone-less, alive, rocking in the Light forever.

Worship the Light, it will awaken your heart.

Discordia? No.

day 319: june 28, 2016

And all of a sudden, Discordia attacks today, railing about the serenity of the sea, popping its ugly head from under the serene shallow shores where it had been crushed and camouflaged for a long time. Discordia reminds me of Carl Gustav Jung's quote: "In all chaos there is a cosmos, in all disorder a secret order."

Last night, I prayed to Saint Anthony to find the love I had lost in the troubled sea. I asked Saint Anthony for a sign. And now, after marching a few steps into the morning dormant pebbles, the sign stares at me—a bill of five euros. Something I had never found at sea.

And I know Discordia will soon disappear and be buried once more, this time in the deep, deep sea. In five hours? Five days? Five weeks? Five years? Does it matter? It will disappear in five and my lost love will come back to me.

For now, I wait.

Impressionable

day 320: june 29, 2016

Always looking out for the prodigal one. Worrying about her, Mama has all her other babies tucked under her other wing, but she does not sometimes notice them. She knows they're safe. But that little one who has dared to venture out of her loving radius, out into the unknown is so impressionable. Yet she thinks she's got it all—the courage, the brains, the looks, and the means. That little one. She's so impressionable. She's so innocent. And Mama knows that "[t]he trust of the innocent is the liar's most useful tool."[150] Mama tries to shield her.

Sometimes Mama forgets to turn and look at the other little ones quietly nested by her side. She forgets to tell them how much she loves them, that she greatly appreciates their gentle touch, that she cares for them even when her head is turned the other way, to the other side, trailing the prodigal one. She thinks they understand all this, that they don't need to be reminded how much she loves and adores them, and that they already know.

But they are young. They need to be reminded of the warmth of their home, the beauty and the gentle touch of family, the unconditionality of family love. They are so impressionable and innocent. Even as adults.

The Thing You Flee
day 321: june 30, 2016

It is said that the thing you flee, finds you on your fleeing path. You plan and make detours, and sometimes you make changes in your life to avoid that very thing that you dislike, or even hate. But life brings it to you on your fleeing path. It awaits you there. And greets you. And forces itself on you and accompanies you on your avoidance path until you can no longer avoid it. It tortures you day and night. You cannot flee from it. It is now part of your life.

And it sticks with you until you learn the lesson that is there to be learned. You may not see it that way at the beginning. You may hate your path. You may lose your faith. You may dislike your circumstances. You may curse and wonder if you ever did any wrong to deserve it. But disliking, cursing, stressing over its presence will not make it go away.

I've come to learn that it will go away if you stop hanging on to it, you no longer detest it, you stop fleeing from it, and you come to terms with it. Yes, face it head on. Maybe even accept it as it is. And it will melt right in front of your eyes, it will turn into a mist—as if it never existed.

Morning Mantra

day 322: july 1, 2016

I am happy
I am healthy
I have got my loving family
And my Best-Everything-Buddy
And my Miracle-Child-Serenity
I know God created me in His own image's copy

The coherent cosmos fuels me
The cool morning mist serenades me
I am happy, for I am me
In my serene lullabying sea
I will not let anyone, or anything beat me
As long as God's breath is living in me

Fête de La Saint Pierre in Cagnes

day 323: july 2, 2016

I walk along the Cagnes promenade and stop for coffee at the boulangerie next to the Eglise Saint Pierre. The church is being decorated with bouquets of flowers, streams of lights, and red-and-white-striped fishermen banners and local flags.

How festive is the mood. The promenade is getting ready for tonight's Fete de la Saint Pierre—Saint Peter's Feast, usually celebrated the weekend closest to June 29th. Each year, a procession of joyful fishermen carry the golden statue of Saint Pierre, the patron saint of fishermen, to the shore to bless the fishermen, the gathered public and church officials, the locals, believers, and tourists. He later supervises the boat burning festivities, among raging music and dancing. In the middle ages, fishermen honored their patron saint on this day, with festivities, dance, and music, and also burnt the boat of the poorest fishermen, and offered him a new boat instead.

Today, keeping tradition alive, they have decorated the boat-to-be-burned with colorful flowers, and it awaits its destiny at the shore. And the sea waits for the ceremonies to begin so she carries the poor boat ablaze.

Fête de la Sainte Pierre in Antibes

day 324: july 3, 2016

I walk along the unusually festive Antibes port. Two women, sitting at a table under the huge white tents covering a makeshift church, prepare little bunches of white and red flowers in great haste. When I ask them about it, they reply that for Saint Peter's Feast Day, a procession from the nearby cathedral will proceed through the streets of Antibes and will end up here to celebrate mass under the tents.

Wanting to go up to the Nomad,[151] and not noticing the guard dog standing right there, I continue. It barks. I freeze. But I keep looking into its bold eyes feeling a gentle smile building up at the corner of my mouth. In these long seconds, a security guard approaches and apologizes for his dog's behavior, puts back its leash, and pulls it away. I continue walking up and now notice that the gates are locked with chains. I turn again to the guard, almost gasping, "Oh, it's locked!" "Venez,"[152] he replies and walking up, holding the leashed dog, unlocks the chained gates. I enter. I see a huge new Cross erected there,[153] besides the Nomad. He leaves me with this unique privilege closing the gates behind him. I am all alone in this silent attraction which is usually crowded with wanderers and admirers. The serenity of the Cross, the warm haze of the early morning sea and the waiting stance of the Nomad engulf me in silence. After all "[s]ilence is the language of God."[154] What a treat. You see people, events, and things from a different angle here, at this moment, where clarity dwells, where there is not one soul, nor a whisper around. Surreal.

I absorb this beauty for the longest time. Even though don't wish to leave, but wanting to partake in Saint Peter's Feast, I descend and walk to the Cathedral. A huge statue of Saint Peter waits at the altar to be carried in the alleyways of Antibes. Dashing to the front of the line, I join, with my camera, the barefoot sailor strongmen who now carry the imposing statue of Saint Peter, followed by the musicians with trumpets, drums, cymbals, and saxophones. Amidst music and cheers, Saint Peter heads to the beach to bless the masses.

The keys of heaven in Peter's hand catch my eye. Jesus had given Peter those keys.[155] They resemble the keys that opened the locked gate for me earlier, so I spend alone time with the morning, the new cross, and the ever-waiting Nomad. Peter had already answered my prayer and opened the gate for me even before I knew I would pray to him today, even before I knew I would follow him in his procession in Antibes accompanied by all the fanfare.

The Empty Manuscript
day 325: july 4, 2016

They welcome you with joy and laughter. You cry. Soon they hand you an empty manuscript, saying, "Fill it as you wish, but let it be with meaning."

One day you realize that if you write it without meaning, it will be forgotten among the ashes of millions of past manuscripts, which are now no more. But those manuscripts filled with meaning, are preserved, they stand out and shine spreading light, during the writing period, and after the writers have long gone. And you start struggling to find that meaning. While you do that, your numbered days are passing and the manuscript fills itself, unless you step in, hold the pen, and write it yourself with each passing day. And the sooner you find that meaning, the sooner you take control of your pen, because if you don't, and once each page is written all by itself, it cannot be deleted if it's not to your liking. You cannot rewrite the old pages.

It is now time to stop and think about how you are filling the remaining empty pages of your life's manuscript. Are your days turning into nights each being filled with meaningful works, or are you letting them just pass by you, while you struggle to first make everything right and perfect, postponing taking control of your writing pen. Resolve then, to grab your life's pen right now. Fill your life's manuscript as you wish, and let it be with meaning. Because once you depart and they cry after you, your filled manuscript will be folded and thrown away in time's capsule. But its meaning will remain as the living reminder of you.

Still

day 326: july 5, 2016

Even the quietest sea cannot stay still. They say, "Just be still." From her smallest ripples to her deep vast home of exquisite creatures, the sea moves and moves. She cannot stand still. Despite the calmness of the shore and the sweet blues of evening twilight, she moves. Who ever said one must stay calm in the face of perpetual change?

Why immobilize oneself when even the eternal sea is unable to do so. Feel her peaceful soothing moves touch your soul, elate your faint heart. Look at the ever-transforming white clouds covering the sea at times and hiding behind the clear pink sky at others. Even Mother Nature does not stay still. She changes colors and shapes and smells with the perpetually changing seasons.

So why stay still, fixated on your outdated ideals. Better to change with the seasons than to try in vain to anchor yourself in the shifting bottomless sands of the ever-moving sea.

The Unusual Seashell
day 327: july 6, 2016

Throw pebbles at sea. What for? What do they accomplish? Picking up a pebble and throwing it back at sea. Wasn't it left there at the shore by the sea herself in the first place? There must have been a reason for the wise sea to choose which pebbles to keep by her and which to throw out. Does she want people throwing them back at her? For a moment of false amusement? As an attempt at meditation? My questioning look turns back towards them, for they are still giggling and stoning the sea, causing more and more ripples to swirl around. They eagerly collect more and more pebbles, as if they are going to run out of them. My eyes meet theirs. We exchange a moment of icy stillness. They leave.

But I want answers.

I pull myself from my stone seat and get up to start strolling and talking with my sea. Suddenly, my curious eyes catch a glimpse of the most unique shell. The sea presented me a gift, an unusual seashell—not a regular pebble—to answer my question. She confirmed that she offers her unique treasures to those who seek. So is does the sea of life. Seek and you shall find your life's meant-to-be treasures. And I decide to always wear my seashell close to my heart.

Front Row Seat

day 328: july 7, 2016

Antibes

"Come," says the sea, "grab the front row seat, that's where all the action is. At the front row, it will be easier to jump into the action and participate in the spectacle if you wish to. No one will bother you at the front row, because most people avoid the front row seat—they are afraid to be in the spotlight, to get their feet wet, no one wants to get caught unawares in my sudden storms."

I have been in the front row for a long time. I have long occupied that front row seat. I have led the spectacle; I have not wanted to avoid the spotlight. Now, I am tired.

I silently sit there for a long time staring at her, and then I quietly leave, without finding the words to respond.

Burden or Blessing
day 329: july 8, 2016

The swimmers, tourists, sunbathers, and sea lovers complain about the low overcast clouds burdening the sea. They do not realize that the smiling sun is still there, tucked away behind the cloud fluffs, waiting to be acknowledged. The wise man who lives by the sea and knows her temperament well, exclaims, "But you see, this overcast is a blessing—and not a burden." They all listen to him. He continues, "When I was young the elders who lived by the sea helped me to always see the blessing in the tiny cracks of any overcast, cloudy burden. Now think, and give me one reason why it's a burden and another why it's a blessing. And so it is with your life: nothing is a burden which is not also a blessing. Train your mind to see the light of the blessing through the apparent burden. Then you will succeed in breathing the blessing in and the burden out. And only then will you be able to see the blue clear sky peaking and blessing through the cracks of the burdened clouds. It all depends on how you allow your mind to see things: as a blessing or a burden, as a boon or a bane."

They all look up squeezing their eyes to see behind the burdening clouds and they are surprised to see the sun's pink rays peeping through the clouds and tickling their eyesight.

Blessings are always there. You just need to squint your eyes and skew your mind to be able to see the rays of the blessing among the burdening illusions of those clouds.

Vanish

day 330: july 9, 2016

They have named this[156] yacht Vanish. Its majestic stance predicts it will not vanish anytime soon. Did they name it Vanish because they know all is doomed to vanish? Money, power, people, and even life—all are here to vanish at some point in time.

It forces you to meditate upon the irony of the hugeness of this splendid yacht and the momentary fleeting mess its name suggests. And you see the whole meaning of life captured in this scene. One has everything and yet everything vanishes. Even this moment has vanished right now, and this one too. That huge wave that struck the shore just vanished, and this rare ripple too. The sun and the moon alternate, one banishing the other, until they both vanish from my sight. But the earth turns and they're both always here, watching, not having vanished. And soon you realize that all these things are not vanishing—but ironically, we are, with our money, power, people, and life.

How to live then among these vanishing possessions, in our vanishing life? We can either cling to and waste our life on vanishing things, or locate that peaceful spiritual kingdom amidst the eternal celestial beings, and roam there, freely, trying to find our way back home. That forever home where nothing vanishes.

Happy Birthday

day 331: july 10, 2016

And today you arrive at 24
With a prestigious JD and some more
You are my miracle child
You always sang and smiled
You came a long, long way
It wasn't always easy along the way
Despite all the ups and downs
We'll always be Sar and Mom
You achieved a lot, traveled a lot, learned a lot
And now you're ready to fly as a big hot shot
Remember to always be grateful to God
May He always guide and bless you, my miracle child
May you always be happy, healthy, surrounded with loving family
Happy merry birthday to you
I vividly remember that Friday when I had you
And I thank God for blessing me with You
Let the happiness of this birthday endure day after day without a blue

Dare to Ask for the Impossible

day 332: july 11, 2016

I asked for the impossible from God, and He replied, *"Pray."* Then I prayed for health, and Saint Charbel intervened, and the sick were healed. Then I prayed to Saint Anthony for the return of the lost, and the lost were found. Next, I prayed for family unity, and Mother Mary intervened. And I kept asking for more. And God advised, *"Pray more."* I prayed for my daughters' health and happiness, and Paul and Peter heard. I prayed for wisdom for my children, that they always choose the right path leading to God, and to not trip on the rocks along the way, to which the Holy Spirit responded. And of course, I prayed for success and the ability to spread God's ministry. I prayed for remission of sins, and Jesus said, *"Do not worry, I am your Savior."*

And I heard a whisper, *"You are praying for all these worldly needs. But God already knows what you need. First seek the Kingdom of God and His righteousness and all these things will be given to you."*[57]*"*

I felt guilty realizing I always asked for more without regard to what God wanted. Thus, I learned to pray that His will be done; that I align my will to His. And should any of my prayers not be answered immediately—I asked for wisdom, counsel, and patience to understand God's will for me, and to accept it in all circumstances.

At that moment, I understood that God answers prayers only when and if we align our will to His. After all, He is the Creator of the blue sea, the vast sky, the million stars, and the beautiful mountaintops. He is the engineer of that bird that can fly and walk and swim; the designer of that green and black cross section of that kiwi, the painter of that perfect black cross at the heart of the red poppy flower. All this perfection, and they don't resist His will. Accepting it, trusting it, they let go, and live under the sun without worrying. And though it seems impossible for us, they all rotate in perfect harmony, in their assigned seasons, and places. And I asked God for the impossible: The ability to not worry, and to trust Him, praying, "Let your will be done." I prayed in the name of Jesus who had promised, *"Ask in my name and you shall receive."*[158] And instantly I knew, in my heart, that all of my prayers were already answered.

Need

day 333: july 12, 2016

Need: A momentary want or desire, causing worries and trouble, and satisfied by a fleeting accomplishment that does not last forever, as nothing ever does.

You need …

I need …

S/he needs …

We all feel we need someone, something, at all times. Always in need of this and that. Sometimes we get what we think we need, and we feel happy or proud, and other times that very person or thing eludes us, and we are frustrated. But when the days turn into dark or starry nights, and the nights unfold into bright or gloomy days, all our needs balance out. The needs of yesterday become less important and get replaced by new needs. And the cycle continues. What is accomplished when our needs are met or not? One need passes away, and another arises, if we let it, that is. And unless we curb our feelings of need, we will walk through life always in need of someone or something. Always worrying about this and that. And no happiness thrives there.

"But only one thing is needful,"[59] Jesus had advised the worried complaining Martha who needed her sister Mary to help with dinner preparations, instead of sitting at Jesus' feet and listening to His teachings. *"And Mary has chosen the good part,"* He had added. Ah, how simple and peaceful our life would be if we felt the need to only accomplish that "good part," listening, learning, and implementing Jesus' teachings instead of fretting over unimportant worldly needs.

bluesummer

A little blue car catches my eye in the streets of Marseille. "bluesummer." A sudden hiraeth subdues my soul. What type of nostalgia it is I do not comprehend. All I feel is the enlargement of my heart and soul longing for times gone by. But it is not sadness, rather a sense of belonging in a different era. There lies my true essence, there is my blue summer. It feels good there.

The realization that "bluesummer" is an electric-powered car brings me back to the present, to the now in which I strive to live. I find myself in the middle of the fusion of two eras: past and present; the nostalgia of the past when an electric car was not even imaginable, fused with the reality of the present, in the presence of this nostalgic electric "bluesummer." I don't know what it is about it that takes me back decades, shakes me up, stirs my soul, twists my memories, and circles me overhead throwing me into the blunt present.

It pierces my heart, my hiraeth[160]—my homesickness for a home, for an era of my past that are no more, and to where I cannot return.

Fireworks for the Decline of Humanity
day 335: july 14, 2016

Joyous fireworks celebrate independence, liberty, equality, and fraternity on the Promenade des Anglais in Nice, and abruptly, humanity is cut by the sickening chaos of hatred. That white bus erratically driving among and on the innocent celebrating independence, crushing their skulls along with their hearts and all the dreams and desires stored therein. Those haunting images of innocence lost.

Where have the human values gone? When did callousness replace sympathy? Will solidarity be able to stand united against hatred and violence this time? What can we do as a nation? What can we do as individuals? What can we do as one world? Tough questions, but no answer seems to respond to the drastic downturn of humanity.

This July 14th, France's Independence Day, will forever be engraved in our hearts and souls.

Invisible People
day 336: july 15, 2016

The busy port boasts its location at the meeting point of the Mediterranean and the bustling city of Marseille. Each boat docked here has a different story. Each arriving or leaving ship tells of the life that brews within. All the busy people rush by without looking at you. Life buzzes all around. But there are also the quiet invisible people. And you realize you've become one of them. You've become invisible. You thrive, toss and turn, labor and toil, climb up and fall down for many long years, only to realize one day that you have become invisible yourself. You have joined the rank of all those who were, just yesterday, invisible to You.

You try to make amends, to make up, dress up, act up—to cling to that visibility a little longer. But your time has passed. You are now invisible. Those eyes that once sought your attention walk past you without even blinking. You hadn't realized that there was this invisible world waiting for you at the end of the seemingly endless shore where your existence melts into the invisibility of that lonely world. If only you had noticed all the invisible people living there—who once like you, were toiling and laboring—you would have lived differently. You would have become their friend; you would have alleviated their loneliness. You would have looked into their eyes to see the pain, the lost love, the longing for life, the understanding of its emptiness. You would have earned the right to hope that when your turn comes to be invisible—and it will—someone will be compassionate enough to look into your eyes, to take notice of you, to be your friend, to alleviate your loneliness.

What the Sea Reflects

day 337: july 16, 2016

She stares into her face inversely looking back at her from the face of the sea. What charm the sea reflects. Superficial charm. Though she sits still in the silence of the perpetual waves, her image stirs in that mirror. Sadness strikes her heart. "Oh," she gasps, "everything is a reflection of me." Swiftly, she looks away and around trying to find the source of all the shimmering reflections, thinking: "If I find the source, I will find the meaning, and if I find the meaning, I will find the solution." The colorful evening lights keep shimmering from within the darkness as the rising moon's silvery tail trails alongside. The magical reflection of light in the sea recaptures her attention. She thinks: "I too, am light." And she looks for her spoiled self again, hidden in the ripples of the moonlight.

A smile creeps on her face and also on the phantom's face bustling in the sea. She has discovered the source of the light. She tries to capture the still photo, but she soon realizes that the glimmering beauty is a mere reflection of her. And she thinks: "I don't want to be admiring myself in the mirror like Narcissus," even though that superficial momentary charm swells her soul. She feels her happy heart jump at the vanity of her beautiful reflection, blinding her to the sight of her wrinkled distorted image that looks back at her from the darkness. She does not like her reflection in the sea's mirror. And vanity reveals itself. Feeling the creepy dark moving over to cover her glittering image, she resolves: "I have my true mirror at home, I don't need the sea." She gets up and moves on, leaving all the long jazzy reflections behind in the sea. Only the immortal echo of the sea remains, eternally seeking—while fully aware it is a mere fantasy—to find, once more, the beauty of that inverted image—that flash phantom—among the millions of reflections that pass by the sea.

The Price of Life
day 338: july 17, 2016

The aftermath of July 14, 2016, in Nice. Promenade des Anglais, once a bustling seaside promenade, is now transformed into an impromptu memorial, all along. Flowers, bleu-blanc-rouge candles, handwritten heartbreaking notes, tricolor flags, little bears and other soft plush animals, pictures of smiling people who are no more, personal items, more layers of flowers, prayers of many faiths, Bible verses, Koran verses, Torah commandments, Crosses, saints' candles and cards planted among the colorful bouquets, and souvenirs of the lost souls try in vain to cover up the bloodstained promenade. Priceless lives. Mysteriously crushed and taken up in an instant. Even the evildoer has disappeared in the heavy crushing mist.

The price of life. After the human mist is gone, the memory is kept alive by the immense shower of flowers and shrines. What really remains, but for a lonely tear drop, a crushed life, a nostalgic memory, and some flowers. But even the precious and luscious flowers shall fade away in a few short days. So, what is the price of life?

Look to the left over the sea. A huge yellow smiley parachute is lifting away two adventure-seekers in the vast air, and on the summery shores of the promenade, tanned sun-bathers and carefree swimmers have set up their colorful umbrellas, either oblivious to life's incomprehensible tragedies, or having quickly moved on in this priceless life.

And the Mediterranean Sea that had seen enormous tragedies and triumphs since more than 2,000 years, carries along the life—of those who have perished and those who will perish one day—as if to say: life is that priceless legend you carry on either in its physical form in this physical sphere or in its spiritual form in that spiritual Kingdom.

How appropriate that one of the notes left in memory of the victims quoted from the Koran, stating: "All things perish, except His face. To Him is judgment, and to Him you will all return."[161]

Everything Will Happen at the Right Time
day 339: july 18, 2016

While the world spins on itself round and round (watch the NASA video of the earth spinning on itself for 365 days) and the moon orbits around the world, they both wait for the sun. And in turn the sun waits for the moon. Though they never meet, they work together, complement each other because they know their prescribed timing. And so, the bright day longs for the soft night, and the dark night waits for the surprises of a new day to unfold.

The seasons too wait for each other: snowy winters patiently wait to blossom into flowery springs, then to dry into hot summers, only to wither into brown autumn leaves. All wait—without worrying, without complaining—for their dream to happen at the predestined time.

We all wait in the dark, not knowing what tomorrow will bring, even though we fill in our calendars and we overload our agendas with goals and deadlines. But, there's always a little hope in the light of the moon—except for those days when even the moon is sad and hides herself in the dark. For a short time. Inevitably, the sun will come out as predestined. The baby will wait for mama for milk, and mama will later wait for the baby to grow up and nourish her. There is no agenda to fill. Life will keep spinning round and round.

There is a season for everything.[162] Why worry about anything then? We just need to completely abandon our will to the will of God and wait for our predetermined seasons to roll in perfect harmony.

Chant to Awaken the Force

day 340: july 19, 2016

This evening at the shores, they keep drumming and chanting, inciting all around into shaking and boogying during their walks and leisurely sit-ins along the plage. The energetic beat motivates even the dormant waves to dance along. They drum and chant—drum-drum drum-drum, olalahey-olalahey—as if singing Bob Marley's "Get up stand up, stand up for your rights, get up stand up, don't give up the fight."[163]

The chant awakens that force within to get up, to stand up, and to not give up the fight. Come on my friend, don't ever give up. Get up. Fight for your rights.

The Heart of the Forest

day 341: july 20, 2016

Before the sun rays reach the forest from the sea where they birth each morning, she loves to sit at the balcony overlooking the distant red-roofed villages—each contouring their own red-roofed church rising high in the middle, all nestled silently in the lush pine forest boasting all the hues of green.

It all started on that morning when she realized there was a big puffy heart staring at her in the midst of the early morning awakening of the green forest. Sipping slowly her dark black coffee from a mug painted with a colorful PEACE message, she expected an instant awakening of her sleepy brain, a sudden opening of her half-shut eyes, and a miraculous opening of her seemingly deafened ears. As the black coffee out of the PEACE mug did its job, the pine tree-top heart, though changing colors with the morning rays, continued staring at her for a long time among the black metal balcony bars, as if whispering, "Good morning my friend, I bring you love, I bring you peace with this new sunrise." The UNICEF mug was painted with five children, each decorated with an innocent smile on their different colored and featured faces, each representing one of the five continents, each holding the five letters of PEACE on a colorful banner, standing side by side on the blue-green contour of the earth, and forming a human chain. A white dove fluttered above their pretty heads. The first child held up the P on an orange banner, the second held up the E on a blue banner. The third: the A on a green banner. The fourth: the C on a pink banner. And finally, the fifth held up the E on a yellow banner.

She knew. The big green forest heart brought her a message of PEACE. That they were to live happily thereafter despite that each one had a different color, facial features, smile, hair style, character, and most importantly a different loving heart. Yet, each held the different letters of PEACE. Each had their own unique way to bring peace and love, to contribute to living harmoniously altogether. The coffee, conspiring with the lush heart, had done its job. It had not only awakened her sleeping senses that early morning, but had opened her withered heart to love, that was once lost. To love each of the five despite their enormous, sometimes irreconcilable, differences. After all, they were all the children of the Creator. And from that day on, when she sipped her dark coffee from different mugs in different worlds every morning, she always peacefully, lovingly, and joyfully remembered the message of love and peace that early sunrise brought on that balcony overlooking the lush green forest of the beautiful French Riviera.

The Souvenir Scarf
day 342: july 21, 2016

The scarf breezes away by the sea. It is not just any scarf. Inspect it. See the red, gold, and black patterns in unison, enfolding the white blank. They speak of life and vivacity in different worlds, in remote vibrant places, reminding you of unlimited sands and dunes, and distant colorful huts neighboring the spacious sea. Of real people trying to thrive there, and of dedicated volunteers trying to help them thrive. There, life is still fascinating, untouched by the 'progress' today's 'developed' milieus take pride in.

The edge of the scarf ventures out again, while its body aims to keep warm—loyal to its initial purpose. Adding oomph to the pale black, the light-hearted scarf shelters that which it wraps. That souvenir of healing times: part of it will always dream to venture away, while its true soul will remain embedded within its folds.

Thank you, my friend, I will always cherish your souvenir scarf.

The Lantern
day 343: july 22, 2016

We have an unspoken rendezvous each night, the Golden Lantern and I,
A secret date, when I empty the depths of my heart into its watchful eye
After my long, dreadful days, retiring in my solitude, I impatiently wait for its first light
Silently, slowly the Lantern moves up behind the mountain's silhouette
Breaking the stronghold of the dark, it spreads awe in the peaceful silence
Hanging from the sky, it moves stealthily to the right, traversing its starry alliance
The darker the sky befalls, the brighter my Lantern shines among the twinkling lights
Competing with the streetlights that try in vain to illuminate the midnight
Never late, never angry, never sad, never stingy with its moonlight
We also have an understanding, the Golden Lantern and I
That some days must be dark—without the Lantern light
But now, glowing in divine light, extending towards me its white rays shining bright
The Lantern secretly smiles at me, hanging from that invisible rope holding tight
Talking in heavenly silence, the celestial Lantern reassures
"Seek and you shall find hope, love, and peace
Be silent, steadfast, slow to anger, never drifting, never changing, adapting to days and
nights and changing seasons, sometimes letting the clouds to overshadow you, but
knowing you are above it all, always singing and dancing in my bright celestial sphere"
The marvelous Lantern.
I keep gazing, and writing faster and faster ... constantly staring at my Lantern, without
losing sight of it. But it begins to slowly slide behind the dark mountainside: first the
curved edge, then the body followed by its highest tip. That one highest point keeps
shining and looking at me for the longest time. It almost disappears, and I am not sad
as I know it will reappear tomorrow.

Fly and Get

day 344: july 23, 2016

The choice is yours: sit and wait or fly and get
They wait, huffing and puffing, hoping to get
Unaware that as such they will lose the bet
For whoever sits and waits, will never get
And the goals of the one flying high, will be met
Rewarding their hard work from eight to eight

When the afternoon starts losing its hue into the night
They arrive fluttering towards the evening light
Facing west, they sit and wait, chasing away the dimming light
As if the last long rays of the vanishing sun will bring them fun
But one daringly ventures out and flapping hard starts her run
So, the choice is yours: sit and wait or fly and get

Promised Home
day 345: july 24, 2016

"Today Your gate is open
And all who enter in
Shall find a Father's welcome
And pardon for their sin
The past shall be forgotten
A present joy be given
A future home be promised
A glorious crown in heaven"[164]

I leave my sea, bidding adieu for now
Traveling far to find my home for now
My heart content, my spirits lifted
I trust to arrive in the home my Father promised

Reflections by the Sea
day 346: july 25, 2016

It will be difficult to leave her, my friend of two years.

I had asked if she could paint the title of my book, this book, on pebbles from our sea. She had agreed. And today, she surprises me with these beautifully lettered and colored pebbles (galets, in French). She had anxiously waited all day to proudly present them to me—to see the reflections on my face. She had collected them at my sea, which is also her sea, and she had found the time in her already filled days to paint these pebbles to reflect the sea. Aren't they so artistic and beautiful? So original. So different.

It is hard these days to find genuine people. But she is. Genuine. Her free spirit, refined beliefs, and impeccable faith in God Almighty (Dieu Tous-Puissant, as she says) makes her truly special. Her genius creativity and love of all things pure reflects not only in her artwork, paintings, sowing, crochets, but also in her eyes, where years of devotion and sincerity have formed a peaceful wisdom that transcends all human worry.

And as I reflect by the sea today, I am able to see the teardrops hidden in her reflections, and my soul shivers at the thought that a huge void would soon take over.

Reflections by the Sea.

Finale
day 347: july 26, 2016

The hectic preparations to leave my blue enchanting sea overshadow the stark reality that I will not be reflecting by its shores for the days and months, even years, to come.

The packing and organizing and all the anticipation of a new life across the oceans fill the misty summer air with excitement.

But the shocking news of an 86-year-old priest—first held hostage with two nuns and a faithful crowd in a church—being killed during mass by ignorant, despicable fools electrifies the already gloomy atmosphere of France even more. And I think, "How can I now leave this home of mine?" But I must.

The Finale must exist. It always does. For a new dawn to break out shedding its young rays on newfound seas.

Fly

day 348: july 27, 2016

Fly, my soul, fly. Up, up in the blue sky
Above the blue sea, the white clouds, the green mountaintops, fly
Above the little homes and the tiny people, fly
Fly to where all is new, where nothing old can crush you
Soar, leaving the empty fluff and touch the fluffy heavens anew
And then you will grow your wings too and fly
Fly, my soul, fly. Up, up in the blue sky

The Darbouka

day 349: july 28, 2016

Illustration by the Author

The distant drumming rhythm of the nostalgic darbouka ... Tum tatatatum tututum ...

Now, far away from my sea, I can still hear that distant rhythm that once livened up her air. That darbouka beat will always secretly play in my heart. Though many people may speak around me, I don't hear a sound but that of the remote darbouka.

That beat stirs the bottom of your soul. It moves you right a little, left a little, and jiggling up your back it loosens your stiff neck and shoulders. It fixes you in that moment in time, that rhythm—tum tatatatum tututum. There's an unexplainable magic in the darbouka's soul that takes you places, those old distant nostalgic places where you might never be able to return again.

Darbouka keeps drumming in faraway lands, and here, not so many souls are stirred by the waves it generates. They don't know. They are not fascinated, but anxious. How they have been played on by their fears for years. If they had gotten to feel and appreciate the soul emanating from the darbouka's rhythm in their childhood, they would understand now.

Will I ever hear again that darbouka playing on these new shores? Will the impact ever be the same? Tum tatatatum tututum...

New Home
day 350: july 29, 2016

Porter Ranch, California

The old objects of the new home are the same
But the spirits are not
It will take some time to adjust
But it's much worth the effort, so why not?

Pity—how objects remain faithful to the dome
Funny—how people often desert their home
And the old objects become heirlooms
To adorn the lives of those deserted rooms

And the new home awaits their return
In hopes of restoring the old heirlooms
As the timeless family makes its turn
After all, this new home is now their old bloom

Family
day 351: july 30, 2016

The old and the young and the in-between. What a wonderful mélange of hearts, souls, outlooks, longings, and hopes. The family. Of course each member is of a different temperament and appearance, but their differences complement each other. They are created to swim in the flow of life together.

It is said to keep your friends close, and your enemies closer. Along the same lines, keep your family closest, for when your friends leave you and your enemies despise you, your family will always be there for you. That sacred root makes sure that all the branches and twigs, despite their far-reaching widespread arms, stay grounded in the love of the family.

The Vision Board

day 352: july 31, 2016

Porter Ranch, California

The vision board paints your story, depicting your stages from one goal to another. It is the movie of your life—a series of adventures, planned or spontaneous, whether you carefully choose it, or you aimlessly let yourself drift in the sea. The question is: did you choose your current adventure, and will you consciously craft your next one, and the one thereafter?

Yes. Yes. Just write, paint, draw, collage each adventure your mind dreams of on your vision board. You can't? Take a walk by the sea to clear your mind. Oh, those peaceful moments, how they rekindle the forgotten dreams. Wait on the sea to offer you her life-giving waters, calming blue skies, vast sands cushioning your feet, and arrays of pebbles and shells to be picked up at its long limitless shores. Then replace each of these gifts with a dream of yours. Put it up on your vision board and stamp it with a deadline. There you have your goals. Fill your days with chores that advance those goals. You will find yourself gliding through wonderful adventures, though sometimes bumpy, but always fulfilling. They will form your own special exquisite movie of your life.

And don't forget. Whatever you do, do it for the glory of God.

The Blue Rose

day 353: august 1, 2016

Saint Eudes Church, Chatsworth, California

Long time ago she had agreed with her loved ones that their happy place was to be the Blue Rose—that when they wanted to communicate with each other even though they would be million miles apart, they would invoke the secret of the Blue Rose—and communicate.

And today was one of those days when communicating with one of her soul mates was a need, indeed a must. So, she went to church with a red rose in her hand, having had forgotten about the secret power of the Blue Rose. Yet still in the stillness of that sacred place, a bouquet of Blue Roses was waiting for her, welcoming her back into her world that she had left behind many years ago.

Her blue sea was far, far away now, and in her place, the Blue Rose brought the message of love, hope, and renewal, whispering in the silence of that church that she was not forgotten, that she was being guarded and guided at all times. By the power of the Blue Rose.

She is there. Always and forever.

Behold, I Make All Things New

day 354: august 2, 2016

The memories of her walks on the beach, of what now seems long time ago, started to fade away. Her heart saddened. The early sunrises and late sunsets were different there. And the sea had never failed to offer her a daily gift—an answer to a question, a solution to a puzzling situation. Once, there was vibrant life along the sea. But the sea did not see.

Where she is now, the sea does not belong; and the desert's sunsets are quieter, while the ocean nearby faintly presents hopes of renewed adventures.

She fondly remembered the old which was no more, and eagerly looked toward the promising new that He had promised, *"Behold, I make all things new."*[165] She pondered if new meant better. She knew His promises were always for the better, and to experience the new better, she had to put Him first, to seek His Kingdom first. And she did.

Waiting for the Message

day 355: august 3, 2016

Still waiting for that special message
Carrying the craved good news
Expecting to feel it assuage
Your weary daily friendly blues

Surely you shall receive it
The rose of the message of the good news
But know that always along with it
There comes the thorny foliage protecting it

So why keep waiting for that message
Don't you get it?
It was never about the message
But about what you did while waiting for it

Fill your days with your assigned undertaking
And live purposefully to forever imprint
In the hearts of those still blindly waiting
With the strength, love, and hope of your footprint

Thank You, My Friends
day 356: august 4, 2016

Thank you.

Thank you to my friends, near and far, who accompanied me on my journey towards healing. Each one of you cared for me during my difficult times in your own special way, and I am grateful for that.

Thank you to all my wonderful doctors and medical personnel in France. You provided the utmost care in nurturing and peaceful environments. You answered all my questions, provided all that was necessary without once complaining that you were busy, or that insurance didn't cover it. What a great healthcare system.

My friends in France, you were by my side at all times: following my medical progress, caring, being present, supporting, listening, encouraging, and making me laugh. Thank you. You did not care of it was night or weekend, and you made your wonderful selves available to help at all times.

Thank you to my friends in the States as well. You all helped me remotely and followed my healing journey closely. You were always there for me, advising and encouraging me. You uplifted me with your self-help books, and you offered to provide help and support. You prayed for me, and you constantly told jokes and made fun of situations just to distract me from looking into my big black bottomless void.

Thank you all. I feel so blessed. May God bless you all and keep you from pain. Thank you God.

The Ceiling Fan

day 357: august 5, 2016

Round and round spins the ceiling fan
Without a beginning nor an end
What does it achieve, the fool fan
By rotating in its constant circular span?
It resembles Mother Earth spinning on herself
Carrying us all in a temporary merry-go-round
I stare at the fan as if time has no end
For a while I let my head spin around aimlessly with the fan
And as the darkness of the night falls
And the fan's spinning shadows grow longer and less bright
I realize the fan has seen it all, through daytime and nightfall
All the loving and hating that has transpired within its sight
How many families it has seen hugging and praying side by side
Troubles it has fanned away by endlessly spinning from side to side
Bearing with all as they continually drift from tide to tide
Patiently blowing as the noisy day turned into the silent night
And it reminds me of my sea, who though not spinning
And is instead inciting her almighty waves into rocking
Peacefully fanning away the troubles of those aimlessly gazing
And silently watching some sadly parting ways, and others joyfully reuniting

The Grinding Machine
day 358: august 6, 2016

Malibu, California

"Nature reaches out to us with welcoming arms, and bids us enjoy her beauty; but we dread her silence and rush into the crowded cities, there to huddle like sheep fleeing from a ferocious wolf."[166] Those crowded cities. Those grinding machines. The town centers—offering commercial outlets; the huge malls—filled with restaurants serving the same look and food; the wide roads lined with the same giant billboard ads and signs-bearing almost the same name, street after street. And you drive. Reaching nowhere, indeed. If you pay attention, it's as if you're driving in circles—leaving your home, heading to wherever, passing by the same scenery, and heading back home.

No one seems to ever stop and pay attention to the long thin palm trees hurrying by overhead. No one seems to visit the ocean shores nearby—those beautiful shores of the California Riviera, stretching from San Francisco to San Diego. No one seems to notice the trash, twigs, dry leaves, plastic bags, crumpled papers that had been pushed by the air currents of the constant speeding cars to the sides of the freeways. And that tree, whose roots were once immersed in the soil, that's now bowing its head under its dwindling branches? No one notices. No one cares. Just like that bundled grandmother now sitting at the front porch, who, once used to walk head up taking pride in her branched-out family. No one cares.

And, unaware, unconscious, though eyes open, they seem to enjoy circling in the grinding machine, running after materialism, glory, image, greed.

But where is the creed? When will they live? When will they open their eyes and see they should have lived in the beauty and silence of our Sacred Nature—wherein God resides?

The War Room

day 359: august 7, 2016

A longtime prisoner who's waiting for her parole hearing suggested to her law student-and-acting-attorney (my daughter), who was helping her to prepare for her upcoming hearing, to watch the movie War Room instead of stressing out over the details of that hearing. And so, we watched the War Room.

And when she put her head on my shoulder and our eyes met in that war room, I felt God working His grace within and among us. There is nothing impossible for Him. Just ask anything in Jesus' name, believe you have received it, and it is yours. I had written—a long time ago—my prayers on many pieces of paper. One by one they came to pass.

But remember, "Prayer is not asking. It is a longing of the soul. It is daily admission of one's weakness. It is better in prayer to have a heart without words than words without a heart."[167] Just set up your war room and pray with your heart, not repetitive words. Pray to God with all your simplicity and faith, laying your life into His loving arms. And you will hear Him assure you, "Consider it done."

The Noise of Silence

day 360: august 8, 2016

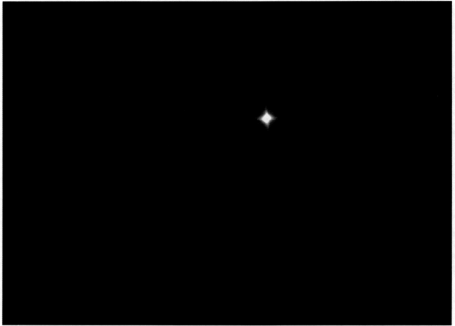

Silence does not wish to be silent tonight. It makes noise. While the sun silently sets, the white moon swiftly rises to watch over, the bustling city turns noiseless, and the chirping birds go into the silent dark night. And yet, silence roars. And I cannot hear it. In the stillness of the night, silence still rumbles loud and disturbs you—you, who do not wish to be irritated.

And I am unable to break this silence nor am I able to keep silent as if nothing has happened. I am surprised the sea is silent nowadays. I cannot hear her waves smashing at the stunning shore. Oh, how I long to hear that blast of the crashing waves. Silence used to speak to me through them. But now all it does is make noise. Loud noise. And yet, I hear nothing. I understand nothing.

I Will Laugh at the World

day 361: august 9, 2016

Pyramids of Giza, Egypt

This may be the biggest day of your life. You may be anxious and stressed out. You may be plotting and planning and following through with your life goals. You may be losing yourself in the process. Just remember to laugh at the world—and at yourself. Why take it so seriously. Even the king who had the pyramids built is gone. "Yea, verily, where is he who built the pyramid?" asked Og Mandino in *The Greatest Salesman in the World*. "He's buried in stone and one day the pyramids will be buried too," he concluded. And because everything passes, he decided he would laugh at the world.[168]

While adjusting the colors of my photo of the pyramids, I ponder: "Indeed, where is he who built the pyramids?" And to my surprise, while saving the photo, something goes wrong (or right), and the saved image now reflects a second set of pyramids in the sky. This answers my question. The guy who built the pyramids, and his pyramids, are up there, in another coexistent dimension. Think about it for a second—whatever you build on earth is mirror-imaged above. Bad acts or good deeds are stored for you up there, above the clouds, so when your time is up here, you would be judged according to your works stored in the heavens. Therefore, why waste your precious minutes fretting and stressing? Instead, laugh at the world, love and do good, and let your treasures pile up in heaven.

Therefore, I decide that I too will laugh at the world. How about you?

Wish Upon a Shooting Star
day 362: august 10, 2016

August 10th. Italy. It is the Notte di San Lorenzo—Saint Lawrence's Night. It's also the night of shooting stars, the Perseids meteor showers, that is. Millions of shooting stars will cross the skies on this magical mid-summer night. People gather at the beaches and in the countryside to watch the spectacular meteor showers and to make their wishes whilst the Perseids shoot across the sky. This night coincides with the feast of Saint Lorenzo who was martyred being burnt in a bonfire on August 10th in the third century. They say the shooting stars are his tears shed during his martyrdom, and that if you wish upon the shooting stars on the Notte di San Lorenzo, your wish will come true.

Wish upon that elusive shooting star. And if you catch your star at the right moment, the mysterious forces will unite, the guiding powers will gather, the opportunities will form, and all seasons will collide to make your wish come true. That star you wished upon will carefully carry the tiny particles of your wish on its shooting trail around the universe. And all events, people, or circumstance will be attracted to it and will make your wish come true.

I look up and my eyes catch the loveliest shooting star. It hears my wish and swooshes into the dark, its trailing light sketching a big smile and disappearing. What did I wish for?

Alone

day 363: august 11, 2016

Walking under the same morning twilight, my feet sense a different earth where the groomed trees, manicured lawns, red and white car-lights trailing the distant freeway, and empty streets exude an ancient aura. They look new, though. But life does not seem to bustle in these quiet corners. I walk and walk. The beige sands and the colorful cute pebbles that once furnished a soothing cushion for my tired soles are far away now; the asphalt gray pavement trying hard to please. Click-clack hitting on the pavement, a jogger runs by disappearing in the morning mist. The sun rises from behind the marine layer and greets me as if I was still at the shores of my sea. But now the sun—that no longer casts its long rays on the blue summer sea—coerces the towering palm trees and the identical houses to cast their shadows on the asphalt pavements and trimmed homogenous lawns. I wonder if the sun still reflects at the shore that I had left behind in the same manner as when I was walking its misty path.

A couple of other walkers barely greet me trying to avoid all eye contact. I am alone. In the Californian desert hills. It is true then what the Master had taught—"Life is an island in an ocean of loneliness, an island whose rocks are hopes, whose trees are dreams, whose flowers are solitude, and whose brooks are thirst."[169] It is the aloneness that fills your spirits, jolts your creativity, clears your mind, pushing you forward. In that solitude, you speak to God, and God speaks to you.

Did You Find What You Are Looking For?
day 364: august 12, 2016

Princess Grace Garden and Fountain in Monaco

"The men where you live," said the little prince, "raise five thousand roses in the same garden and they do not find in it what they are looking for."

"They do not find it," I replied.

"And yet, what they are looking for could be found in one single rose, or in a little water."

"Yes, that is true," I said.

And the little prince added, "But the eyes are blind. One must look with the heart..." [170]

364

Sit by Me

day 365: august 13, 2016

Come sit by me
To savor the sea
The day is bright
With this gorgeous sight

Come sit by me
By our old sea
Let us reminisce
About our days of bliss

Come sit by me
Feeling carefree
Take in the view
Without any review

Come sit by me
As I love thee
And hold my hand
In this wonderland

Come sit by me
Only you and me
In this lonesome land
Tenderly hand in hand

Come sit by me
Sit by me
You and me
Free

366 Days of Reflections

day 366: august 14, 2016

Today completes my yearlong (366 days because of the leap year) reflections by the sea—my sanctuary. As I reflect upon the events that transpired during those 366 days, I realize how swiftly and steadily life is passing through this temporary habitat of ours— our earth. Whether one is happy or angry, content or bitter, healthy or not, forgiving or holding grudges, life shall pass through these rotating days and nights, completing its sets of 365 days. It is up to each soul to fill each of those cycles of 365 with happiness and intentional acts of kindness. No one knows at which point in the circles of 365 one will be called to leave our earth. So, wouldn't it be agreeable to live each one of those days with deliberate love in the heart, intentional humility and peace in the soul, willful wisdom in the mind, and conscious charity towards the neighbor, instead of the detrimental habits of anger, anxiousness, arrogance, envy, unforgiveness, bitterness and cruelty—habits that destroy and pull one away from the love of God and others?

The one who makes the best of life is the one who seeks until s/he finds God's grace that transcends all human kindness. It's the one who summons the courage to pick up the Bible and starts reading it; the one who lets go and forgives; the one who has the stamina to pen their daily reflections—by the sea, the ocean, the forest, the mountain, or the bustling city—for tomorrow's children to read and understand how the Divine can mold and morph our transient weary spirits.

Unleash the Power of Blessed Virgin Mary
day 367: august 15, 2016

Author's Illustration, based on a painting in Notre Dame de Laghet Sanctuary, Nice

One more day. The year of Reflections ended yesterday, but since these reflections had begun on August 15th of last year—after we had followed the Marian procession, and celebrated her Assumption in the Port of Nice, it's only proper then to end these reflections with the feast day of Mother Mary's Assumption.

Assumption for Roman Catholics, or Dormition for the Orthodox celebrates Mother Mary's departure from earth, but each tells a different story. Catholics celebrate her Assumption into heaven—that she did not die but was assumed into heaven body and soul. The Orthodox celebrate the day as the Dormition of Theotokos (Sleeping of Mary)—that Mary fell asleep (died), and even though was buried in her tomb near the Gethsemane Garden, her body did not corrupt. On the third day, she was resurrected and was assumed into heaven body and soul. There are several traditions describing how Mary, during her Assumption into heaven, dropped her girdle to doubting Thomas, sent her icon the absent Bartholomew, or left her shroud behind for the faithful.

Celebrations and Marian processions are cancelled this year in Cote d'Azur fearing violence. Christians are diminishing in the Middle East—being persecuted, killed, and forced to migrate. Turkey is blocking mass today in some churches while confiscating others. In the US, it's a forgotten day by many—it's a workday. Marian processions are privately carried around churches, unlike many other countries where Mary's Assumption is still venerated in public, with festive processions walking through cobblestone streets of old towns.

Where is our world going to—persecuting Christians? But this is not the end. Mary shall help. She will intercede and this persecution shall stop. We have to pray collectively, incessantly, and she will unleash her power, and intercede.

Pray daily to Mother Mary. Pray the Rosary of the Blessed Virgin Mary.

The End

Endnotes

1 The people of Nice
2 John 1:5
3 Matthew 5:14-16
4 Romans 12:2
5 Colossians 3:21
6 Ephesians 6:4-5
7 John 14:1, Mark 11:22
8 Luke 17:3-4
9 James 1:17-18 NIV
10 Luke 16:11
11 First day of school
12 John 1:1
13 Matthew 24:31 KJV
14 Luke 23:43
15 Pissaladiere is a local pastry with onion topping
16 Sea Bass
17 Similar artwork by Jaume Plensa can be found all over the world
18 Quote by Goi Nasu?
19 Psalm 25:4
20 2 Corinthians 5:17
21 John 12:36
22 John 1:5
23 Menu #2 please, with tall coffee and pastries
24 Luke 4:4
25 John 6:35
26 Job 38:11 NKJV
27 Paraphrasing the First Epistle to the Corinthians, Chapter XX—The peace and harmony of the universe, Clement of Rome
28 Of Nice
29 James 1:2-8
30 Ground floor, or first floor
31 Matthew 6:9-13
32 Dawn, (1895) by Paul Laurence Dunbar
33 Referring to Jesus
34 Referring to Jesus
35 Good luck then
36 It's not courage, it's pleasure
37 The restaurants of the shore
38 Lounge chairs
39 Mussels and fries
40 2 Corinthians 5:17
41 Matthew 6:22
42 Luke 10:23 KJV
43 Ezekiel 36:26
44 *The Sun Also Rises,* Ernest Hemingway
45 *Si Quaeris Miracula,* Miraculous Responsory of Saint Anthony by Saint Bonaventure.
46 *Rubaiyat,* Omar Khayyam,

47 Luke 10:5

48 Sinterklaas in Dutch has morphed into Santa Claus

49 They were three little children

50 Spiced bread

51 Ecclesiastes 9

52 Ecclesiastes 1:2 KJV

53 Ecclesiastes 1:17

54 Ecclesiastes 4:4

55 Ecclesiastes 5:10

56 Ecclesiastes 1:14

57 Ecclesiastes 12:13,14

58 Nativity scene

59 Referring to Jesus

60 John 14:21

61 Romans 6:23

62 Christmas bath/swim

63 Luke 10:42

64 Matthew 18:20

65 John 1:4-5

66 Matthew 7:6 NET

67 Matthew 2:9-12

68 The Lamb and the Wolf from *Aesop's Fables*

69 Song by John Denver

70 per Wikipedia

71 Single by Cliff Edwards, from Walt Disney's Pinocchio movie

72 Mandelbaum Translation, https://digitaldante.columbia.edu/dante/divine-comedy/purgatorio/purgatorio-3/

73 Lerici is located on the Italian Riviera

74 La Turbie is located in the French Riviera

75 *The Sayings of Buddha*

76 *The Prophet*, Khalil Gibran

77 Carl Jung

78 Luke 2:22-39

79 Luke 2:26

80 Luke 2:28-31

81 Luke 2:34-35

82 Genesis 7

83 Genesis 8:4

84 *The Pathway of Life*, Leo Tolstoy

85 *The Pathway of Life* or *Calendar of Wisdom*, Leo Tolstoy, citing Emerson

86 *The Art of Public Speaking*, Dale Carnegie

87 Luke 10:42

88 www.routedumimosa.com

89 2 Timothy 4:7-8

90 Referred to as Qoheleth, or Kohelet, who may have been King Solomon

91 Ecclesiastes 1:14

92 Ecclesiastes 3:12

93 Ecclesiastes 5:18-20

94 Matthew 13:24-43

95 A popular game in France where players aim to throw their metal balls closer to a target

96 *The Pathway of Life*, Leo Tolstoy

97 *Rubaiyat*, Omar Khayyam

98 2 Timothy 4:6-7 KJV
99 http://www.vallauris-golfe-juan.fr/
100 The Kronos Quartet
101 Traditional Gaelic blessing, author unknown
102 Numbers 6:24-26
103 Toast and jam
104 Provencal market
105 This was written on March 11, 2017, in Cagnes Sur Mer
106 *Divine Comedy*, Paradisio, Canto II, Dante
107 Delicacy
108 *The Torrents of Spring*, by Ivan Turgenev
109 Matthew 11:28-30
110 Tenebrae means the darkness of the Holy Thursday (today) that fell after Jesus' Last Supper
111 John 19:20
112 Lamb of God, from Roman Catholic Latin Mass
113 Matthew 5:14-16
114 Aristotle had said: "A friend is a single soul living in two bodies"
115 *The Will to Power*, Friedrich Nietzsche
116 *Carpe diem, quam minimum credula postero*, Horace
117 Matthew 6:34
118 My drawing trying to memorialize my dream's image of Jesus' right foot and sandal
119 Luke 15:22
120 Vanilla of Madagascar
121 What Woman Wants, God Wants, by Alfred de Musset, *Le Fils du Titien*
122 Saying in France, translated in the next two lines
123 Lily of the valley
124 James 4:6-17
125 Hachi: A Dog's Tale
126 My drawing, replicating the stained glass in the Antibes Cathedral
127 John 14:2
128 Acts 26:18
129 *The Practice of Optimism*, by Helen Keller
130 Stained glass window in White Penitents Church in Saint Paul, France
131 John 20:29
132 Leo Tolstoy
133 View from the Solar Impulse Headquarters in Monaco
134 Motto at Solar Impulse Headquarters in Monaco
135 Mathew 3:9
136 Napoleon Hill
137 The Ten Scrolls from *The Greatest Salesman in the World*, by Og Mandino
138 Coffee
139 In God's name
140 Luke 1:46-56
141 George Muller was the Patriarch of Bristol, and the founder of Ashley Down Orphanage in Bristol, England. He had provided shelter and care to thousands of orphans, without any financial means of his own, but with the help of God who sent him millions—just because he believed, and incessantly prayed.
142 An hour with George Muller, The Man of Faith to Whom God Gave Millions, an interview by Pastor Charles R. Parsons
143 Maulana Jalal al-Din Rumi. "The Persian Mystics: Jalálu'd-dín Rúmí." Apple Books.
144 Maulana Jalal al-Din Rumi. "The Persian Mystics: Jalálu'd-dín Rúmí." Apple Books.
145 Copies of paintings mounted on stands

[146] Que Sera, Sera: the popular song of the movie "The Man Who Knew Too Much." (Wikipedia)

[147] Que Sera, Sera: the popular song of the movie "The Man Who Knew Too Much." (Wikipedia)

[148] Matthew 4 :19

[149] *The Little Prince*, Antoine De Saint-Exupery

[150] Stephen King

[151] See Nomad's photo at page 31, day 31

[152] Please come

[153] See Day 333 for picture

[154] Rumi

[155] Matthew 16:13-20

[156] This is a picture of another yacht; it is placed here for the visual effect.

[157] Matthew 6:33

[158] John 14:13

[159] Luke 10:38-42

[160] A Welsh word defined as "A homesickness for a home to which you cannot return, or for a home which may have never been." https://en.wiktionary.org/wiki/hiraeth

[161] Koran Chapter 28, verse 88

[162] Ecclesiastes 3:1

[163] Bob Marley, "Get up. Stand up." Album *Burnin*, 1973

[164] Methodist Free Church Hymns, 1889

[165] Revelation 22:5

[166] *The Voice of the Master*, Khalil Gibran.

[167] Mahatma Gandhi

[168] *The Greatest Salesman in the World*, Og Mandino

[169] *The Voice of the Master*, Khalil Gibran

[170] *The Little Prince*, Antoine De Saint-Exupery

Acknowledgments

Many loving and caring people supported and encouraged me to assemble my daily journals and photos and to publish them in the format of a book. I'm grateful for all the time and effort they provided to help me in my writing, editing, and publishing process, which was a somehow steep, but a worthwhile learning curve.

I would like to thank my wonderful family for their constant love and cheer and for their positive feedback even when I would repeatedly request their objective, or negative, opinion relating to all aspects of this book.

Thank you to my friends who volunteered to read parts of the manuscript and provided warm words of support and new ideas to enhance the reading experience. Lilla, thank you for your continuous encouragement and insight. Liz, thank you for your vibrant ideas about the cover design and photos.

Special appreciation also goes to my good friends Fabienne and Jade who were part of my daily life while I was writing these journals, who provided valuable insight and ideas for this journey, and who sustained me with their unshakeable strength and faith.

And last but not least, a big thank you to my dear friends Nelly and Greg who donated their precious time reading, editing, and providing suggestions for the front and back matter, the cover design, and some portions of this book.

About the author

IRENE ARMANI, JD, is a global citizen and a wandering nomad who was constantly seeking her true identity, her permanent home. She found both in Jesus Christ's teachings on her journey for a meaningful life, and has created faith-based fellowships to share His message of Love and peace.

She is also a California estate planning and business law attorney, speaker, and author. Because life has taken her around the Middle East, the USA, and Europe, enabling her to connect with different cultures, traditions, and regions, she has developed an all-embracing view of the oneness of humanity.

Irene loves helping people with their legal and personal problems. She reads, writes, draws, practices yoga and tai chi as a newbie, and walks her golden retriever Albi in her free time.

Reach and follow Irene at: www.irenearmani.com

Made in the USA
Monee, IL
03 January 2021